ORDER OF ISSHIN-RYU
ONE FAMILY – ONE DOJO

History and Teachings of Master Toby Cooling
and a Promise Made to the Founder

by
Dan Popp

www.OIKarate.org

Copyright © 2018 by Dan Popp

Front and back cover graphics and design by Jerry Robinette
Website: jerryrobinette.com

Kanji / front cover: *Kazoku* (family)
Kanji / back cover: *Seizan* (quiet mountain)
Brushed November 2017 by the author

All rights reserved. No part of this book may be reproduced in any form or by any means, electronic or mechanical, including photocopying, recording, or by any information storage and retrieval system, without permission in writing from the author and Kamel Press.

PHOTO CREDITS
See Appendix III

Proudly Published by Kamel Press, LLC.
Visit www.KamelPress.com/Popp for more from this author!

Library of Congress Control Number: 2018946486

978-1-62487-071-2 – paperback
978-1-62487-072-9 – ebook

Printed in the United States of America

Let us run with endurance the race that is set before us, looking unto Jesus, the author and finisher of our faith.

Hebrews 12:1-2

DEDICATION

To Denshi

Your dedication to the martial arts has and continues to serve as a guide and inspiration to countless karate-ka. You have far exceeded your promise to Grandmaster Shimabuku of creating a martial arts 'family' as the Order of Isshin-Ryu has changed countless lives and developed bonds to last a lifetime.

TABLE OF CONTENTS

Note to the Reader 7

Foreword 9

Messages to Denshi 15

Introduction 21

Chapter 1 - History of Isshin-Ryu Karate 25

Chapter 2 - History of the Order of Isshin-Ryu 51

Chapter 3 – Black Gi: History and Evolution 97

Chapter 4 – Family 107

Chapter 5 – Shiai and Dai Sempai 119

Chapter 6 – Sempai – Kohai: The Teacher-Student Relationship 125

Chapter 7 - Three Arrows of Isshin-Ryu 137

Chapter 8 - Overcoming Obstacles 153

Chapter 9 – Philosophy and Training 161

Chapter 10 – Budo of the Order of Isshin-Ryu 183

Senior Dan Bios 205

Order of Isshin-Ryu Inducted into the Hall of Fame 249

Memorial: Order of Isshin-Ryu Members Who Have Passed 251

Special Memorials 265

Conclusion 269

Acknowledgments 273

Special Recognition 277

Appendix I: Alphabetical Listing of Order of Isshin-Ryu Yudansha 279

Appendix II: Lineage Tables – Order of Isshin-Ryu Black Belts 287

Appendix III: Photo Credits 317

Appendix IV: Sources 319

NOTE TO THE READER

There are several possible ways to present or spell the system of martial arts for which this book is about: Isshinryu, Isshin Ryu, Isshin-ryu, and Isshin-Ryu. You will likely find books and videos on this system of karate using each of these examples. In the case of Master Toby Cooling's organization, the preferred spelling is "Order of Isshin-Ryu." Therefore, for ease of presentation to the reader, I've chosen to use "Isshin-Ryu" as the presentation throughout this book. If you come across one of the other spellings, just know I am talking about the same style of martial art and in no way do I wish to offend any other Isshin-Ryu organization or practitioner. The reader will also see the acronym "OI" from time to time. This is the acronym for "Order of Isshin-Ryu."

FOREWORD

This is the story of a modern American karate master and the organization he built. While there are many associations of like-minded practitioners of karate who network and support each other to varying degrees; the Order of Isshin-Ryu is rather unique in that its members can still interact with its founder, Grandmaster Toby Cooling.

Too often, the biography of a martial arts leader is written by a well-meaning author who has no actual first-hand knowledge of the subject matter. His writing must rely on second or third-hand accounts of events that occurred and facts that have been altered or fabricated after the main subject is no longer present to refute or acknowledge the events as recorded. This is certainly not the case with this work. This book and its writer have the approval of Grandmaster Toby Cooling. The author, Master Dan Popp, is not only a celebrated martial arts practitioner of multiple disciplines but also an "insider" that is a member and teacher in Grandmaster Cooling's organization, the Order of Isshin-Ryu (OI).

I first met Grandmaster Cooling in the mid-1980s while serving on the Isshin-ryu Hall of Fame board of directors. When invited to attend an OI event as a guest, I was immediately impressed with the caliber of his students, their physical skills, and dedication to their karate "family." The Order of Isshin-Ryu adhered to some of the highest standards for promotion and consistency of training that I have witnessed in any organization. This can be attributed to the unwavering dedication of the senior black belts of the OI who wish to preserve the legacy of their founder and sensei, Toby Cooling.

Over the years, my relationship with Grandmaster Cooling and the members of the OI has deepened from respect to friendship; to being mentored by him; and to being accepted into the OI brotherhood as an honorary member. For many years, he has visited Tennessee and mentored and shared his instruction with me and my students, as well as countless others as far away as Australia, who have taken advantage of the opportunity to meet, converse, and train with him.

I am honored to recommend this book to every practitioner of Isshinryu karate and to those who desire insight into the life and legacy of an American karate icon.

Butch Hill, Ku-dan
Isshinryu Cross Training Alliance (ICA)
October 8, 2017
Nashville, Tennessee

*****

Foreword

One day, not long after my brother and I opened a dojo in Roseville, California, a gentleman entered the school and sat down on the window bench. It was exciting to have a potential student walk in and sit since we were trying to grow our student base. After introducing myself, the man started asking questions about the school and the type of karate we taught. After answering a few initial inquiries, it was my turn. First question, *"Have you ever trained in karate?"* He replied yes. Next, *"What style of karate?"* He said Isshinryu Karate. I then asked, *"Who is your sensei?"* His answer was Tatsuo Shimabuku.

That conversation took place in 1994. It was quite a thrill to have Grand Master Toby Cooling, an Isshinryu icon, in the dojo. Over the last 23 years, he has visited often to share his knowledge and a valued friendship developed.

Who is Grand Master Toby Cooling? He was a young man who trained originally with Tom Lewis, then the legendary Don Nagle. Later, after receiving permission, he went to Okinawa to train directly with the founder of Isshinryu Karate, Grand Master Tatsuo Shimabuku. He lived and trained with Shimabuku for three months and was awarded his 6th degree black belt.

After returning to the United States, he started the Order of Isshinryu (OI), an elite group of martial artists recognized as a tough group who are also quite proficient in joint manipulation, pressure points, traditional Okinawan weapons, and firearms. Toby Cooling is an accomplished expert in all these areas. Grand Master Cooling honed his knowledge and technique on the streets against the bad guys while working for the Sheriff's department in both Maryland and Nevada. Lastly, becoming a Douglas County Nevada Constable. He is the real deal!

There is more to the man than just his martial abilities. Master Cooling keeps you in stitches as he shares his in-depth knowledge with witty anecdotes. The integrity level of this man is such that if he tells you something you can count on it being so. A rare and special quality.

David Joslin, Ku-dan
V.P. Karate International Association of Isshinryu (KIAI)
December 16, 2017
Roseville, California

*****

When I think of a true master, I think of the Samurai warrior's code. I also think of our dojo's code of God, family, job, karate, honesty, integrity, loyalty, tenacity, and never giving up.

On our dojo wall has a saying that many only recite: *"The ultimate aim in karate lies not in victory or defeat but in the perfection of one's character."* I have known Grand Master Toby Cooling for more than 30 years, and he lives this. He has been helping people perfect their character during his long Isshinryu journey. He shows no ego… in fact, he encourages others to show what they know and makes them feel good about themselves. He is very giving of himself to others, never asking for anything in return, except that his students practice his teachings. This book is an inside look at his story.

It is an honor for me to say a few words about Grand Master Cooling's story. He was first a friend, then a mentor. When in Okinawa, O'Sensei Tatsuo Shimabuku asked him to "go back to the States, teach good Isshinryu, and make happy family." Promising to do as asked, he returned to the United States and has since fulfilled his promise beyond expectations. He continues to fulfill his promise, traveling extensively to teach Isshinryu and increasing the family ties of his organization, the Order of Isshinryu, with many other Isshinryu organizations.

Grand Master Cooling's influence on so many martial arts practitioners and his leadership and contributions to Isshinryu are making a difference today and will undoubtedly stand the test of time.

Bob Kristensen, Ku-Dan
Texas Isshinryu Karate Kai
Grapevine, Texas
December 17, 2017

*****

Foreword

You can recognize the traits of greatness in the developmental stages of a person's potential, but it is still difficult to predict what level of greatness a person can achieve. Toby Cooling was born in 1944. His mother and father wanted their baby boy to grow into something they considered as great in life—being a successful doctor, attorney, or businessman. Young Toby had his own plan for greatness in his life—he chose the martial arts.

Master Cooling recognized his purpose and spent his life making his dreams a reality for so many people, many of whom weren't yet born when he started his martial arts journey but have shared in his dream of becoming a great martial artist. He is a man who understands the meaning of God's promises— "Let us not become weary in doing good, for at the proper time we will reap a harvest if we do not give up," (Galatians 6:9 NIV). In holding fast to his dreams, Master Cooling has grown the Order of Isshin-Ryu from a front yard martial arts school into an international martial arts family, bringing a community of people together with his skillful leadership, immeasurable integrity, tireless dedication, and clever jocularity.

This one man, Walter "Toby" Cooling, has impacted so many martial artists by keeping a promise to Chief Grandmaster Shimabuku, who tasked him with making the Isshinryu karate family strong. No matter what challenges have confronted him in life, he has never moved away from this promise or grown weary in his well doing. He has been more than a karate master. He is a Sensei to all he meets— a counselor, teacher, business partner, and loyal friend. He has mentored people beyond his community and socioeconomic status, and his genuine teachings have been a cutting-edge formula for the thriving Isshinryu family that we know today—Order of Isshin-Ryu: One Family, One Dojo.

Carl Martin, Ku-dan
Traditional Okinawan Karate Institute (TOKI)
October 30, 2017
West Chester, Pennsylvania

*****

I am honored to have my thoughts mentioned in this book as I have a 50-year relationship with the art of Isshinryu karate. Toby Cooling was on the testing board for my Sho-dan examination, along with Kichiro Shimabuku. This was a day I will never forget, as my school was very much 'old school.' My instructor at that time was Mark Wzorek, one of master Nagle's top fighters. After testing was over, the names of the new black belts were called out one-by-one, but my name was not called. The gymnasium was quiet. Then Sensei Wzorek and Master Shimabuku go to the center of the floor and finally my name is called. As I face Sensei Wzorek, he commanded me to kneel and told me to take off my brown obi. He knelt, removed his obi, and put it on around my waist. Sensei Cooling, Sensei Wright, and Master Kichiro Shimabuku were all part of this ceremony. I found myself speechless as I know what an honor this truly was. That was August 1971.

As time passed, the Order of Isshin-Ryu was born, and Sensei Cooling became Master Cooling. He traveled to Okinawa to train with Soke Shimabuku and was elevated in rank to Roku-dan, 6th degree black belt, and wore a red and white obi. Our friendship grew, and our schools had schools under us. Isshinryu continued growing and becoming recognized as a force to deal with in any competition.

The spark of Isshinryu in Elkton, Maryland has since spread to Pennsylvania, Tennessee, Michigan, New Jersey, New York, Canada, Nevada, Texas, Florida, Alabama, Ohio, Illinois, and many more parts of the United States. Toby Cooling is a recognized Grandmaster of Isshinryu and is part of our history. I am honored to know him and call him my friend.

Ralph Passero, Ku-dan
Don Nagle's American Okinawan Karate Association (AOKA)
October 24, 2017
Toms River, New Jersey

MESSAGES TO DENSHI

*"Let your light shine before men, that they may see
your good works and give glory to your Father in heaven."*

Matthew 5:16

Grandmaster Toby Cooling... you will always be recognized and remembered as a leader, a teacher, a friend, and a true sensei in the world of Isshinryu. Grandmaster Harold Long thought very highly of you. Your lineage of karate-kas will always leave an imprint on whatever event they happen to be. My best wishes.
    Maurice Msarsa, Ku-dan, International Isshin-Ryu Karate Association

Denshi saved my life. Meeting him was like turning on the ignition I needed to become what I am today.
    Barry Smith, Ku-dan, Order of Isshin-Ryu

I want to thank Grandmaster Cooling for carrying on Master Shimabuku's vision and direction to come back to the United States and teach No. 1 Isshin-Ryu.
    Danny Cross, Roku-dan, Order of Isshin-Ryu

Grandmaster Cooling... if it wasn't for you, I would not be where I am today.
    Sotiere Nicholson, San-dan, Order of Isshin-Ryu

Grandmaster Toby Cooling, is the founder of the Order of Isshin-Ryu martial arts organization and a nationally known and respected leader in the Isshin-Ryu world. But most of all, he has devoted himself to be the mentor, confidant, teacher, and soul of the OI for every student that has walked through those doors from the past, in the present, and into the future.
    John Costanzo, Hachi-dan, Order of Isshin-Ryu

Grand Master Cooling... a sincere and heartfelt thank you for the gift you've given us. For many, this is the only family known, for others, it has been an opportunity to be part of something much bigger. It is said, we may never know how we have impacted others or society and, if we can have the opportunity to impact just one individual in our lifetime, we will have accomplished something special. You, sir, have had the opportunity to accomplish both. The Order of Isshinryu has withstood the test of time, and each of its members has been influenced and molded by you personally and throughout Isshinryu community.

Lawrence Waldridge, San-dan, Order of Isshin-Ryu

Some men make a mark, some men leave a mark, and some men are marked by destiny. You accomplished all. Your forever loyal student.

Larry Sica, San-dan, Order of Isshin-Ryu

I have been blessed to call you Sensei for the last 37 years. Your integrity and dedication to your students set the bar for all Sensei.

Ron Tyree, Hachi-dan, Order of Isshin-Ryu

Grandmaster Cooling is a man of honor, a man of his word. If he says it, it will happen. Who can you trust? This man.

Dave Joslin, Ku-dan, American Okinawan Karate Association

Thank you, Denshi, for allowing me to share the OI path and your friendship for the last 49 years. You are a master in the true sense of the word.

Tom Sanson, Yon-dan, Order of Isshin-Ryu

Your friendship over the years has meant much to me. Sensei Mitchum thought highly of you too. Your organization has done much to preserve and protect the foundations of Isshin Ryu karate. I appreciate not only your friendship but your dedication to a cause bigger than any one person.

Just before his passing in 2016, Sensei Mitchum intended to sign your certificates; unfortunately, we lost him before that could happen. As a senior Yudansha in Isshin Ryu, you have continued your quest to preserve, promote, and protect our style. In an era of self-proclamation, you simply want to be a good Sensei. You work and improve so that you might help others do the same. Your actions should inspire others to do likewise. Thank you for keeping things simple.

Dan Holloway, Hachi-dan, United Isshin-Ryu Karate Association

Messages to Denshi

Grandmaster Cooling (Denshi)... you are indeed the "Sensei of the Sensei." You always square your actions, you always keep your word, and you're always on the level. Thank you for the Order of Isshin-Ryu and for bringing us all together as one family "Domo Arigato Gozaimasu Sensei"

Ronnie Cimorosi, Nana-dan, Order of Isshin-Ryu

Congratulations Master Cooling on a lifetime of dedication to Isshinryu Karate. I have known you most of my time in Isshinryu. You are a great leader, great person, and a true ambassador of Isshinryu Karate. All the best.

Steve Young, Ju-dan, American Okinawan Karate Association

My relationship with Master Toby Cooling goes back a very long time. I believe we first met when I was only a very young 17-year-old, and that's why he calls me Donny. Now in my mid-sixties and he has always believed in me. Anytime in my karate career, if I needed help I knew he would be there as he's been there for many others. I remember when Master Don Nagle passed away and we (AOKA) had a meeting to see who was going to replace Master Nagle. We had Master Cooling's name on the list. Just for that, he should be proud that Master Nagle thought enough of him to be someone to take over the Nagle lineage.

Don Nash, Ku-dan, Don Nagle's American Okinawan Karate Association

Denshi... the strongest influences that I had growing up were my parents, other relatives, and the OI family. The discipline, confidence, tenacity, and respect for all others that I learned as a member of the OI, has and will continue to guide my decisions and actions daily. The OI is the everlasting legacy that you have built. I am proud to be a small part of it and grateful that, thanks to you, my children have the opportunity to grow up within the OI family, too.

Mico Slijepcevic, Sho-dan, Order of Isshin-Ryu

Master Cooling... your vision for a new martial arts organization and courage to create it are truly inspirational. The creeds and codes established and embodied by all in the OI provide for lifelong values and lessons for all to follow. Finally, thank you also for being a regular guy... approachable, honest, and sincere!

John McNair, Ni-kyu, Order of Isshin-Ryu

Denshi... thank you for your dedication and leadership all these decades. You founded the Order of Isshin-Ryu and through much long-suffering have kept it alive and doing

well. I personally thank you for your guidance, training, and teaching that has positively impacted my life. God's grace to you!

Ken Varney, San-dan, Order of Isshin-Ryu

Grandmaster Cooling... thank you for your lifetime commitment to teaching Isshin-Ryu karate. It is an honor to be a part of the Order of Isshin-Ryu and train with such talented martial artists and great people.

Gregory LeBlanc, Ni-kyu, Order of Isshin-Ryu

I was one of the very lucky ones. As a young man in the late 60s, I began taking karate classes at Harford Community College in Maryland taught by a young, dynamic, enthusiastic instructor named Sensei "Toby" Cooling. As a sensei, a mentor, and a friend, he had a profound influence on my life as he doubtless has for many, many others. I'm sure I can speak for all in offering Master Cooling our sincere gratitude, appreciation, and respect for all he has accomplished and all he has given to others over these many years.

Tom Miller, Ni-dan, Order of Isshin-Ryu

To the man who taught me the true meaning of on-giri, congratulations on the publication of the OI history. I wouldn't be who I am today otherwise.

Steve Dawson, Yon-dan, Order of Isshin-Ryu

Grandmaster Cooling... thank you for everything you have done for the Order of Isshin-Ryu and the world of Isshin-Ryu. Without you and the OI, who knows where I would be. I've cherished all the times we've spent in and out of the dojo. Thank you for everything.

Chris Harris, Go-dan, Order of Isshin-Ryu

Denshi... I believe that you and the Order of Isshin-Ryu family have been a major contributor to the woman that I have become. I want to express my deepest gratitude for teaching me that hard work and perseverance are key factors in success. You have inspired me, not just within the dojo, but in all aspects of my life. I truly value all that I have learned from you and the life-long friendships that being a part of the Order of Isshin-Ryu have fostered.

Nikolina Novakovic, San-dan, Order of Isshin-Ryu

Master Cooling and the Order of Isshin-Ryu has made a definite and long-lasting impression on my life. The high standards, discipline, and camaraderie are highly commendable. The encouragement and support I have personally received is greatly appreciated.

Bob Cole, San-dan, Order of Isshin-Ryu

Thank you, Master Cooling. The Order of Isshin-Ryu has given me a martial arts foundation, developed my moral character through its teachings, and given me the opportunity to create lifelong friendships. All of these will last me a lifetime. I cannot thank you enough for being a large influence in my life.

Wayne Brittingham, San-dan, Order of Isshin-Ryu

To the boy on a downward spiral... he gave a positive direction and an absolute role model.

   To the man... he shared his wisdom and never-ending support.

   For this, I am now and forever grateful.

Jeff Bracone, San-dan, Order of Isshin-Ryu

Grandmaster Cooling... thank you for creating an organization devoted not only to the teaching and advancement of martial arts but also to the promulgation of an ethos of personal development through a dynamic process. One life-changing paradigm shift for me is your observation that "slow learning is not poor learning." Reading this statement in the OI pamphlet and seeing it in practice has completely changed my attitude toward teaching and learning. The concrete manifestation of this changed attitude is the growth and improvement of my musical practice and performance allowed by a newfound patience with personal shortcomings. More significantly, I've become a much more effective, patient, compassionate, and joyful music instructor for my own students. Thank you for everything and congratulations on the OI publication.

Aaron Walker, Ni-dan, Order of Isshin-Ryu

You always say that you can't choose your family. We believe that you can't choose your relatives, but you can choose your family. You've created a network of friendships and family bonds that will last a lifetime. Thank you for all that you have done to make this world a better place!

Gerri Ankers, San-dan & Pete Ankers, San-dan, Order of Isshin-Ryu

Your knowledge, talent, and efforts made you a great martial artist, but your visionary leadership has made you the OI family's patriarch. Congratulations for a super job fostering unity and brotherhood between all members. I am proud to be part of your extended family.

Maria Kristensen, Nana-dan, Texas Isshinryu Karate Kai

I'll never forget my first tournament in Elkton, MD. I was in the locker room changing around a bunch of people I had never seen before. A guy started joking with me and simply introduced himself as "Toby." Moments later after I shook his hand, I found out who he was. It was a great honor that at my first tournament the first hand I shook was Grandmaster Cooling.

           Danny Warner, Go-kyu, Order of Isshin-Ryu

Master Cooling... thank you for your life-long dedication to the Order of Isshin-Ryu. This organization has truly saved my life.

          Mark Fellenbaum, Ik-kyu, Order of Isshin-Ryu

Grandmaster Cooling... take time to smell the roses and enjoy the legacy you created within the Order of Isshin-Ryu. You have affected many lives in a positive way; we are better for having known you.

          Buster Hash, San-dan, Order of Isshin-Ryu

Denshi... you always said that "you don't have to be in the dojo to practice karate." As a young man - I never could have envisioned how true was such a statement and how impactful on my life this would be. Whether on patrol in my 20s or in a boardroom negotiating a contract in my 40s, karate has been and continues to be practiced every day. Ironically, outside of the dojo much more than inside of the dojo. The values you instilled in us are not only practiced in a gi (uniform) but have become part of our DNA. I cannot summarize in a few sentences the impact that growing up in this organization has had and continues to have upon my life, but summarily, a heartfelt THANK YOU for your selfless pouring into many of us.

          Kurt Kline, Nana-dan, Order of Isshin-Ryu

Denshi... "The teaching that came from his mouth was true. Nothing unjust was found on his lips. He lived with me in peace and honesty and turned many people away from iniquity."

 [Mal 2:6] A prophet..a legend..or an illusion..it doesn't matter the memories will stay alive.

         Juan D. Lopez, Roku-dan, Order of Isshin-Ryu

INTRODUCTION

Isshin-Ryu karate is one of the world's most popular martial arts due to its efficiency of movement and straightforward training methods. The system gained popularity rather quickly once it reached U.S. soil due to the efforts of many United States Marines who learned directly from the system's founder while stationed on Okinawa. There are numerous Isshin-Ryu organizations across the world. As of this writing, there are 20-plus major organizations teaching Isshin-Ryu karate, all with slightly different standards and requirements.

There are many books in print today on the subject. A search of Isshin-Ryu karate on Amazon will yield various titles to choose from to further your research into this style. All of them are outstanding works and provide quite a bit of information the reader can read over time and again to further their understanding of this excellent martial art. So why another one? Many of those books were written by first-generation American students of the founder of Isshin-Ryu karate. Sadly, the pioneers of this incredible art are beginning to pass away. Don Nagle, Harold Long, Steve Armstrong, and Harold Mitchum – the "Original Four" – are all now deceased. As of this writing, there are very few first-generation students still alive such as A.J. Advincula, John Bartusevics, Toby Cooling, and Tom Lewis just to name a few.

Toby Cooling was an American who studied with the founder on Okinawa. He has a considerable amount of knowledge to pass along. His thoughts and words coupled with those of his students who have gained recognition and respect in their own right can serve to bridge the gap from Master Cooling's original students to the next generation of Order of Isshin-Ryu karate practitioners as well as the entire Isshin-Ryu community.

The Order of Isshin-Ryu was founded by Grandmaster Toby Cooling on January 15, 1971. This date happens to coincide with the 15th anniversary of the founding of the system of Isshin-Ryu karate by Grandmaster Tatsuo Shimabuku on the island of

Okinawa on January 15, 1956. Grandmaster Cooling traveled to Okinawa to train with the founder in December 1969, and prior to his departure back to the United States, Grandmaster Shimabuku said to Toby, "Go back and make happy family." This was his way of telling him to begin teaching Isshin-Ryu karate upon his return home and develop a strong organization that would treat each other as a family, creating strong bonds that would last a lifetime.

Grandmaster Cooling has more than lived up to his sensei's simple request. On the surface, such a request is simple, but it is really quite the opposite. To foster and grow an organization where members are there for one another through thick and thin, using Isshin-Ryu karate as the binding activity, is no easy task. It takes someone with the ability to lead beyond the normal call of duty; someone who not only sets the example by action, but also has the ability to listen. A person who makes the difficult decisions and knows that not everyone will be happy all the time. A leader who gets everyone involved and makes everyone, even down to the newest student, feel welcome and a part of something bigger. Grandmaster Cooling has shown these traits time and time again for over five decades of martial arts practice and research.

The Order of Isshin-Ryu is now approaching 50 years old; therefore, it becomes imperative to preserve the memories of this organization for future generations of the Order of Isshin-Ryu family. I would encourage other Isshin-Ryu organizations to also publish their histories and teachings for the benefit of future generations of this art as well. It would further propel understanding among the various Isshin-Ryu organizations and also honor Grandmaster Shimabuku's teachings in a deep and personal way.

All things are incomplete. Isshin-Ryu karate is no different. It will, and should, forever evolve and improve as with all martial arts. There are generations of Isshin-Ryu sensei and karate-ka yet to be known. Hopefully, this publication will preserve the thoughts, experiences, knowledge, and ideas of Master Toby Cooling, as well as his students, which may provide a springboard to future generations of Isshin-Ryu practitioners.

I cannot take credit for being the sole author of this book. I had the help of many of my fellow Order of Isshin-Ryu karate-ka. Frankly, this is how it should be. The Order of Isshin-Ryu is more than a fraternity of men and women who practice and study the art of Isshin-Ryu karate. The Order of Isshin-Ryu is a family, as the founder of our organization wanted it to be. How exactly does an organization evolve into a family? This would appear to contradict the average mindset of a group practicing martial arts. The student makes payment to the instructor for lessons and in return anticipates moving up the ranking structure to hopefully one day be awarded his or her black belt. Well, this is not always true. Not all answers should be simply given

Introduction

and clearly, rank should never be conferred by expectation from monetary payment. They must be earned for the student to fully understand and appreciate the knowledge being imparted.

The following pages contain nearly 50 years of the history, stories, philosophies, and training methods of the collective efforts of the Order of Isshin-Ryu. To capture everything in this span of time is clearly next to impossible. However, I have done my best to interview as many of my fellow family members as possible to honor Grandmaster Cooling to the best of my abilities. I hope you enjoy all this book has to offer and that you always train your mind, body, and spirit to its fullest – which takes nothing short a lifetime.

This book will hopefully provide a glimpse of what a martial arts family is all about. What is a karate family? Read on and hopefully you can see for yourself how truly special this family really is – this family called the Order of Isshin-Ryu.

Dan Popp, Roku-dan
Order of Isshin-Ryu
August 7, 2016

Chapter 1
HISTORY OF ISSHIN-RYU KARATE

"Self-observation brings a man to the realization of the necessity of self-change. And in observing himself a man notices that self-observation itself brings about certain changes in his inner processes. He begins to understand that self-observation is an instrument of self-change, a means of awakening."

George Gurdjieff

The historical aspects of any endeavor are important to provide perspective, to assist in fully absorbing what it is you are studying or practicing. Many famous athletes are true historians of their craft. Pick a top athlete from any sport and if you research their background, you will come to realize they have a very good grasp of the historical figures who came before them. Watch an interview with any of these and others who take their practice seriously, and you'll see the depth of historical knowledge they have for what they are doing. They not only know the names and dates of past athletes, they also go farther to understand and appreciate the personalities of those who helped shape and define their respective sport.

The same holds true for a serious martial arts practitioner. Having a solid grasp of historical facts adds to understanding your art. But you shouldn't stop there. Consider going beyond mere names and dates and try to understand the personalities of the key figures not only in your art but other martial arts as well. Try to understand the period in which they lived, possibly the cultural norms and if egos surfaced, the root causes.

Considering the amount of history involved with the evolution of martial arts, from the Shaolin monks in China to the present day, the process of research into the history of Isshin-Ryu karate and other arts cannot truly happen over a few years.

It takes dedicated effort in tandem with your physical practice to fully absorb the history of your art.

On a working trip to Los Angeles in 2006, I visited The Japanese Garden located in Van Nuys on my last day there prior to returning home. This 6.5-acre public Japanese garden is located adjacent to Woodley Park and was created between 1980 and 1983. The gardens were incredibly serene and maintained meticulously. In one of the buildings, a short movie documented the life of Gichin Funakoshi, the founder of modern karate. Part of the film told the story of how Funakoshi and one of his contemporaries, Choki Motobu, were often seen in heated debates over various aspects of karate. Although Motobu has a distinct part of the eventual formulation of Isshin-Ryu karate (he was one of Master Shimabuku's instructors), I had no idea these men did not necessarily care for one another. This was a revelation to me mainly because my historical research into my art had fallen off. We are all human, and sometimes this level of research can fall off the student's radar. Once you are a student of the martial arts, you should always remain a student.

Master Cooling requires everyone within the Order of Isshin-Ryu family to, at a minimum, have a solid grasp of the history of Isshin-Ryu karate. If questioned, students should be able to express this history clearly and concisely whether in the dojo, to seniors, or to the public. Of course, I'm talking about the overall general history of Isshin-Ryu and not the detailed fine points that a dedicated historian would be able to recite. It takes considerable time and patience to trace the full scope of history behind the history of any martial art. But on a high level, the OI expects a certain degree of understanding behind Isshin-Ryu's evolution.

Not having this basic knowledge can serve as a point of embarrassment. Someone with no knowledge of martial arts may ask, "Tell me, what is the background of your karate? Where did it come from?" The OI wants everyone to answer these questions with confidence. Clearly, you don't need to be an expert on Japanese or Okinawan history or be able to speak the native language from where karate was invented. However, you should have some grasp of these concepts. As martial artist and author Dave Lowry writes in his book, *The Essence of Budo*, "A study of that art [Japanese budo] will always be more thorough and broader in perspective when it is taught by a person who has additional knowledge and understanding of the place where that art originated." Having a good understanding of your art's history as well as the ability to speak the words and phrases correctly of Okinawan karate-do is essential if you want to be considered a serious student.

Any publication on a specific martial art system such as Isshin-Ryu requires some level of historical background to lay the baseline of where the system originated, who is responsible for the development of the style, when events took place that were key to the eventual establishment of the system, and so forth. This type of information is essential for the reader, hardcore practitioner, or passive reader to understand not only where the martial art came from, but also where it is going in the future.

Isshin-Ryu karate is one of the world's most popular martial arts and is studied and practiced across the globe. It was officially founded on January 15, 1956, by Tatsuo Shimabuku[1] (1908 – 1975) on the island of Okinawa, Japan. Okinawa is one of over one hundred islands in the Ryuku chain that extends from southern Japan to Taiwan.

Figure 1: Okinawa and its surrounding islands.

Brief History of Karate

The origins of martial arts as we know it today stem from nearly 1,500 years ago. To encompass the historical activity of this span of time is next to impossible. The author Andreas Quast in his book *A Stroll Along Ryukyu Martial Arts History* provides a detailed account from this history of Okinawa based upon actual historical documents. Perform a search of books on Amazon of authors such as Patrick McCarthy to discover a treasure trove of published material on Okinawan karate and the history behind various masters responsible for the development of karate as we know it today.

In an article from Black Belt magazine, author James Melton provides a concise summary from this beginning up to the point where the Okinawan people

---

[1] The more formal surname or family name is Shimabukuro.

developed their system of fighting, called *Te* (pronounced 'tay', meaning, 'hand'). Here is the opening paragraph of that article.[2]

> About 1,400 years ago, an Indian monk named Daruma (or Boddhidharma), the founder of Zen Buddhism, left western India by crossing the Himalayan mountains. He made the difficult, several-thousand-mile journey alone and on foot. His purpose in traveling to China was to present lectures on Buddhism. Eventually, his travels in China led him to the Shaolin Temple in the Hunan Province. There, legend has it that many of his students were unable to keep up the training because of their poor physical condition. To develop their physical strength, Daruma taught them a method of physical conditioning contained in the *Ekkin Kyo*. Through this training, the monks recovered their spiritual and physical strength, and eventually became the subject of legend for their courage and fortitude. Eventually, this method of training spread and came to bear the name of its origin, *shorinji kempo*. This method was then brought to the Ryukyu Islands, where it developed into *Okinawa-te*, the forerunner of present-day kara-te.

The traditional methods of karate we know today were formed on the island of Okinawa, a small island of approximately 466 square miles in size located 400 miles to the south of Japan. In Harold Long's book *Isshin-Ryu Karate – The Ultimate Fighting Art*, he states, "The most significant progress in the development of modern karate took place on the island of Okinawa beginning in the 1600s. However, for almost 300 years, karate was practiced in secrecy due to the Japanese occupation of the island. History and forms were passed from teacher to student without any written record ever being made."

---

[2] The Evolution of Karate – From Fighting Method to Art, Sport and Self-Defense System, by James R. Melton. Black Belt Magazine (Active Interest Media)

History of Isshin-Ryu Karate

Figure 2: Okinawa's proximity to China and Japan.

Figure 3: 1992 - Master Bill Sullivan, then a san-dan, performing Chatan Yara no Sai kata.

Okinawa is the largest of the Ryukyu Islands of Japan and is also about the same distance from China as it is from Japan. This location provides for quite a diverse cultural exposure and influence. The fighting techniques from Okinawa were heavily influenced by China and other countries due to the proximity of Okinawa to those countries in the South China Sea. Long goes on to write, "Chinese martial arts such as Kung Fu, Wushu, and Chuan' Fa had a major influence in the development of karate."

Various proponents of Okinawan martial arts either traveled to foreign lands or studied directly from legendary fighters traveling to Okinawa. This is chronicled in Richard Kim's book titled *The Weaponless Warriors*. His book provides several examples of these 'travels' where learning and exchange of knowledge took place. Yara, from the village of Chatan on Okinawa, studied some 20 years in China under Wong Chung-Yoh. Kim's story of Yara states, "His (Yara) uncle, a trader, had convinced Yara's parents after a long talk that their little son, who was strong as a bull, would make a great martial artist. They agreed with him that China was the place to learn." Kim goes on to explain in the notes to his story on Yara that a great number of Chinese families settled in Okinawa.

The Chinese influence lasted until the reign of Emperor Sho Tai (1848-1879). Although the Okinawans had their own fighting methods, they were clearly heavily influenced by the many styles of Chinese fighting arts. One who has either learned or watched the sai kata named after Yara, *Chatan Yara no Sai*, can see for themselves these influences in the circular, flowing movements of this form.

Another example of an Okinawan seeking influence by systems of martial arts outside of the island is Sokon "Bushi" Matsumura. In his book, *Shotokan's Secret*, author Bruce Clayton, Ph.D. indicates, "Matsumura made trips to China and Japan to study their martial arts, including a pilgrimage to the Shaolin Temple (Henan Province, China[3]). He allegedly brought back several kata including early forms of *naihanchi, seisan,* and *gojushiho*, among others."

Figure 4: 1992 - Sensei Mike Goodyear performing Chinto kata at an OI shiai.

As for Chinese visiting Okinawa, either on purpose, by accident, or by divine intervention, there is the famous kata found in Okinawan karate called *chinto*. Bruce Clayton, Ph.D. says in his book, "Most accounts agree that Matsumura created the kata called *chinto*, using techniques he learned from a shipwrecked Chinese martial artist in Tomari."

To understand the development of karate, you must have some level of understanding of the history of the island of Okinawa and its people. Since ancient times, Okinawa has been a crossroads of Asian cultures. This was due to Okinawa's central location in the East China Sea, making it an excellent trade center for goods moving to and from China, Japan, Indonesia, Malaysia, Vietnam, and the Philippines.

---

[3] https://en.wikipedia.org/wiki/Shaolin_Monastery

According to Wikipedia, Okinawa's population is known as one of the longest living in the world. In fact, there are 34 centenarians per 100,000 people, which is more than three times the rate of mainland Japan. And martial artists from the island of Okinawa are no exception. This issue is presented in *Shotokan's Secret*, a book in which Bruce Clayton, Ph.D. conducted research about how long karate masters on Okinawa lived. He notes Japanese emperors lived to around 35 years while Americans in 1850 lived to approximately 40 years of age. At the same time, many Okinawan masters lived much longer including: Peichin Azato – 78, Tode Sakugawa – 82, Anko Itosu – 85, Gichin Funakoshi – 89, and Sokon Matsumura – 97.

These results can trace back to a major root of karate stemming from ancient China. A monk named Daruma Daishi (Bodhidharma) developed eighteen exercise forms for the use of the Buddhist monks living at the Shaolin Temple. These exercise forms eventually became known as Shaolin *Kempo*, meaning "Way of the Fist." The exercise discipline concentrated upon the art of learning to control and master the body, mind, and soul. Through physical exercise, coupled with proper breathing, improvement of mental awareness and the diet on the island, the practitioners of Okinawan karate could clearly see the benefits of a longer life.

Since ancient times, the Okinawan people practiced a system of self-defense referred to as *Te* (pronounced 'tay'), meaning "hand," the second root of modern karate. Three main styles of *Te* existed on Okinawa, each named after the town that originated the system: Shuri-te from the town of Shuri (later named Shorin-ryu), Naha-te from the town of Naha (later named Goju-ryu), and Tomari-te from Tomari. Harold Long notes in *Isshin-Ryu Karate – The Ultimate Fighting Art*, "Tomari-te was a mixture of both (Shuri-te and Naha-te) and was practiced mostly by farmers and fisherman."

Karate master Darryl Baleshiski studied under Shorin-ryu grandmaster Eizo Shimabukuro (younger brother of Tatsuo Shimabuku). In his book, *My Journey of Practice* he writes, "Shuri-te is said to be more formal or elegant as it is from the Shuri Castle area, while Tomari-te is more of a rough and tumble as it is around the port city of Tomari." Both Shimabuku brothers, Tatsuo and Eizo, studied under Chotoku Kyan.

Tatsuo Shimabuku's Instructors

Chotoku Kyan
(1870 – 1945)
Shorin-ryu

Chojun Miyagi
(1888 – 1953)
Goju-ryu

Choki Motobu
(1870 – 1944)
Shorin-ryu

Shinken Taira
(1897 – 1970)
Kobudo

Kyan did not prefer the Shuri-te style. Bruce Clayton, Ph.D. notes in his book *Shotokan's Secret*, "Later in his life, Kyan apparently abandoned Shuri-te completely and taught only pre-Matsumura kata and techniques." Both Tatsuo and Eizo Shimabuku studied under Kyan during his later years, so it seems quite logical that the creation of the Isshin-Ryu system has a very heavy dose of the 'rough and tumble' martial arts practiced by the farmers and fisherman of the Tomari region of Okinawa. This is further supported by the fact Tatsuo was so influenced by Kyan that he originally termed the art he formulated using the nickname of Kyan: Chan Migwa-te.

During the years of trade and cultural exchange, the Okinawans were exposed to Shaolin Kempo. Over many years, they synthesized these two martial traditions into what we know today as *karate*. The term originally translated to "China hand" in the late 1800s and in the early twentieth century the translation became "empty hand." This was done by Gichin Funakoshi upon moving to Japan to teach Okinawan karate to the Japanese. Bruce Clayton, Ph.D. writes in his book *Shotokan's Secret*, "Funakoshi changed the first kanji character of "kara te do" to mean "empty-hand way" instead of "Chinese-hand way." This was part of his campaign to make karate seem more Japanese and less foreign." He said Funakoshi also changed the name of the kata to more politically correct Japanese names: naihanchi became tekki, seisan became hangetsu, and kusanku became kanku.

In the 14th century, during the reign of King Sho Shin, the private ownership of weapons and the use of armed retainers by lords were first prohibited. Through this, the nobility was able to gain complete control over the citizens, which, in turn, fueled

History of Isshin-Ryu Karate

the desire for empty-hand fighting systems. During the 17th century, Okinawa was overrun and occupied by the Satsuma Clan of Japan. Okinawa was never to be independent again.

All weapons on Okinawa were confiscated, and people were forbidden to own, use, or carry any weapons. The edict issued in 1609 also forbade the practice of martial arts. Again, this was to completely subjugate the Okinawans. Faced with the necessity of defending themselves and their people from their oppressors and pirates and having only their bare hands with which to fight, the citizens on Okinawa turned to the ancient forms of *Te* and *Kempo*. In those desperate years, they developed and refined the techniques until their bodies were as deadly and effective in their defense as had been the swords that were taken from them. Karate was

Figure 5: Karate (empty hand).

taught in secret and was known only to the nobility. Where and how it was taught was a mystery to most Okinawans, for to be introduced to the discipline of karate was to be marked as one of the most poised and trusted human beings and was an honor as high as any that could be bestowed.

For over 300 years, karate remained secret and known only through word-of-mouth on the island of Okinawa. Masters taught only small groups, usually family members and relatives. Each family developed their own personal method of training; thus, many styles of karate came into being. Karate became a course of exercise valued for its health and character building.

In 1875, the Satsuma occupation ended, and Japan officially recognized Okinawa as a prefecture. The need for secrecy ended. In 1902, Anko Itosu, a master of Shuri-Te, gave the first public demonstration of karate on Okinawa. Later, both he and Master Kanryo Higashionna (sometimes spelled *Higaonna*) introduced karate into the public-school system.

In 1917, an Okinawan school teacher by the name of Gichin Funakoshi, who had studied karate in Shuri, Okinawa, gave a series of karate demonstrations at the Butokuden in Kyoto, Japan. The Butokuden is the government sanctioning body for all martial arts prior to WWII. These demonstrations could well be

Figure 6: Gichin Funakoshi, founder of modern karate.

the most historic event in the history of karate, for this was the first time that this fighting system was demonstrated outside of Okinawa. In 1921 he was asked to give a demonstration at Shuri Castle for visiting Crown Prince Hirohito. The prince was so impressed that he mentioned it in his report. This led to Master Funakoshi being invited to give a demonstration to the Ministry of Education in Tokyo, leading to the adoption of karate as part of the school system in Japan.

After World War II, Okinawa was occupied by the United States. Our military servicemen, a long way from home and looking for something to occupy their free time and to perhaps stay in good physical condition, discovered karate. Those men returned home and opened their own karate dojos in various locations throughout America. Thanks to them, karate is now studied and practiced throughout the United States.

Brief Story of Tatsuo Shimabuku - Founder of Isshin-Ryu Karate

Shinkichi Shimabuku was born in Chan, Okinawa on September 19, 1908. He began his study of karate at a young age, training under the instruction of his uncle. Several years later, feeling that he had taught Shinkichi as much as he could, his uncle sent him at the age of 18 to study with Chotoku Kyan. Sensei Kyan was already famous throughout Okinawa as an instructor of Shorin-ryu Karate. Being a poor farmer, Shinkichi walked the long distance to study with Sensei Kyan for several hours each day, then return home to complete his chores. He did this for approximately four years. He later studied karate with Chojun Miyagi of the Goju style of karate, learning at least two kata that he later incorporated into his own Isshin-Ryu system: seiuchin and sanchin.

Harold Long notes in his book *Isshin-Ryu Karate - The Ultimate Fighting Art*, "By 1940, he was recognized throughout the Ryukyu Islands as the foremost proponent of Shorin-ryu and Goju-ryu karate. He was the first person ever to master both systems." He also trained with Choki Motobu, who was one of the greatest fighters in the history of Okinawa, learning naihanchin kata. He also took up the study of Okinawan weaponry such as the bo and sai, as well as the tuifa forms from Taira Shinken, one of Okinawa's leading kobu-jutsu instructors.

It is interesting to note that Master Shimabuku began his study of these weapons in 1959 at the age of 50[4]... several years after the official formulation of Isshin-Ryu. He

---

[4] https://en.wikipedia.org/wiki/Isshin-ry%C5%AB

had mastered both Shorin-ryu and Goju-ryu and was one of the highest sought-after instructors on the island at that time, yet he was humble enough to begin training in another system of martial arts called Kobudo. He continually searched for a variety of techniques to complement and blend with his Isshin-Ryu system. As all true martial artists do, he constantly explored and expanded his capabilities and skills.

During and after WWII, he and his family lived in Japan. He returned to Okinawa in 1947 and began teaching karate. It was also at this time, at the age of 39, that he took the name *Tatsuo*, meaning "Dragon Man." The taking of a karate name is an Okinawan custom. During the next nine years, Tatsuo experimented with a variety of karate techniques. He was an innovator, not being satisfied with following the crowd. Originally, the method of karate that he formulated was called "Chan Migwa-te" to honor his teacher, Chotoku Kyan. On January 15, 1956, he held a meeting to discuss his new style of karate, which he decided to call *Isshin-Ryu*, a blend of techniques from the various systems he trained in and instructors with which he trained.

Figure 7: 1960 - Agena, Okinawa. Grandmaster Shimabuku performing demo in Agena Village. He is driving a nail into a block of wood with side of his hand. Photo attributed to Jake Eckenrode.

Master Shimabuku's movement toward his own method or system of training and not following the crowd aligns with highly proficient martial artists of earlier times on Okinawa – masters such as Tode Sakugawa, Sokon Matsumura, Anko Itosu, and others. As Bruce Clayton, Ph.D. explains in his book *Shotokan's Secrets*, "The old masters were completely different from their modern followers. A master might study with a karate organization, but he would never join one. The "real" masters of karate were Okinawans who studied many arts with many teachers. They moved freely from one teacher to another, cherry-picking the techniques and skills that they thought useful." This is exactly what Tatsuo Shimabuku did by combining elements of both Shorin-ryu and Goju-ryu, along with various other techniques from the instructors under which he trained.

However, Shimabuku stayed true to tradition in some respects. For example, the *seisan* kata is the first form learned in the Isshin-Ryu system. While other styles on Okinawa opted for a more basic kata to begin their curricula, Shimabuku stuck with *seisan* as taught to him by his instructor Chotoku Kyan, as did his brother Eizo Shimabuku in the Shorin-ryu system.

Bruce Clayton, Ph.D. says the *seisan* version that Kyan taught Shimabuku is "based on older versions of Okinawan kata instead of the forms modified at Shuri… the Isshin-Ryu kata are in a time capsule showing karate before Shuri-te." While Shimabuku made some rather innovative changes to his system of training, such as the vertical punch instead of usage of the traditional twisting or corkscrew punch, he maintained some of the historical traditions passed down to him by his instructors.

Figure 8: Formal portrait of Grandmaster Tatsuo Shimabuku, founder of Isshin-Ryu Karate-do. This photo is typically found at the front of all Isshin-Ryu karate dojo.

Many of the senior instructors of karate on Okinawa at the time did not agree with Master Shimabuku's decision to combine elements of various systems and instructors or his new style of karate. Although he was sometimes shunned, and Isshin-Ryu was not officially recognized for many years, he persevered. It did not help the cause when Master Shimabuku's students won local matches and fights.

During the 1950s and 1960s, Master Shimabuku was hired to train the U.S. servicemen stationed on Okinawa. Our U.S. military servicemen were looking for opportunities to learn fighting methods and continue their physical training programs outside of their daily activities on base. Their quest brought them to Master Shimabuku in relatively short order. This is noted in the book *Tales from the Western Generation – Untold Stories and Firsthand History from Karate's Golden Age* where author Matthew Apsokardu states, "Military leaders quickly realized that karate could be used to enhance the skills and fitness of their servicemen and set about hiring reputable instructors from nearby towns. Shimabuku sensei quickly became one of the most active instructors." Apsokardu goes on to note, "Shimabukuro Tatsuo was one of the first major instructors on Okinawa to establish a contractual relationship with the Americans."

Master Shimabuku continued to experiment and challenge the traditional concepts of karate until he retired from active teaching in 1971. Those fortunate Americans who were able to travel to Okinawa and train with him will tell you of a man who enjoyed sake and cigarettes and loved to joke. They will also tell you of a phenomenal martial artist, who struck awe in his students. Master Tatsuo Shimabuku passed away on May 30, 1975.

Isshin-Ryu karate made its way to the United States when U.S. military servicemen who trained with the founder on Okinawa returned home and opened their own dojos to continue their practice and research into their martial art. Subsequent visits back to Okinawa as well as various trips made by Master Shimabuku to the United States further solidified the bonds between the founder and his American students.

Translation of Isshin-Ryu

It is widely accepted Isshin-Ryu literally translates to "one heart way." The kanji for Isshin (一心) breaks down into *Ichi* (一), meaning "one" and *Shin* (心), meaning "heart" or "mind" or "spirit." Together the Ichi and Shin kanji form Isshin to mean "one heart."

The second part of the name is *Ryu* (流), meaning "tradition" or "school." As noted by author Dave Lowry in his book *Sword and the Brush*, the warrior clans of Japan formalized their various ryu, or schools, during the Muromachi period (1300 – 1600). Lowry writes, "…warrior clans began to organize their professional skills, to polish those that were most effective, and to transmit them to other clan members. Such evolution allowed learning from the accumulated experiences of others." Thus, Isshin-Ryu is the formal system of accumulated experiences of Tatsuo Shimabuku.

Note that *Ryu* doesn't translate to "way" as is often used by the vast majority of Isshin-Ryu practitioners. The word "way" in kanji comes from the character *Do*,

Figure 9: Isshin-Ryu (one heart method).

(道), pronounced *doe*. This kanji is often used with the word karate to signify the "way of empty hands," or karate-do. Irrespective of these subtle differences and nuances, the common interpretation is "one heart way." The Order of Isshin-Ryu uses "one heart method."

There is an interesting correlation with the purpose of karate training and the name for which Shimabuku ultimately settled upon for his new system - Isshin-Ryu. Upon being questioned why Master Shimabuku chose the name he replied, "Because all things begin with one.[5]" Martial arts training is intended to unify mind, body, and spirit into a singular demonstration of achievement. Goju-Ryu karate pioneer and author Peter Urban writes in his book *The Karate Dojo*, "Karate can be considered as a philosophy based on the belief that a sound mind is achieved through the development of a virtuous character. A sound body is achieved through rigorous training. The natural result of sound mind and sound body is "oneness." Perhaps Master Shimabuku wanted to tie the goal of karate training to naming his system. Considering the worldwide growth of Isshin-Ryu and the many highly-skilled proponents of the art, there may be something to this theory.

The Original Four

There are four men largely responsible for the proliferation of Isshin-Ryu karate in the United States. Not to disrespect or leave out any others who were on Okinawa around the same time as these four, but these men are commonly regarded as the "Original Four" American students of Isshin-Ryu on Okinawa. Upon their return from duty in the U.S. Marines, each man opened an Isshin-Ryu dojo in their respective locations. Their efforts provided the solid roots of Isshin-Ryu on American soil. No book on Isshin-Ryu karate would be considered complete without some type of information on these four men.

---

[5] Reference social media by A.J. Advincula.

I had the distinct honor of meeting each one except for Master Steve Armstrong. After reading numerous books about the background and history of these important martial artists, I must admit it was a bit intimidating at first to meet them. However, all of them couldn't have been easier to approach and talk to about, not only martial arts, but life in general. These were extremely rugged, honorable, and proud Marines. They were as respectful and pleasant to be around as you could imagine. Deep down, I feel they understood we are all a part of something bigger – Tatsuo Shimabuku's Isshin-Ryu karate system. As such, they wanted to make me feel important and let me know, in the way they talked and treated me, that they were appreciative and thankful for carrying on Isshin-Ryu to the best of my ability.

Below is a brief biography of each of these four legendary martial artists (in alphabetical order). *Note: The source for each bio is from the Isshin-Ryu Hall of Fame website (www.theihof.com), changed slightly to fit the format of this text.*

Steve Armstrong (1931 – 2006)

Figure 10: 1973 Chattanooga, TN. Steve Armstrong (center in white gi) was one of the main pioneers of Isshin-Ryu karate in the United States. L-R: Bob Hill (Bando system), Ed McGrath, Armstrong, U Maung Gyi (Bando system), Don Bohan, Toby Cooling

Steve Armstrong began his study of karate at the age of 16. He continued his training while in the U.S. Marines and notes the following from those early days, "I was a young Marine a long way from home, and I was looking for something to do during my off-duty hours. I watched a group of Japanese Karate-ka through the window of a dojo in Kobe, Japan and decided to go in and show them a thing or two."

Armstrong grew up in Texas where he had 72 amateur boxing matches, winning 68 of them. This set the stage for the eventful day in Kobe, Japan, in 1948. Things just didn't go right for young Armstrong because when he started in Karate he was not quite willing to accept that Karate was a self-defense and that the object was to avoid fighting if possible. His belief at this time was summed up as: "Why do all this training if you were not going to fight?" He studied at a dojo not far from a nearby train station in Kobe, Japan.

In 1949, he had to take some time out for a trip to China. His tour of duty would be up later that year. At that time, having achieved a black belt and after spending a year and a half in the Orient, he was really looking forward to a tour of duty in the United States. After a 30-day leave, he found himself once again back in Japan. This time he was stationed at the Marine Barracks in Yokohama, Japan. Again, he started his studies in Karate, but this time, he was required to begin anew as a white belt as this was different from his original style of Karate. He continued to study Karate in the area and achieved Black Belt status in this new discipline.

Then one day in July 1950, his outfit left for the Korean War. Time passed. After having served in Korea, Sensei Armstrong returned to the U.S. to be stationed at the world famous Marine Barracks in Washington, D.C., where he found himself on the Presidential Honor Guard for President Truman. During these years, he continued his studies in Karate on his own. Finally, he decided to leave the Service to go to college at the University of Texas.

After leaving school, Armstrong re-enlisted in the Marine Corps. This time, he was stationed on the Japanese island of Okinawa where he met a man that would change his life: Master Tatsuo Shimabuku, Founder of Isshin-Ryu Karate. Although already a Black Belt in two different styles of Karate, Armstrong was again required to start as a white belt. Sensei Armstrong has "flatly" stated that while under the tutelage of Master Shimabuku: "This is where I started learning karate and what it is all about. My other instructors were good, but I wasn't a good student. Karate was only a method of fighting for me until I met Shimabuku." Prior to leaving Okinawa for the last time, Sensei Armstrong had become Shimabuku's number two student, second only to Harold Mitchum.

Harold Long (1930 – 1998)

Figure 11: Elkton, MD. L-R - Danny Cross, Harold Long

Harold G. Long was one of thirteen children who attended Central High School in Wartburg, Tennessee where he excelled as a football player. In 1949, Mr. Long joined the United States Marine Corps but was not called to duty until 1950. He was sent to Paris Island, South Carolina where he completed his basic training, and then went to Camp Lejeune, North Carolina, where he completed advanced training. Shortly thereafter, the Korean conflict broke out, and he was transferred to Camp Pendleton, California, to bring the 1st Marine Division up to strength. In 1950, as a young marine in Korea, he fought in the battle of the Chosin Reservoir against the Chinese Army.

In the mid-1950's, Mr. Long was stationed on Okinawa. He always had the desire to study martial arts and inquired who was the best karate instructor on Okinawa. He was told that in Chun Village there was a teacher by the name of Tatsuo Shimabuku, who had the reputation of being the top karate instructor on Okinawa. After three visits to Master Shimabuku's dojo, he was accepted as a student and began training.

Upon returning to the United States, he was stationed at Twenty-nine Palms, California, where he opened his first dojo in his backyard. After his discharge from the Marine Corps, in July 1959, he returned to East Tennessee and opened a dojo at the Marine Reserve Training Center. In 1974, Mr. Long returned to Okinawa to visit with Grand Master Tatsuo Shimabuku. During this visit, he received permission to start a new Isshin-Ryu karate association in the United States.

In December 1995, Master Long closed his dojo in Knoxville, Tennessee, and retired from active teaching. He moved into the U.S. Naval Retirement Home in Gulfport, Mississippi, in 1996. He remained active representing Isshin-Ryu Karate at tournaments, clinics, seminars, and special events.

Harold Mitchum (1933 – 2016)

Figure 12: August, 2005: Master Harold Mitchum with UIKA senior black belts. L-R: Cindy Ingram, Dan Holloway, Mitchum, Tom Lewis, John Ingram

Harold Mitchum spent over seven years studying karate under Master Shimabuku on Okinawa. In 1961, he was appointed by Master Shimabuku as the first president of the American Okinawan Karate Association. While on Okinawa, in addition to studying Isshin-Ryu, Sensei Mitchum studied Shorin-Ryu. His relationship with his teachers was very close, and he learned well. After serving in Korea,

Okinawa, and two tours in Vietnam, Sensei Mitchum returned to the South as a First Sergeant with twenty years in the Marine Corps. After retiring from the military, he opened a dojo.

His philosophy of karate is:

(1) "I personally think that tournaments have terribly distorted the public image of what karate really is."

(2) "I stress hard the very basics of karate and kata, and that when people have the perseverance to stay with karate long enough, they will know without having to demonstrate to themselves or anyone else when they have reached a high degree of enlightenment and ability. I believe in Master Funakoshi's philosophy that the ultimate aim should be the perfection of one's character."

Don Nagle (1938 – 1999)

Figure 13: July 14, 1999 - Elkton, MD. This is widely considered as the last time Grandmaster Nagle wore a karate gi.
L-R: Ralph Passero, Don Nagle, Denny Shaffer, Toby Cooling, Butch Hill, Jung Kim

Don Nagle grew up in Jersey City, New Jersey. While still in high school, Master Nagle began his martial arts training by studying Goju-Ryu karate until his graduation from high school. From there, he joined the United States Marine Corps and was sent to Parris Island, South Carolina for his boot camp. He then transferred to the Advanced Infantry Training School at Camp Lejeune, North Carolina. Within a few months, Master Nagle was transferred to the Third Marine Division, on the island of Okinawa. Within days Sensei Nagle had discovered Soke Tatsuo Shimabuku, the creator of Isshin-Ryu karate. This was in late 1955 in the Kyan (or "Chun") village, on Okinawa. At that time, Okinawa was in the hands of the United States government, since the end of World War II, but within several years would be handed back to the Japanese.

The young Marine, who was probably seventeen at this time, applied as a student of Soke Shimabuku and was eventually accepted after Soke detailed his daily chores, which had to be finished prior to karate studies. It would immediately have been self-evident to Soke that he had a prodigy in his student, Don Nagle. As a white belt, Sensei began to form the fighting style that would become famous throughout the karate world and was so natural and instinctive that, with little change, he would use for the remainder of his life.

According to all who knew and trained with or under him, Sensei Nagle personified economy of movement, who innately understood his opponent's intentions as soon as the opponent's brain created the first and slightest measure of movement in his body. His Isshin-Ryu was an immediate, devastating, and preemptive retaliation to movement. Unless he wished it, his fights lasted but seconds. As the Okinawans meant it to be, he fought in your face, often in a position oblique to your stance and suffocated any techniques that you attempted. He had unlimited speed, whereby his adversary rarely saw, detected or knew what blow ended the match, or where it originated. When you felt that you had trained to the point where you had equaled his speed, he did not just notch it up a bit, he made a quantum leap. He embodied speed. His balance unbalanced your stance and created the errors of which he took full advantage.

Within the eighteen months he spent training under Master Shimabuku, Don Nagle won matches throughout many dojos on Okinawa and finally, he won the legendary Okinawan Championship as a white belt. This was accomplished against the best Okinawan black belts of the time. At this point, he was promoted to 5th degree black belt. Then with his tour of duty up, he was transferred back to the Second Marine Division at Camp Lejeune, North Carolina.

The Nagle dojo turned out numerous fighters and teachers, who in their own right would become part of the legend of Isshin-Ryu karate. Among those students were people such as Rick Niemira, Jim Chapman, Ed McGrath, Don Bohan, Ralph Bove and Lou Lizzote.

Grandmaster Nagle passed on on August 23, 1999. He left behind a legacy of perfection as the only goal, through dedication and perseverance.

The Isshin-Ryu Karate Symbol

The patch or symbol formulated for the Isshin-Ryu karate system contains quite a bit of symbolism. All published accounts of the formulation of the symbol indicate this overall vision as depicted in the photograph below came to Tatsuo Shimabuku in a dream at the time he was formulating his style of martial arts. Isshin-Ryu karate practitioners throughout the world wear a patch on their gi that contains all the elements of Shimabuku's dream. There are several versions of the patch. The number of stars could be either three or five depending on your affiliation. Most patches are oval; however, some organizations utilize a shape that resembles the outline of a vertical fist – one of the main hallmarks of the Isshin-Ryu system.

The figure in the center is half woman and half sea dragon and is called either *Mizu-gami* or *Me-gami*, depending on the organization of Isshin-Ryu karate and what they teach. She represents quiet character and her left hand is open in a universal sign of peace while her right hand is closed in a fist representing strength if evil prevails.

In Asian mythology, the sea serpent is born at the bottom of the sea and ascends to the heavens as depicted by the small dragon above her head. The churning sea and the gray background represent a typhoon. Mizu-gami represents a mother taking care of her child, calm and gentle as a mother would be under these circumstances, but ready to unleash the same amount of fury a mother would if her child was harmed in any fashion. The three stars represent the three arrows of karate: physical, mental, and spiritual.

Figure 14: The Isshin-Ryu Karate Symbol/Patch, one of several versions.

The kanji on the left-hand side means "Isshin-Ryu Karate-do." The words *Isshin-Ryu*, when translated from the Okinawan language, literally means "One Heart

Way". [Note: The word *shin* also means "mind", so it is common you may see translations as "One Heart/Mind Way".] *Karate-do* is translated to mean "the way of empty hands."

The oval shape of the patch is said to represent one of Master Shimabuku's largest innovations in his style of martial arts – the vertical fist of the Isshin-Ryu punch. Okinawan karate systems incorporate a 'twisting' punch whereby the palm side of the hand faces upward in the 'chamber' position on the hip. When the punch is delivered, the fist rotates 180 degrees until the palm side of the fist faces downward upon impact to the intended target. Shimabuku removed this motion when formulating Isshin-Ryu, and the practitioner keeps the fist in a vertical position throughout the execution of the punch. This is considered more efficient and powerful and allows for a 'snapping' motion that is essential in the process of damage to bone targets of the opponent.

Harold Long notes in his book *Isshin-Ryu Karate – The Ultimate Fighting Art*, "The next morning when Master Shimabuku awoke, he felt that his dream had been a divine revelation. He met with his top student, Eiko Kaneshi, and told him of his dream and his desire to break away from Okinawan tradition and start a new style of karate." The symbol was drawn by Kaneshi's uncle, Shosu Nakamine.

Figure 15: Master Bud Ewing at Hombu dojo - Elkton, MD - October 2007. Standing in front of Mizu-gami and OI Torii painting.

Members of the Order of Isshin-Ryu do not wear the patch or symbol of Isshin-Ryu karate that many other organizations wear. There was a period when this was not the case. The 'standard' patch worn by nearly every Isshin-Ryu practitioner was worn by the OI up until 1983.

In a formal letter dated July 19, 1983, from Master Cooling to all OI black belts, it was directed to all members of the OI to remove the Isshin-Ryu patch as a new patch was being developed. The decision to remove the patch took over two years to make as it could not be agreed upon what would replace the Isshin-Ryu patch. This decision was not a popular one. Denshi wrote in his letter, "I realize that this is a very emotional thing and one that is not easy to perform.

Please keep in mind that Master Shimabukuro stated 'Isshin-Ryu Karate is an ever-changing, living thing.' Our new patch will be the growth of his teachings." Soon after Denshi's letter, the OI went back to the original Isshin-Ryu patch but also include a smaller patch with the words *Order of Isshin-Ryu* just above the Mizu-gami patch. That decision was announced formally in a newsletter dated September 15, 1984.

However, in 1994 the practice of wearing the Isshin-Ryu *Mizu-gami* patch was discontinued and has been in effect ever since. When Master Cooling started his Isshin-Ryu training under Tom Lewis in 1966, the Mizu-gami patch was not in use. The founder of the Isshin-Ryu system never wore the Mizu-gami patch, ever. There was much debate by the senior ranking members of the OI around the time Denshi finally decided to remove the patch. The debate continued until Master Barry Smith asked Denshi during a black belt meeting, "Do you want the patch on or off?" After a few seconds, Denshi replied, "I'd like to take it off." Master Smith stood up, turned to everyone in the room and declared, "Take off the patch!" He sat down, looked at Denshi, and casually asked, "Next?"

Figure 16: Nikolina Slijepcevic-Novakovic competing with Chinto kata - 1991. Note the updated Isshin-Ryu patch with the words "Order of Isshin-Ryu" over the Mizu-gami.

The Mizu-gami patch is still worn by the vast majority of Isshin-Ryu karate-ka worldwide. The Order of Isshin-Ryu is not opposed to this practice and many friends of our organization still wear this patch. However, it must be noted and understood that whether someone wears the patch symbolic of Isshin-Ryu karate on their gi does not indicate their level of Isshin-Ryu skill, knowledge, nor respect for the founder of the system. It is simply a tradition chosen by the organization's leader to wear the Mizu-gami patch, if they wish to do so.

Although not worn by the Order of Isshin-Ryu, members are expected to know the history and meaning behind the Mizu-gami.

Shimabukuro – A Karate Family

Tatsuo Shimabuku (formal name is Shimabukuro) came from a family with a rich tradition of martial arts heritage. While he was just eight years of age, he began studying under his uncle. Harold Long writes in his book *Isshin-Ryu Karate – The*

Ultimate Fighting Art, "He walked several miles to the home of his uncle, Urshu Matsumura[6], who was a Shuri-te instructor. He studied informally with his uncle for several years." He soon moved on to study with the leading masters on the island of Okinawa at that time.

Other members of the Shimabuku family attained worldwide notoriety in the martial arts arena and are still actively teaching to this day.

Eizo Shimabuku (1925 - 2017) is the younger brother of Tatsuo and studied under many of the same instructors as his older brother. Among them being Chotoku Kyan and Choki Motobu of Shorin-ryu, Chojun Miyagi of Goju-ryu, and Taira Shinken of Kobu-jutsu. Eizo founded the Shobayashi branch of Shorin-ryu karate. According to Wikipedia[7], in 1959 at the Kodokan in Japan, Kanken Tōyama promoted Eizo Shimabukuro to 10th Dan at the age of 34. This made Eizo Shimabukuro the youngest person ever to receive such an honor. Eizo studied often with his older brother Tatsuo, which may explain why the kata are so similar and Eizo retained Sanchin and Seiunchin from Goju-ryu, in the same fashion that Tatsuo did for Isshin-Ryu.

Tatsuo is one of the first, if not the first, Okinawan instructor to institute free-sparring using full Kendo protective armor to allow for full-contact training while minimizing the risk of injury[8]. This is an interesting point. His younger brother, Eizo, was dan ranked in Kendo and one could speculate that Tatsuo got the idea of using Kendo armor from watching his brother train in Kendo. In fact, Kendo training by some of Okinawa's highest-ranking masters became more and more common as pointed out by contemporary Shorin-Ryu master and author George Alexander in his book *Okinawa: Island of Karate*. Shoshin Nagamine was dan ranked as well in Kendo, and other masters such as Zenryo Shimabukuro and Shigeru Nakamura utilized the armor worn by Kendo-ka in their free sparring practice similar to Tatsuo Shimabuku.

---

[6] According to Wikipedia, the name of Shimabuku's maternal uncle was Shinko Ganeko.
[7] https://en.wikipedia.org/wiki/Sh%C5%8Dbayashi_Sh%C5%8Drin-ry%C5%AB
[8] https://en.wikipedia.org/wiki/Isshin-ry%C5%AB

Figure 17: Actual Kendo protective armor which Master Cooling brought back from Okinawa in 1970.

Kichiro Shimabuku (b. 1939), is the eldest son of Tatsuo Shimabuku. Harold Long states in his book *Isshin-Ryu Karate* that he turned over the system to Kichiro upon his retirement from active teaching in early 1972. Kichiro continues to head the Isshin-Ryu World Karate Association (IWKA) from Uruma City, Okinawa and travels frequently around the world, including the United States, to teach Isshin-Ryu. He was inducted into the International Isshin-Ryu Hall of Fame in 2012.

Shinso Shimabuku (1942 - 2006), was the second son of Tatsuo Shimabuku. He began his training in Isshin-Ryu karate under his father when he was 14 years old. Nicknamed "Ciso" he was remembered as being a critical member of his father's dojo by helping to teach in the early years of Isshin-Ryu when the dojo became quite busy with numerous American servicemen coming to train. Shinso was inducted into the International Isshin-Ryu Hall of Fame in 2009.

Angi Uezu (b. 1935), married Tatsuo Shimabuku's third daughter Yukiko. In 1987, he founded the Okinawan Isshin-Ryu Karate Kobudo Association (OIKKA) which continues to this day. Master Uezu has traveled extensively throughout the world to spread the art of Isshin-Ryu. In 1996, he passed the leadership of the OIKKA to Tsuyoshi Uechi. Angi Uezu was inducted into the International Isshin-Ryu Hall of Fame in 1997.

Chapter 2
HISTORY OF THE ORDER OF ISSHIN-RYU

"For any art to remain dynamic, it must be granted the freedom to grow and develop."

Grandmaster Toby Cooling

Toby Cooling started his martial arts career by studying Judo at the age of 16. The doctor told his mother that since he was anemic, he needed to participate in some type of physical activity. As Denshi recalls, "I was too small for football and basketball, and I was terrible at baseball. In the 1960s, Judo was the major form of martial arts offered in the United States, so I gave it a try and quickly realized I found what I was looking for." During this time, Master Cooling would head to the local newsstand and pick up the latest issue of Black Belt magazine. In 1966, one of those issues included an advertisement on a form of karate called *Isshin-Ryu*. As fate would have it, the Isshin-Ryu karate dojo of Tom Lewis happened to be a block away from where Denshi bought the magazine in Salisbury, Maryland. So, at 20 years of age, Master Cooling began his Isshin-ryu training under Master Tom Lewis at 714 E. Main Street in Salisbury, Maryland.

Figure 18: Sample cover of Black Belt magazine from 1966.

He continued training in Isshin-Ryu and earned his black belt under Master Lewis in 1967, after only nine months of dedicated study. His Isshin-Ryu training also involved training under such early Isshin-Ryu notables as Don Nagle and Joel Buchholtz. Eventually, Toby established a martial arts program in 1964 in Cecil County[9] and became the first to open a karate school on the Upper Eastern Shore of Maryland in 1967.

Master Cooling visited the dojo of Master Don Nagle in Jersey City, New Jersey frequently over the years. Denshi recalls, "When I heard that Master Shimabuku was still alive, I had to make a trip to Okinawa to train with him. I was single at the time, and I had the resources to make it happen." He goes on to say, "The way I see it, if your training means anything, you go to the source. If Master Shimabuku lived in Florida, I would've traveled there. But he happened to live in Okinawa. It didn't matter, I had to train *with* him wherever he was." It became Toby's mission to travel to the land where the system he trained in was developed. He wanted to get there and train and learn under the direct instruction of the founder of the Isshin-Ryu system, Tatsuo Shimabuku. Before traveling to train with the founder, he had all the Isshin Ryu kata, except for *shi shi no kun dai*, or the third and final bo form.

When he arrived on Okinawa, he called home to let his parents know he arrived safely. When they asked where he was, they thought he was in Oklahoma instead of Okinawa, Japan! He laughed it off and said he would be home in a few months. Denshi recalls meeting Master Shimabuku at his dojo with a letter of introduction in hand prepared by both Don Nagle and Steve Armstrong where he explains, "I sent a copy of each letter to him before I went to Okinawa. And then brought a copy with me to hand to him once I got there." When Denshi arrived at the dojo and, upon request, performed several kata, Master Shimabuku said he would accept him as a student.

Denshi recalls from the initial meeting, "The dojo was his home. I walked in across the floor and I thought it was his garage, but it was the dojo. He must have gotten the concrete for free because it was far from an even floor. I walked up to a sort of 'stage area' with my shoes on. He looked at my shoes and shook his head 'no' since, as many know, the custom in the Orient is that shoes are not worn in the house. I finally realized it wasn't a garage but was actually part of his house." Soon after removing his shoes, Shimabuku grabbed a western-style chair sitting near his desk. Sitting down, Master Shimabuku said, "Soke catchy Toby-san karate-do." When asked what he meant by 'catchy' Master Cooling stated, "He spoke very broken English. I didn't really understand it at first either. But based on his gestures I

---

[9] *Karate: An Art of Excellence,* by Frank Williams. Cecil Whig, August 31, 1989.

could tell he wanted me to demonstrate some Isshin-Ryu for him since he knew I was a black belt based upon the letter he had from Nagle and Armstrong. I figured he was speaking of himself (soke) and he wanted to 'catch' whatever I could demonstrate for him so he could evaluate my karate at that point and see if he wanted to take me on as a student."

For several minutes Denshi showed him everything he could think of. Finally, Shimabuku simply said to him, "Ok. I teach." Denshi said, "It was an exciting moment in my martial arts as I felt privileged to learn and study from the founder of my style, even though I knew it was only going to be for a short amount of time. Master Shimabuku was lightning fast, just like Don Nagle. When you fought Sensei Nagle, all you saw was the punch going back. You could never catch up to it."

Denshi lived in an apartment right behind Shimabuku's dojo, maybe 30 feet or so away. The Mayor of Agenda owned the apartments. He rented two rooms, one with a bath. Shimabuku started every class by saying, *yasume, kiotske, rei*, essentially meaning attention and bow. Denshi explains, "He'd then go have a domino cigarette. If mama-san wasn't around, he'd have a shot of sake, if she was in the house he'd opt for tea instead. He'd say *steps* and you would run around the dojo for a while. Sometimes I'd lead the class. You would run through techniques and exercises. Eventually, you'd take a break due to the heat, and then practice kata to finish off the workout. I always tried to sneak up next to Master Shimabuku when practicing my kata, so he'd see how I performed. If he looked at it and thought it was good enough, he'd show you a few extra moves. If he didn't like your performance, he would shake his head and let you know it wasn't good enough and show you the proper way to do it."

During class time, Shimabuku was in gi. He always would begin and end every class with gi and proper rei or bow to show respect. When asked about the amount of time in the dojo, Denshi remembers, "I was in the Air Guard (not active duty), so I went over to Okinawa as a civilian. Therefore, I could go into the dojo during the day and train all by myself, hoping he would look over and notice in order to get some private lessons. On one particular day, I was doing kata and for whatever reason, I simply couldn't get through a sequence. I tried over and over and nothing was registering. I just couldn't get it down." After watching for a bit, Master Shimabuku finally said, "Toby-san, nobody home. Nobody home today. You go. Come back tomorrow." He was telling Denshi that, mentally he was not having a good session and he should try again the next day.

Regarding Shimabuku's family and whether Denshi had any chance to interact with them, Denshi recalls, "I would see mama-san all the time. I also trained with Ciso (Shimabuku's son) here and there." Shimabuku's English was broken, but that didn't create a hurdle for Denshi since karate terms were well-known. Learning was a combination of pidgin English, karate speak, and physically showing the students right from wrong.

"One afternoon I walked in and Kanei Uechi[10] was visiting with Master Shimabuku. Nobody else was there. I just turned about face and walked out, that scared the heck out of me seeing two 10th dan black belts sitting around talking. I didn't want to stick my head where I didn't think I belonged." After class, students would often sit and drink with Master Shimabuku. Shimabuku called Denshi "cake[11]-boy" because he didn't drink alcohol. If you didn't drink alcohol the custom was to eat cake.

Denshi relates a story where one time he got into a confrontation in Koza. As Denshi recalls, "When I got back, Shimabuku and mama-san were there at the dojo, and he started giving me the once over where he essentially was telling me, 'You give Isshin-Ryu a bad name!' After mama-san left, he leaned into me and asked, 'Toby-san, did you win?'"

Figure 19: 1970 Okinawa. L-R: Kichiro Shimabuku, Toby Cooling, Tatsuo Shimabuku

The last class Denshi attended on Okinawa, Master Shimabuku called him to the front of the class. He had a good idea he was likely getting promoted; however, he was hesitant at first since that was not the reason he wanted to train in Okinawa. He didn't go there for rank, he went there for knowledge. Upon receiving his promotion to roku-dan (6th-degree black belt), Master Shimabuku said to him, "Toby-san, go back and teach good Isshin-Ryu. Make happy family." This was a directive that Master Cooling took seriously. He made it a personal vow to do just that, teach sound Isshin-Ryu karate to those with a true commitment to Isshin-Ryu

---

[10] Kanei was the son of Kanbun Uechi, founder of Uechi-ryu karate, one of the primary styles of karate on Okinawa.
[11] Denshi pronounces it 'kay-kee' as Shimabuku would have at the time.

and foster growth within the members of his organization – or more appropriately stated, his *family*.

After returning from Okinawa, Master Cooling visited and stayed with Master Steve Armstrong for about a week and taught some of his classes. Denshi wore the standard black belt during all the classes. Armstrong eventually pulled Denshi aside. The conversation went something like this:

Armstrong – "I understand Master Shimabuku promoted you to sixth-degree black belt. But you're not wearing a red and white belt. How come you're not wearing it?"

Cooling – "I feel I'm too young for that."

Armstrong – "Well, he is betting on the come."

Cooling – "What do you mean?"

Armstrong – "Yeah, you're not a red and white belt now. But he may never see you again. He feels strongly enough about you and he's betting that you will eventually come up to that rank. If you don't want to wear that belt or you're ashamed to wear the red and white belt that Shimabuku gave you, leave it in my dojo. I can use an extra red and white belt. You *should* wear it everywhere you go."

The following excerpt is directly from the current OI student manual:

The Order of Isshin-Ryu was founded on January 15, 1971, and is a fraternity of the students of Toby Cooling.

Purpose: The Order of Isshin-Ryu was created to:

Eliminate any and all political feelings involved in Isshin-Ryu Karate;

Provide and support *shiai* for members;

Keep the cost of student participation low;

Regulate the quality and fairness of judging;

Maintain the value of the black belt by strict rules and regulations to obtain the rank;

Unite for unification of standards; and

Teach Isshin-Ryu kata and knowledge of karate as taught to us by Master Cooling.

The Order of Isshin-Ryu is comprised of karate-ka who believe in the honor and ethics of the martial arts. A member's word is their bond; when they say they are going to do something, they do it, otherwise, they are in the wrong organization. The Order of Isshin-Ryu is not a religious organization – it is a way of life that holds a common bond for many people from different walks of life.

- Toby Cooling, 1971

The Early Days of the OI

Toby Cooling was the first to bring Isshin-Ryu karate to the upper eastern shore of Maryland. The OI dojo found many homes. The first five students to train with Master Cooling were Richard Krischbaum, Cliff Beck, Johnny Dolar, Leroy Sewell, and Bob Foard who was 12 years old at the time. Krischbaum was the first black belt ever awarded in the Order of Isshin-Ryu. Master Cooling recalls, "I was a brown belt at the time. Master Tom Lewis gave me permission to begin teaching students, and we trained on my parent's front yard in Chesapeake City." Foard recalls, "The dojo moved around quite a bit back then. From his Dad's house, it moved into the elementary school in Elkton, then the Holly Hall building behind what is now Elk Mall, then into a building next to Hershey's Restaurant on Main Street, and finally to its current home in the rear of Jayco Liquors, which sits along Rt. 40 in Maryland."

In the summer of 1970, Tom Sanson met Master Cooling for the first time after a job offer in Towson, Maryland forced him to move to the area from Pittsburgh,

Pennsylvania. At the time, Tom was training under Bill Duessel[12]. He also had trained under other early Isshin-Ryu black belts in the late sixties including James Morabeto. Tom missed training with the founder by several years as both Duessel and Morabeto were the first to sponsor a trip by Shimabuku to the United States in 1964[13]. Traveling to the U.S. was a rarity for the founder as he only made the trip on two occasions – in 1964 and 1966.

Prior to Sensei Sanson's move to Maryland, Mr. Duessel provided several names for Tom to seek out for continuing his Isshin-Ryu training. However, he was very emphatic for Tom to meet Toby Cooling. After several attempts to meet up, they finally connected and from there started a very long martial arts training relationship. At the time, Denshi was finishing up his degree at the University of Baltimore. Tom helped with transportation and Denshi provided karate instruction.

Another of the earliest members of the Order of Isshin-Ryu was Buster Hash. In his hometown of Joppatowne, Maryland, Hash started his martial arts training at 17 years of age in the rugged style from Japan called

Figure 20: 1972 - Tom Sanson in Pittsburg, PA. The OI attended a tournament held by George Dillman.

Kyokushinkai, founded by legendary martial artist Mas Oyama. After enlisting in the Army and being deployed to Seoul, South Korea, Sensei Hash later earned his black belt in Song Moo Kwan while training under SGT Hong Kyung Wan, a 5th degree black belt. SGT Wan was assigned as a Korean Augmentation United States Army (KATUSA). In 1970, Buster competed as a red belt (brown belt) in a national Song Moo Kwan Tae Kwon Do tournament placing 3rd overall in the black belt division. Mr. Hash eventually competed for and was awarded a first-degree black belt in

---

[12] Bill Duessel, inducted into the Isshin-Ryu Hall of Fame in 2000, would later receive 10th dan ranking from Kichiro Shimabuku at the 2013 Isshin-Ryu World Karate Association tournament in Akron, Ohio. Grandmaster Duessel passed away in 2014.

[13] https://en.wikipedia.org/wiki/Tatsuo_Shimabuku

Taekwondo at the Song Moo Kwan school in Seoul in 1970 and was recognized by the National Tae Kwon Do Association later that year.

Returning to the states in 1970, Buster searched for a Taekwondo school in the Edgewood area. At that time, Jhoon Rhee was the big deal in the DC area but had no schools in the Edgewood, Aberdeen area. Buster was working on his Associates Degree at Harford Junior College and found a flyer announcing a karate class to be held at the school in early January 1971. He dug out his old white belt, took off his Taekwondo patches, and showed up for class on a cold January night. The classes were being taught by Isshinryu brown belts out of Elkton, MD; John Patti and Dennis Longo, and a guest brown belt were visiting; his name was Tom "Buffy" (short for buffalo) Sanson. He immediately connected with Sanson, and they have been great friends ever since. Buster recalled from those earliest training sessions, "One day during class, a guy named Toby Cooling showed up with one of his students, John King. We sparred for the longest time. I decided these are the people I want to train with."

In those early days of the OI, Buster remembers classes were lopsided towards kumite since that was what everyone preferred to do in their training. Everyone just wanted to spar the entire class. He recalls kata was a necessary evil. You did kata because you had to. He remembers, "That was one of Denshi's biggest frustrations. He could never quite get his students to perform kata exactly the same. His goal was to make all of our kata identical." Sensei Hash received san-dan (3rd degree black belt) from Grandmaster Cooling in 1983; however, career and family took him away from his continual training and study in the OI. Regardless, Sensei Hash to this day still attends OI functions such as the shiai and black belt testing. He puts it in this context, "It's not about rank. If you're here for belts or rank, you're missing the point of being a part of this family."

Barry Smith remembers going to college with Denshi at the University of Baltimore. He notes, "We trained constantly. And then one day he tells me, 'I'm going to Okinawa to train with Shimabuku.' I couldn't believe it! The semester was still going and he just up and leaves for Okinawa." After several months of intensive training with the founder of Isshin-Ryu, Master Cooling returned home. Smith not so fondly recalls, "When he came back from Okinawa, he demoted me from Ik-kyu (the rank just below black belt) back down to green belt. No reason. No explanation. He just told me one day before class to put on a green belt."

Smith eventually started the Cambridge, Maryland dojo as a brown belt. He tells of the way Master Cooling taught his students. "Denshi had students punching cinder block walls. Once I was hardly tapping the wall, and he came up behind me and said, 'Hit the wall!' I gave him a look like he was insane. After a few minutes, he said to everyone, 'Okay, let's fight.' That's how those workouts went back then."

The first two women to receive sho-dan ranking in the Order of Isshin-Ryu happened in 1969. This was two years before the actual formulation of the OI. According to Denshi, Lois Drummond and Theresa Nickle were solid karate-ka and rightfully earned the honor to wear the black belt of Isshin-Ryu karate. Both women eventually earned their ni-dan (2nd degree black belt) rankings prior to becoming inactive in their training.

The highest-ranking female in the Order of Isshin-Ryu is Diane Ortenzio. Currently holding hachi-dan ranking (8th degree black belt), Diane is still extremely active in martial arts and going very strong. Few women in the entire world have even seen 8th dan black belt level, much less remain diligent in their ongoing training and learning. Master Ortenzio has extended her training into other arts such as Modern Arnis and Kombatan, both arts originating from the Phillippines (reference Chapter 10). She is truly making a name for herself in those systems in tandem with her Isshin-Ryu experience where she was inducted into the Isshinryu Hall of Fame in 2003.

Shiai

The word *shiai*, in general, means "game" or "competition." *Shi* translates as "test," or "to test." *Ai* translates as "join," "gathering," or "meet." In terms of karate, shiai stands for "a meeting to test" the current skills of those gathered. Presently, the OI gathers three times a year for competition among its members. These shiai, or competitions, are held in Chesapeake City, Maryland at Bohemia Manor High School. Prior to that, the shiai was held at Cecil Community College.

Current students of the OI might probably think these locations were always used for OI shiai; however, this is not the case going back to the early days of the OI. According to Sensei Tom Sanson, the annual shiai within the Order of Isshin-Ryu were often held at the old dojo on Front Street across from the Veteran of Foreign Wars in Elkton, Maryland. This was just a two-room storefront. Generally, the participants consisted of one or two green belts and several brown belts. Back then, the group consisted of Bucky Garrett, Buster Hash, Barry Smith and John King. Tom Sanson recalls, "You were almost assured of placing just by showing up." The black belts were John King and Richard Krisbaum, both of ni-dan ranking. Later, the shiai was moved to the grade school in Chesapeake City, Maryland.

Back then, the OI was obviously a small group; however, everyone got along very well. The shiai consisted of sparring and kata. Sanson notes, "It was a time

Figure 21: Two of the earliest OI members. L-R: Charlie Deitterick, Master Barry Smith.

of **no egos.** Everybody had different backgrounds but just enjoyed doing karate. I am not glorifying that time, it was a fairly small group, and it just worked. Barry Smith was a tough brown belt as was Bucky Garrett. Buster Hash introduced high kicks. John King had a slow method of sparring that confounded everyone. It was a time when Denshi on down to all of the black belts invited you to their house for dinner, and amazing friendships grew. Friendships that last to this day."

At one of the earliest OI shiai held in June 1972 at Bohemia Manor High School, Buster Hash, Bucky Garrett, and Bob Burns were promoted to sho-dan (1st degree black belt). Master Cooling recalls, "They were all brown belts and doing extremely well. The number of students participating and competing at the shiai started growing, and I needed corner referees. So, I promoted all three of those guys to black belt."

Another early student of the OI, Charlie Deitterick, recalls those shiai as well. Charlie's first sensei was Tom Miller and remembers the dojo at the University of Maryland, "We would travel up to Elkton to train with Toby. I was in my early twenties back then, and I didn't care too much for kata. I preferred to spar and just enjoyed being with the other guys and training hard. Everyone got along well, and we all clicked."

In the early 70s, there were no set number of shiai held every year as there is today where the shiai are held in the Spring, Summer, and Fall of each year. But 45 years ago, the shiai were held when Denshi sent out a handwritten note to all dojos and black belts informing them he wanted to hold a shiai. At one point, the shiai was held in the backyard of black belt Bucky Garrett's (*see figure 22*) house. It was at this location where Tom Sanson earned his san-dan (3rd degree black belt) via a black eye administered by Master Cooling.

Figure 22: 1971 – Elkton, Maryland
Seated front row L-R: Bud Ewing (far right)
Kneeling 2nd row L-R: unknown, Kenny Hopkins, unknown, Bailey Russel, Curtis Jones
Standing L-R: John Nichol, Ronnie Gray, Phil Stanley, Bill Spence, unknown, unknown, Bucky Garrett

Times were different back then. Although padding used for kumite or sparring, was available the usage of this equipment was minimal or non-existent. The use of protective gear was pretty much a dojo-by-dojo judgment call, something not exactly enforced in the strictest sense. However, lawyers and insurance concerns have certainly made an impact on those earlier days, and now the use of sparring equipment is mandatory.

Figure 23: May 1977 – Elkton, MD. John McDonald (on right) during kumite match with an unknown opponent at the annual OI shiai. Note that hand and foot padding were not in use around this time. Toby Cooling serving as center referee on the left. Bob Whited (black gi to the right of McDonald) is serving as corner referee. Larry Jackson is seated to the right of Whited. Bob Burns is seated in bleachers at top right of photo.

Figure 24: 1973 - Bel Air, MD. Line up of black belts at a shiai held at Bel Air Armory. L-R: Malachi Lee, Maria Melendez, John Remick, Bob Burns, Barry Smith, Buster Hash, John King, Tom Sanson, Tom Miller, Bucky Garrett, unknown.

At that time in the OI's history, the organization of these events were not as formalized as they are today. There simply wasn't as many members back then. The OI was only several years old. As such, students stepped up and offered locations to hold events. The shiai in 1973 was one such location where Charlie Deitterick (blue belt at the time) provided a location at the Bel Air, Maryland armory. In terms of numbers, there were about 12 black belts available to judge 20-30 students. According to Sensei Deitterick, this is when Malachi Lee started to attend the OI shiai, traveling down from New York City.

In the 80s, whenever students from Puerto Rico were able to make the trip to Elkton, Maryland, Denshi had them stay at the homes of various OI members. Sensei Kurt Kline recalls while being a blue belt, "Everyone from Puerto Rico stayed with me. At that point in time, nobody got a hotel. Ever since then, every year they would stay with me. They would teach me Spanish, and being a teenager, I fumbled through it. Sensei Jiménez enjoyed playing chess, and he always lost to me."

The Order of Isshin-Ryu shiai continues to this day. Currently, there are three shiai held every year. One of the unique aspects of the shiai is there are no 'women's divisions.' Women compete right along with the men in every division. Master Cooling attempted many times to have a separate women's division to foster, as much as possible, fairness of competition; however, the feedback was always the same: women are more likely to be attacked by a man on the street, so it makes more sense to compete against the men in all categories – weapons, kata, and kumite, or sparring.

Kata Clinics

The OI also held outdoor kata clinics in various locations such as Calvert Hall, Maryland, or Denshi's front yard in Chesapeake City, Maryland. Back in the early 1970s, the OI dojo consisted of Hombu dojos in Elkton, Calvert Hall, University of Maryland, and Cambridge, Maryland where Barry Smith had his dojo over a foundry. Charlie Deitterick opened a dojo in Edgewood, MD as well. Just prior to going into the Army, Sensei Deitterick was at one time teaching classes at three different dojos. Malachi Lee, who started his Isshin Ryu training under Ed McGrath, joined the Order of Isshin-Ryu in 1972. His students followed him into the OI fold, including notables such as Isham Latimer, Maria Melendez, John McDonald, and eventually John Costanzo.

Tom Sanson notes, "I do not remember what fostered the clinics, but it is probably in some way the result of building on the sparring.

Figure 25: 1974 kata clinic at the residence of Bucky Garrett in Elkton, MD. L-R: Malachi Lee, Bucky Garrett, John King, John Remick. Standing: Bill Spence

One night in the early 70s, Denshi and I sparred for an hour and 20 minutes. A few weeks later, Denshi and Mr. Hash went about an hour and 45 minutes. It was a time of brotherhood and for the most part, we just got along." Sensei Sanson goes on to state, "Denshi always said 'who do you think I learned from'? It was us, but it took a while to figure that out. And, he could spar at whatever level was needed. If he sparred with me at brown belt, it was like sparring with an opponent two levels above. Denshi did not push us verbally. He didn't have to. We wanted to train and train hard. However, he was always there with whatever we needed next. It seemed that Denshi had the OI in mind early on." Sensei Sanson was a brown belt when students from northern New Jersey and New York City started to come down and visit. Tom recalls, "Some black belts were serious, and some were not, but Denshi always seemed to know the difference."

Figure 26: 1974 – Master Cooling during a break for a kata clinic at the residence of black belt Bucky Garrett in Elkton, MD.

Communication from Denshi to all black belts during those early years was through the good old U.S. Postal Service as the internet was futuristic technology. Denshi informed black belts of upcoming OI events such as the shiai (competition) and information for public demonstrations using standard mail. A listing of OI black belts from 1976 looked like this:

Walter Cooling	Milledge Murphey
John King	Maria Melendez
Tom Sanson	Bill Spence
William Garrett	Perry Hall
Barry Smith	Bud Ewing

Tom Miller	Charlie Deitterick
Charles Hash	Dale Stanton
John Nickle	John Judway
Bob Burns	Juan Lopez
Bob Whited	Jose Diaz
John Remick	

Bud Ewing recalls from the early days, "Toby and I became the best of friends. He taught me a lot of martial arts over the years. I'm not necessarily creative, and I've learned from many people over the years, but everything I know and have in martial arts is because of Master Cooling. The best thing about meeting up with Toby was his father. His father taught me everything about business. About accounting and book work, on how to run a business. He taught me how to be a person in business, still be a nice guy but also get things done. Without the martial arts, I would never have had that opportunity to be who I am today in business."

Sensei Charlie Deitterick remembers from the earliest days of OI training, "For one, I wasn't looking for rank. I just enjoyed the workouts and particularly, the sparring aspect of training. I didn't want to have anything to do with any sort of politics. Denshi kept everything straightforward. When I went up for black belt, nobody told me anything. I had no idea I was about to test. My sensei, Tom Miller, just walked over and asked me 'Are you ready?' I said, 'Ready for what?' And I looked over and the judges were lined up waiting for me."

Open Tournaments

The late 1960s and early 1970s saw the beginnings of sport karate competition take hold across the United States. In 1964, Ed Parker, the founder, and pioneer of Kenpo karate in America, organized a highly successful tournament in Long Beach, California and The Long Beach International Karate Championships continues to run to this day. Parker's tournament is where Bruce Lee was famously discovered by movie executives after demonstrating his Jeet Kune Do system[14].

On the east coast, major competitors made their way to New York City for a tournament held by Aaron Banks whose first show premiered in 1966 and eventually became so popular it was held in Madison Square Garden and televised on ABC's Wide World of Sports. During his life, Banks promoted 352 karate tournaments[15].

---

[14] https://en.wikipedia.org/wiki/Long_Beach_International_Karate_Championships
[15] https://en.wikipedia.org/wiki/Aaron_Banks

Another big tournament was held in Washington D.C. sponsored by Maung Gyi, the founder of Bando, which is a martial art from Burma. In the 1960s Gyi began teaching Bando at American University[16] in Washinton, D.C. Master Cooling made a point to attend his tournament and over time, they became good friends.

Another big tournament at this time was the East Coast Nationals held in Ocean City, Maryland by Harvey Hastings. In attendance and competed were the likes of Chuck Norris, Bill Wallace, Fred Wren, etc. At that point in time, it was one of the biggest tournaments around. Hidy Ochiai was the main forms competitor. This tournament is where Order of Isshin-Ryu would often attend and compete considering the proximity to many OI dojos at the time.

Charlie Deitterick recalls from the 1974 Ocean City event, "I competed in kumite as a brown belt. At that time, the pads became a requirement, but I didn't have any. Jhoon

Figure 27: 1974 - East Coast Nationals in Ocean City, MD. L-R: Charlie Deitterick, Toby Cooling

Rhee's equipment was becoming popular. I explained to the judges that I was without any gear, and at first, they weren't going to let me fight. I pleaded my case and they eventually let me slide. This would never happen today. But back then, things were different."

Demos

Demonstrations are often a necessary element of any dojo to generate interest in the dojo and seek new enrollees to build up the student base. Demos at community events, local schools, after-school activities such as boy scouts and girl scouts, the list is limited by the dojos' imagination. Denshi remembers, "That's how we would get students in the old days. You would have to go out and put on demonstrations. We would do all sorts of crazy stuff. Use bull whips, lay on a bed of nails, break

---

[16] https://en.wikipedia.org/wiki/Maung_Gyi

boards. Someone who I used to buy liquor from (Denshi owned a liquor store in Elkton, MD, which is now owned by Bud Ewing) would help us with the bullwhip segment. He would stand with both arms extended to the sides and hold rolled up newspaper in both hands." For the reader with limited knowledge of martial arts training, bear in mind there is no requirement to train with, let alone become expert in using a bullwhip. However, back in the 1970s, you needed to do *something* to draw attention and bring in students. Martial arts was simply not that popular to the masses at this point. As Denshi puts it, "I said to Bud, 'Go find a bullwhip. I have something I want you to practice.' So, he did. He came back to Jayco with a whip and started practicing outside. He hit everything but the target almost every time, including himself."

Figure 28: 1974 Elkton Days Festival. Master Cooling breaking boards being thrown.

At another demo, Denshi cut a watermelon on the belly of Jimmy Nicholson, black belt Sotiere Nicholson's father. As Denshi tells the story, "Jimmy asked me, 'How many times have you done this?' I replied, 'This is my first time Jimmy.'"

The demonstrations proved successful. Many students came to join the Elkton dojo. In those early days, Denshi had an open-door policy. Anyone who wanted to take karate had the opportunity to train.

Matching Superfoot

Bill 'Superfoot' Wallace was an outstanding martial artist who became the middleweight world full-contact karate champion in 1974[17]. He retired an undefeated 23-0 from the full-contact ring and became highly successful running kicking and stretching seminars across the world. Wallace began to study Judo in 1966 and was forced to discontinue because of an injury he suffered to his right knee during practice. He then began to study Shorin-ryu karate in 1967 while serving in the Air Force. Superfoot earned his nickname for his tremendously fast roundhouse and hook kicks using primarily his left leg, which was clocked at about 60 mph. His prior injury in Judo to his right knee ended up allowing him to develop his kicking skills with his left leg to a point that nobody had ever seen before.

In the early 80s, Bud Ewing attended one of Superfoot's seminars along with a few other OI members. Master Ewing explains, "I was there working with my seminar training partner, just trying my best to practice the kicks and concepts Wallace was teaching. Then at one point when he stopped the seminar to explain another technique, he told me to come up front with him and be his partner. Apparently, he noticed my kicks and told me, 'I want you up front with me.' He demonstrated a kick and then asked me to perform it against him. So, I did. We then went back and forth with various kicks. He wanted to show the audience what I was doing and, I guess, give me some of the spotlight because he liked what I was doing." Getting emotional, Master Ewing confessed, "That was one of the highlights of my karate career."

The Maryland Dojo

The OI was founded in Elkton, Maryland. As a result, the state of Maryland has seen the most activity with respect to the opening of dojos and the change of instructors. To document the history of all dojos within the state of Maryland since 1971 would be a monumental task at the very least. The table below provides an idea of the various dojos and sensei over the years.

---

[17] https://en.wikipedia.org/wiki/Bill_Wallace_(martial_artist)

Year	Location	Sensei
1971 – present	Cambridge	Barry Smith
Unknown	Hartford Community College	Tom Miller
Unknown	Baltimore	John Remick
1972 – 1974	Edgewood	Buster Hash Tom Miller John Patti
Unknown	Various	Charlie Deitterick
1979 – 1985	Baltimore Highlands	Jeff Bracone
1981 – 1987	Beltsville	Ken Varney
1987 – 1990	College Park	Ken Varney
1978 – 1986	North East	Bailey Russell
1986 – 2015	North East	Mike Goodyear
1989 – 1991	Elkton	Curtis Jones
1991 – present	Elkton	Ronnie Cimorosi
1993 – present	Elkton	Ron Tyree
1992 – 2012	Easton	Bill Sullivan
2012 – present	Easton	Mike Magill
1999 – 2014	Olney	Alan Jenkins
1996 – 2013	Baltimore	Pete & Gerry Ankers

Coming Into the OI Fold

Joining the Order of Isshin-Ryu is not an automatic process. Merely being an Isshin-Ryu karate practitioner is not enough. You don't simply pay a membership fee and gain acceptance. One must formally request consideration to join. The OI is family. As such, its members are highly protective of current family members. I can attest to this personally. Upon meeting Denshi for the first time, he explained the 'process' to me. I thought, in my mind, okay I'll ask him if I can join the OI. Upon verbalizing my wishes, Denshi simply said, "Thanks for your interest, Sensei Popp. Make sure you come to the next shiai." That's it. Little did I realize I had to make a positive impression on *everyone*, not just the head of the organization.

The list of honorary members of the OI is short, to say the least. In the nearly 50 years of the OI's existence, the following is this list:

Butch Hill

Carl Martin
Frank Hastings

Recently, Master Bob Kristensen of Grapevine, Texas and his organization, Texas Isshinryu Karate Kai, have come into the OI fold, yet they retain their autonomy as a karate school. They have traveled in tandem with OI members to visit Sensei Jesús M. Jiménez in Puerto Rico along with being frequent guests of the annual OI shiai.

As Denshi relates, "I don't care the size of the package or the color of the wrapping paper of the package, I care about what's inside." These men are decent human beings who I'm proud and honored to be associated with."

****

There are various OI dojos within the state of Maryland where the OI was founded; however, there have been sensei and dojos outside of the 'home state' that have joined the ranks. Below is a brief discussion on those dojos that have gained acceptance into the OI family.

New York

The New York dojo entered the OI family early in the 1970s. According to Master Cooling, Dennis Bootle told Malachi Lee about this Isshin-ryu guy from Maryland that Malachi should meet. Denshi tells the story this way:

"I was fresh from being back from Okinawa and at a workout in New York. Malachi walks over to me and asks, 'Are you Toby Cooling?' I responded, 'Yes I am and you're Malachi Lee.' Malachi said, 'How'd you know my name?' to which I said, 'Well, you're the only 6'7" black guy in the room!' We both laughed, and I then asked him, 'How did you know I was Toby Cooling?' Malachi replied, 'Because you were the only one in the room watching everything I was doing.' We instantly connected from then on."

Sensei John McDonald recalls, "After about my first year of training, around 1972, I walked into the dojo one day and Denshi was there. Sensei Lee introduced him to everyone. The next thing I knew, we attended a shiai in Maryland, and soon after, we were a part of the OI."

Isham Latimer took a slightly different route into the Order of Isshin-Ryu. He started karate training in 1972 and attained black belt three years later in another Isshin-Ryu organization in Huntington, New York. He then went on to do some 'renegade' training in various systems of Kung Fu, at Adelphi University, and then trained with one of the top instructors of Grandmaster Moses Powell (1941 – 2005), in the Sanuces Ryu Jujitsu system.

Although Latimer enjoyed the variety of different arts available in New York City, he still wanted to find a good Isshin-Ryu school to continue his studies in that system. After a meeting with Ron Taganashi, who trained in Nisei Goju Ryu, and discussing his interest in joining another Isshin-Ryu school, but had no luck finding an Isshin-Ryu instructor, Sensei Taganashi smiled and said, "I happen to know someone you might want to check out." That person was Malachi Lee.

Figure 29: Sensei Malachi Lee. Sensei Lee was elevated to 6th dan black belt at his funeral in 1975.

Sensei Lee and his students so impressed him during his first visit to the dojo that he made up his mind to join that very evening. He remembers that when he entered the dojo that night, everyone was serious and busy and that was before the sensei even walked on the floor. This was also Master Latimer's first introduction to the Order of Isshin-Ryu. He remembers telling one of the other students in the dojo that Isshin-Ryu was definitely "sweet for the street." Master Latimer petitioned to join Lee's dojo and was accepted. Sensei Lee knew of his previous Isshin-Ryu black belt status and asked what belt he wished to wear in his dojo. Master Latimer replied, "I'll come in as a white belt under you; promote me to what you feel is appropriate."

About his training there, Master Latimer remembers thinking, "That man has got to be crazy! He would work you beyond your limits and then bring you back. He had a lot of energy and would bring the same out in you." Latimer then recalls, "About eight months after that time, traveling by train from Long Island to Manhattan to train on a consistent basis, and then after watching me spar Aston Hugh (one of Lee's top students), he told me to wear a brown belt.

Master Latimer had the privilege of being Sensei Lee's student until Lee's untimely death in 1976. He made sho-dan soon after, under Sensei Maria Melendez.

Shortly after joining the OI, Sensei Lee passed away and Sensei Maria Melendez and Tom Campfield took over the dojo and kept it running. Sensei Melendez subsequently promoted Master Isham Latimer and Sensei John McDonald to sho-dan (1st degree black belt).

Maria subsequently started to train in another Isshin-Ryu organization under Lewis Lizotte. During this time, she seriously injured her knee and eventually fell out of training in martial arts. However, Master John Costanzo recalls, "Maria Melendez trained all the big names that came out of the New York dojo – Isham Latimer, Aston Hugh, John McDonald, Jose Diaz – and she was their sensei. In my mind, that alone puts her on a very special level."

Puerto Rico

Juan F. "Paco" Lopez and Juan D. Lopez were originally students of Sensei Jaime Acosta and Sensei Eduardo Caro. Both of those karate-ka were black belts in Isshin-Ryu and were students of Russell Best.

As Sensei Jesús M. Jiménez recalls, Eduardo Caro went to Santo Domingo to study medicine and Jaime Acosta went on to study Goju-ryu from Kimo Wall. Both Lopez brothers were brown belts at the time and wanted to continue their Isshin-Ryu study; therefore, they traveled to New York in the early 1970s to look for Don Nagle and petition to become his students. Paco and Juan didn't realize the size of New York City and struggled a bit in their quest.

Figure 30: 1980 Puerto Rico. L-R: Juan D. Lopez, Bobby Gonzalez, Master Cooling, Paco Lopez, Eduardo Gonzalez

On their way to search for Grandmaster Nagle, they entered an Isshin-Ryu dojo, which happened to be the dojo of Malachi Lee. They watched Sensei Lee, talked with him several times, and eventually saw him hitting a heavy bag in the dojo one day. At that point, both knew this was what they were looking for. They remained in New York and worked at Lee's dojo for about one month.

Eventually, Sensei Lee traveled to Puerto Rico and worked in the dojo with Paco and Juan. He reviewed their kata in detail and soon promoted both Lopez brothers to brown belt (again). At this point, they officially became students of Malachi Lee within the Order of Isshin-Ryu. Sensei Jiménez recalls that later, when Sensei Lee was about to promote them to black belt ranking, Lee passed away.

Shortly after Lee's passing, Master Cooling made the trip to Puerto Rico to train and teach in the Puerto Rico dojo. He elevated Juan F. "Paco" Lopez to sho-dan (1st degree black belt). A short time later, both Juan D. Lopez and Eduardo Gonzalez received their sho-dan rankings. After these gentlemen, those who earned their black belts in the OI were Bobby Gonzalez and Jesús M. Jiménez. Many more excellent black belts have come out of the Puerto Rico dojo, and Sensei Jiménez continues to produce outstanding karate-ka, including Efrain Rivera.

Michigan

Karen Bronson's dojo was in Traverse City, Michigan. She was associated with Isshinryu Hall of Fame member Norbert Donnelly. Master Cooling was instrumental in getting Master Donnelly back into the dojo training to pass on his extensive knowledge and experience to the Isshinryu community. Sensei Bronson was looking for a solid Isshin-Ryu dojo to continue her training in the system, which she devoted her life to, and at some point, she got word of the Order of Isshin-Ryu.

Many OI black belts traveled to work with Sensei Bronson to get her requirements in-line with OI standards. Sensei Kurt Kline was there for a week and taught classes. Several other OI notables made the trip, including Master Ron Tyree and Sensei Jesús M. Jiménez. Sensei Bronson petitioned for acceptance into the OI, and she was eventually tested and graded as a sho-dan. Her time with the OI was cut much too short as she eventually succumbed to cancer. Through her association as an OI member and her battle with illness, she demonstrated to everyone how a true warrior fights.

Pennsylvania

There are several OI dojos within the state of Pennsylvania. One of the earliest members of the OI, Sensei Buster Hash, ran a dojo in Shrewsbury, PA from 1980 through 1984. This was likely the first Pennsylvania dojo representing the Order of Isshin-Ryu.

The dojo, run by Sensei Kurt Kline and Sensei Adam Knox, are extensions of the hombu dojo in Maryland as both men originally started their training and earned their black belts while training at the hombu dojo in Elkton, Maryland.

Kurt Kline started his first dojo in 1991. The dojo didn't really gain traction until 1993, when Matt Scarborough joined. Sensei Kline and his students originally trained at the Universtiy of Delaware until black belt Chris Taggart joined, after which the dojo alternated between the University and Sensei Ronnie Cimorosi's school on Blue Ball Road in Elkton, Maryland. Sensei Kline vividly remembers discussions with Denshi, "While I was still in high school, Denshi and I spent a lot of time together. You were around karate all of the time. We went to dirt track races, shot pool, went to the gun range to practice shooting skills, and worked on his home on Lewis Shore road. Others like Sotiere Nicholson helped as well. I and all my friends would be together doing odds and ends with Denshi; that's just what we did back then."

Sensei Dan Popp was a black belt from another Isshin-Ryu organization and joined the Order of Isshin-Ryu by formal petition in 1996. Richard Muhs, a student under Master Mike Goodyear, would eventually start his own dojo in Allentown, PA.

The Media Hook and Ladder dojo started in September 1995 by Sensei Larry Sica. As Sensei Sica was a volunteer firefighter and EMT, it was a natural progression to begin offering classes above the fire station in Media, PA. Under the permission of Master Cooling and Sica's sensei, Danny Cross, Mark Fellenbaum was the dojo's first student. Todd Stare and Christy Mandes started training shortly thereafter. As Sica recalls, "Many came and went but several remained for many years. Mr. Stare was my first black belt, who I awarded my original black belt. Christy Mandes became my second black belt not long after. Mr. Fellenbaum achieved brown belt at the Hook and Ladder dojo and is

Figure 31: October 2000 - Media, PA. Sensei Danny Cross working with Sensei Larry Sica's daughter, Margo, at the Media Hook and Ladder Dojo.

currently training at the Elkton dojo in Maryland." Due to Sensei Sica's health issues, the dojo formally closed in 2004.

Florida

In 1991, Sensei Larry Jackson moved to Florida and opened the Naples dojo. Sotiere Nicholson subsequently moved to Florida and took over as sensei of this dojo in 1994. Currently, Sensei Nicholson has a good core of five students working with him, and they continue training hard. As Sotiere indicates, "Denshi changed my life. Therefore, I always try to do things the right way, and my loyalties will always lie with the OI."

Australia

In January 1999, Master Cooling and his wife, Master Diane Ortenzio-Cooling, visited Australia at the invitation of Sensei Robert Slywa and provided several seminars in the Sydney, Australia area. They were guest instructors at many dojos, including: Sensei Arthur Moulas (Uechi Ryu), Sensei Doug Turnbull (Kyokushinkai), Sensei Nick Donato (Tae Kwon Do/Jujitsu), and Sensei Peter Mylonas (Kempo Ryu).

Several years later, one of the attendees from those seminars, Sensei Danny Goding, reached out to Master Cooling to request acceptance of his dojo under the OI umbrella. Various trips by members of the OI were made to Sydney, Australia to work in Sensei Goding's dojo in Liverpool, a suburb of Sydney. The kata of Sensei Goding and his students needed to be reviewed in detail to ensure standards met those of Master Cooling and the OI.

Master Bill Sullivan and Sensei Kurt Kline made the trip in March 2001. Over nine days, they reviewed each of the eight empty-hand kata, with some of the training sessions lasting over 10 hours. This trip was highly successful, and the dojo in Australia was left with the necessary hand kata, information, and techniques to become part of the Order of Isshin-Ryu.

Various members of the OI made subsequent visits, including the sensei and several students of the three Pennsylvania dojos: Allentown, Harrisburg, and West Chester. They further reviewed the skills and technical requirements for Sensei Goding and his students. The motto of the OI has always been:

Never lower the standards for the student.
Always work with the student until they can meet the standards.

The Australia dojo eventually moved away from the OI to pursue their training on other terms.

Figure 32: 2001 - Bill Sullivan and Kurt Kline visit the Australia dojo of Danny Goding.

Afghanistan

The Afghanistan dojo was formed in 2014 by Sensei Luis Aponte upon serving in the U.S. Marines. Sensei Aponte, a student of Sensei Jesús M. Jiménez, opened the dojo there while on active duty. He is now a civilian and still running the dojo on the military base in Afghanistan. To date, he has produced several brown belts.

Denshi's Move to the Western Frontier

In 1995, Master Cooling and his wife, Diane Ortenzio-Cooling, moved west to Nevada. Denshi has always said that he's a cowboy at heart, so he wanted to experience the West while there was still time. He's lived there ever since, yet he has attended nearly every shiai from the time he moved (the OI holds three shiai every year).

Figure 33: Sensei Luis Aponte with student in the OI Afghanistan dojo.

According to Denshi, "I got tired of the politics of Maryland and the taxes and how they are distributed across the state. I was also tired of the restrictions on gun ownership there. I wanted to experience the West." They considered moving to Florida, but Diane didn't want to move there. And Denshi says that Washington state is too liberal. He goes on to explain, "I can make it from Nevada to Elkton, Maryland within a day. So, it's no problem getting back to my roots."

Surely, a void has occurred since Denshi moved from Elkton; however, he is continuously in contact with his martial arts family. At the same time, he doesn't rest for too long at home as he constantly is in demand for seminars across the United States as well as his regular attendance at the OI shiai.

A Scare in Venezuela

Note: the following is an article written by Wendy Gilbert included in the September 2001 edition of the OI newsletter, The Gateway. The author has made slight adaptations.

In 2001, Master Cooling and Sensei Juan Lopez traveled to Caracas, Venezuela to train with a karate sensei living there, as well as a Christian mission that Sensei Lopez wanted to carry out. The beginning of the trip turned out quite different than expected for both men. The following email thread to members of the OI was sent by Master Cooling's wife and stated the following:

> Got a call from Denshi this morning. He and Sensei Lopez arrived safely in Caracas, Venezuela yesterday. That's the good news. The bad news is that the karate instructor who sponsored them is nowhere to be found. Denshi reports that Venezuela is a third-world country in every sense of the word. They are staying at the YMCA, which locks down after dark and has bars on the windows. They awoke around 1 a.m. this morning to the sound of gunfire. They would have rented a car to sightsee, but there are no street signs – anywhere.
>
> The people there are extremely poor. Denshi and Sensei Lopez are determined to make this a grand adventure and have fun. They found a karate school to visit tonight.
>
> Diane

When both men arrived in Venezuela it was a democratic country. By the time they left, it was a communist country. Keep in mind that Sensei Lopez, who once lived in Cuba, is very familiar with the Fidel Castro regime and the communist way of life about to overtake Venezuela. Denshi remembers, "I was very concerned, especially with the anti-American sentiment, and here I was – my only amigo is Juan 'The Crazy Cuban' Lopez, who has sworn to kill Castro on sight."

Being in the middle of a communist take-over is risky business at any time, but they couldn't just turn around and go home. There was a mission to complete since Sensei Lopez was on a pilgrimage to deliver 2,000 medals to be distributed to Catholics attending a large festival at the edge of the Amazon river.

Figure 34: Puerto Rico dojo. L-R: Sensei Jesús M. Jiménez, Sensei Juan D. Lopez

Denshi and Sensei Lopez arrived in a country in turmoil. The unions had been disbanded, the churches were closed and surrounded with barbed wire and, of course, honest citizens were allowed only very restricted access to firearms. "But all the criminals had fully automatic weapons," Denshi recalls. Over the course of the weekend prior to their arrival, there had been over 200 people killed in Caracas; 350 killed country-wide. A travel agent got them to a YMCA deep in the 'Red Zone.' Denshi remembers, "We went up to our one-room suite that had a 40-watt light bulb, a toilet, sink, shower, and two narrow beds. There was no hot water, and we had to throw our toilet paper in the trash can."

During the entire trip, Denshi pretty much kept quiet the entire time, lest his lack of the Spanish language draw attention to the fact he was a gringo. He didn't comb his hair and scuffed himself up as much as he could. They heard gunfire every day, and two days prior to their leaving, the U.S. military was ousted from the country. Castro and the presidents of Venezuela and Brazil made an agreement of some sort, and now the second largest oil exporter in the world is on the brink of becoming a communist country.

Each night they stayed at the YMCA, they had to trek the 90 plus steps to their room in darkness. "I carried a big switchblade and brought one along for Juan. One night, he heard mine click and asked, 'What was that?' I said, 'If I were you, I'd open mine.' A second later I heard *click*," Denshi fondly recalls.

They finally journeyed to a Catholic shrine in Las Trekas that featured bleeding communion bread. In 1917, a documented miracle occurred during a communion service, which caused a consecrated piece of bread to bleed like Christ's wounds. As luck (and prayer) would have it, the convent they stopped at for directions was now the keeper of the sacred bread. "It was like we were directed there in spirit," Denshi stated. From that moment on and throughout the rest of the ordeal of getting out of the country, Denshi said, "Everything worked like clockwork. If one thing had gone wrong, we'd still be there." At any one of the checkpoints, they could have been refused egress from the country. "The guy who picked us up to leave at 4 a.m. ran seven red lights, he was so afraid to stop. I was prepared to hijack a car. I'd put a knife to a guy's throat in a minute to get us out of there."

Isshin-Ryu Leadership

The topic of leadership for the Isshin-Ryu system is tense and controversial, to say the very least. There are quite a few 9th and 10th degree black belts at this point in the history of Isshin-Ryu karate. This book is not intended to debate this topic nor to debunk any other organization's claim of the leadership of the Isshin-Ryu system. To attempt such a thing, frankly, isn't necessarily time well-spent nor would I believe the founder, Tatsuo Shimabuku, necessarily would endorse such activities. Simply stated, there are numerous practitioners within Isshin-Ryu karate with an extremely high level of knowledge and experience about which Master Shimabuku would be very proud. The student of Isshin-Ryu karate should seek out as much information as they can regarding all these men and their histories to become as well-rounded a martial artist as possible.

In June 1992, three men were promoted by Don Nagle and Harold Long to ku-dan (9th degree black belt) in a ceremony at the Order of Isshin-Ryu summer shiai: Toby Cooling, J.C. Burris, and Joel Buchholtz. The following letter from Harold Long was published in Long's book *Who's Who in Isshinryu* and indicates this promotion:

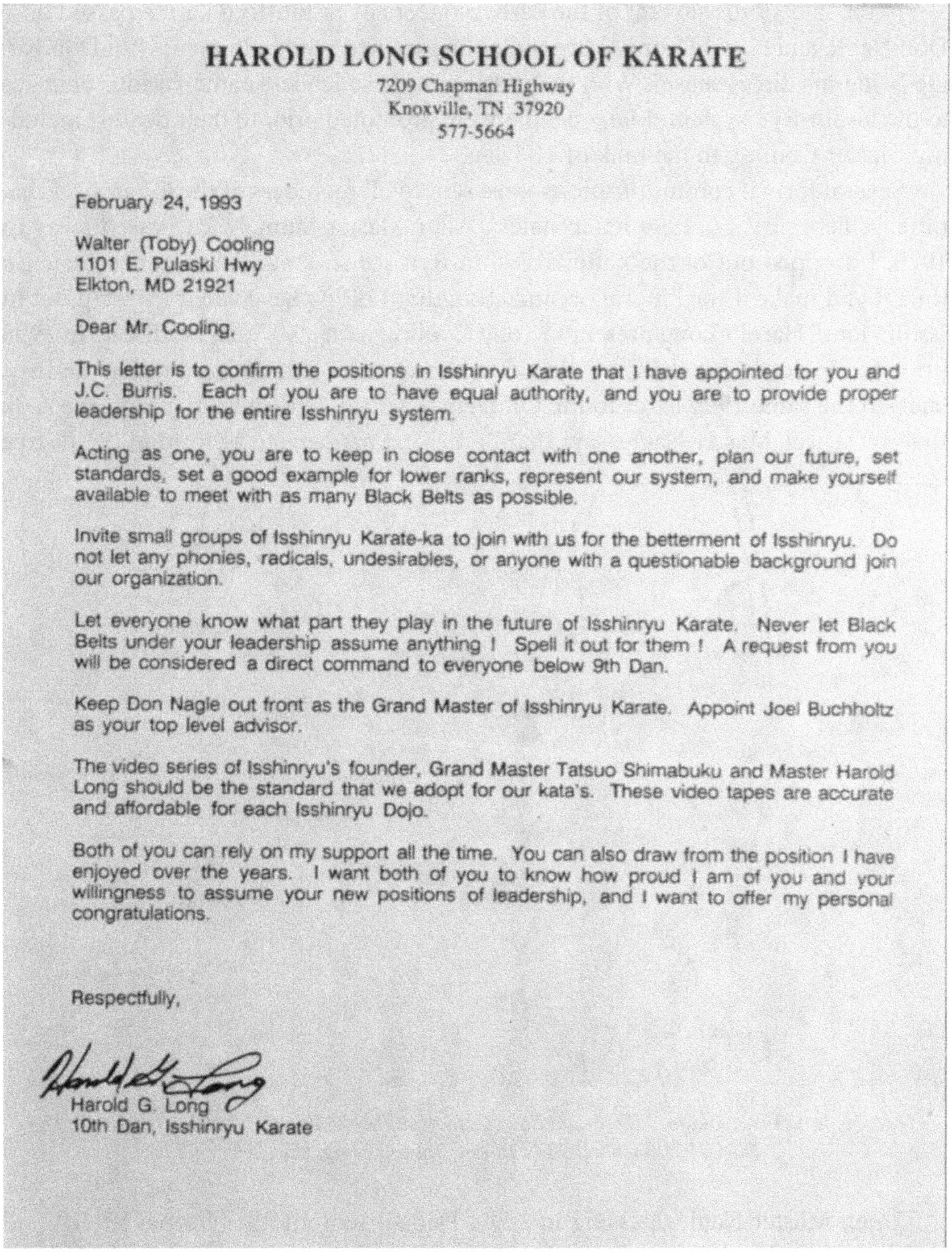

HAROLD LONG SCHOOL OF KARATE
7209 Chapman Highway
Knoxville, TN 37920
577-5664

February 24, 1993

Walter (Toby) Cooling
1101 E. Pulaski Hwy
Elkton, MD 21921

Dear Mr. Cooling,

This letter is to confirm the positions in Isshinryu Karate that I have appointed for you and J.C. Burris. Each of you are to have equal authority, and you are to provide proper leadership for the entire Isshinryu system.

Acting as one, you are to keep in close contact with one another, plan our future, set standards, set a good example for lower ranks, represent our system, and make yourself available to meet with as many Black Belts as possible.

Invite small groups of Isshinryu Karate-ka to join with us for the betterment of Isshinryu. Do not let any phonies, radicals, undesirables, or anyone with a questionable background join our organization.

Let everyone know what part they play in the future of Isshinryu Karate. Never let Black Belts under your leadership assume anything ! Spell it out for them ! A request from you will be considered a direct command to everyone below 9th Dan.

Keep Don Nagle out front as the Grand Master of Isshinryu Karate. Appoint Joel Buchholtz as your top level advisor.

The video series of Isshinryu's founder, Grand Master Tatsuo Shimabuku and Master Harold Long should be the standard that we adopt for our kata's. These video tapes are accurate and affordable for each Isshinryu Dojo.

Both of you can rely on my support all the time. You can also draw from the position I have enjoyed over the years. I want both of you to know how proud I am of you and your willingness to assume your new positions of leadership, and I want to offer my personal congratulations.

Respectfully,

Harold G. Long
Harold G. Long
10th Dan, Isshinryu Karate

Figure 35: Formal promotion announcement of Toby Cooling to 9th degree black belt from Harold Long.

In the late 1990s several of the early pioneers of Isshin-Ryu karate passed on – Don Nagle and Harold Long. Master Cooling trained with both men, with Don Nagle being his direct sensei. With the passing of these leaders came various changes to the Isshin-Ryu system. Many people were promoted prior to their deaths, including Master Cooling to the rank of 10th dan.

Several formal communications were sent to all members of the OI around that time. A February 11, 1999 letter states, "After Master Shimabuku passed away in 1975, I dropped out of the national Isshin-Ryu scene. I wanted to concentrate on the OI and make it the kind of organization that I didn't have when I started out in Isshin-Ryu." Harold Long presented Toby Cooling with a 10th dan certificate in 1998 prior to his death; however, he did not recognize this promotion until some time later. In the same 1999 letter to the OI, Denshi writes, "I believe that I am the rank that my sensei, Master Nagle, says that I am. That happens to be ku-dan (9th degree black belt)."

Figure 36: June 1992, Elkton, MD: Promotion ceremony of Isshin-Ryu system leadership. L-R: Don Nagle, Joel Buchholtz, J.C. Burris, Toby Cooling, Harold Long.

Upon Master Nagle's passing in 1999, Denshi sent another formal letter to all OI black belts dated October 8, 1999. This letter indicates Master Nagle considered Toby Cooling his senior 9th dan; however, Denshi informed him he did not plan to spend any time supervising another organization in another part of the country when he had his own organization centered in Elkton, Maryland. Master Nagle responded, "Then do your own thing; you already have a diploma for 10th dan from Harold Long." Master Nagle then asked Denshi to keep his legacy alive and do what he felt was best for Isshin-Ryu. This is a crucial point to be made. There are many, many organizations in existence currently representing Isshin-Ryu karate-do, along with many 9th and 10th degree black belts. Rather than worry about who the sole leader of the system should be, or what rank should be recognized by other organizations, Master Nagle simply requested Denshi to do what was best for Isshin-Ryu. This shows the total respect Master Nagle had for the founder of Isshin-Ryu and what Isshin-Ryu karate-do had meant to him and his life. Everyone needs to take a cue from Master Nagle's request. There is no need to waste time and effort arguing over who is the leader of Isshin-Ryu. The bottom line is Tatsuo Shimabuku produced several highly skilled, high ranking martial artists. They, in turn, developed many of their own quality martial artists, and all of them have a considerable amount of talent and knowledge to offer. If all of us simply train hard, teach Isshin-Ryu karate to the best of our abilities, and recognize the tremendous abilities Tatsuo Shimabuku had as a martial artist, then we cannot go wrong.

The March 26, 2000 shiai of the Order of Isshin-Ryu marked Master Cooling's 40th year in the martial arts. A special gathering and ceremony was held to honor Denshi and recognize him as a ju-dan (10th degree black belt). In attendance were Masters Joel Chandler, Lonnie Workman, Carl Martin, and Sensei Dennis Sammartino. A letter of congratulations was also read from Master Denny Shaffer.

Torii – The Symbol of the Order of Isshin-Ryu

The Order of Isshin-Ryu uses the Japanese torii as the symbol to represent the members in good standing to our organization. This is depicted by the OI patch, which is worn by all members of the OI on the right sleeve of their gi, or uniform, and currently is the only patch worn by members of the OI.

Figure 37: The Torii patch worn my all members of the Order of Isshin-Ryu

The torii patch is not issued automatically upon joining the Order of Isshin-Ryu. Students must earn it. New students generally train for a period before they earn the right to wear one. The waiting period is determined by the sensei of each respective OI dojo. Some dojos may require a set amount of historical knowledge before issuing the patch.

I petitioned to join the OI in the summer of 1996. At the time, I was ranked as go-dan (5th degree black belt) from another Isshin-Ryu karate organization. Denshi spent the better part of a full Saturday reviewing my kata at his home in Elkton, Maryland. He appeared to accept my abilities as a martial artist, and I was hopeful to receive admittance along with the OI patch. No chance. He said, after he reviewed all my kata, "Mr. Popp, you will need to travel around and visit as many of my black belts as possible and work with them. Once they indicate to me that you meet the OI standards, then I'll be happy to bring you into my family." Based on that response, I could tell immediately that he didn't care about quantity of students, but rather he expected quality, and his black belts provided a sort of barometer to let him know if the quality was there or not. I knew I was traveling along the correct road in my karate training.

Figure 38: October, 1996 - Elkton, MD. The author receiving his OI Torii patch and promotion to nidan (2nd degree black belt).

I knew I had been accepted as one of Denshi's students, albeit informally. I didn't receive my OI patch on that day, and I dared not even ask! The way of thinking should be this: if you're going to join a karate organization, then simply ask to join and train as hard as you can. Don't be concerned with patches, rank, certificates or whatever. If you came seeking those things, then you're not likely going to grasp the essence of what is offered. I figured when the time was right, and Denshi felt I earned the distinction of wearing the patch, he would offer it up.

Today, the only member of the OI who doesn't wear the torii patch is Master Barry Smith. This is not in any way a show of disrespect as nothing could be further from the truth. Barry Smith and Toby Cooling have a deep friendship and respect one another. As Master Smith puts it, "Denshi has given me a lot of [grief] over not wearing the patch. But I've told him I don't need to wear a patch to show I'm a member of the OI. The OI, the torii, and what it stands for is in my heart."

The definition or translation of the word torii is "bird abode," and these structures are most commonly found at the entrance of or within a Shinto shrine. Shinto is a Japanese religion dating from the early 8th century and incorporates the worship of ancestors, nature spirits, and a belief in sacred power (*kami*) in both animate and inanimate things. Shinto was the state religion of Japan until 1945. The torii symbolically marks the transition from normal or flawed thinking to sacred. Torii are also a common sight at Japanese Buddhist temples, called chinjusha, and are usually very small.

In Asian cultures, the torii is a gateway built at the entrances to temples, schools, and harbors. The torii represents a gateway to higher learning or a safe place. For the Order of Isshin-Ryu, by making the torii our symbol, we look upon it as an endeavor by us to obtain higher learning through working together under our sensei. We do not recognize or follow any religious connotations with the torii being our symbol. We simply use it as a reminder of the purpose of our organization: to denote the goal of continuous learning and improvement while representing the Order of Isshin-Ryu positively and professionally.

Interestingly, there are other organizations that use the torii as a symbol in non-religious contexts. The Marine Corps Security Force Regiment and the 187th Infantry Regiment, 101st Airborne Division, and other U.S. forces in Japan, also utilize the torii as a symbol.

Figure 39: The famous torii at Itsukushima Shrine in the city of Hatsukaichi, Hiroshima Prefecture in Japan.

There is no universal agreed-upon theory on the origin of the torii. Instead, various theories abound on this subject. What we do know is that symbolic gates are used widely throughout Asia. These structures can be found in many countries such as India, China, Thailand, and Korea. As such, historians believe they may be an imported tradition for Japan. The oldest existing stone torii was built in the 12th century and belongs to a Hachiman Shrine in Yamagata prefecture. The oldest wooden torii can be found at Kubō Hachiman Shrine in Yamanashi prefecture built in 1535.

Torii were traditionally made from wood or stone, but today they can be also made of reinforced concrete, copper, stainless steel, or other materials. They are usually either unpainted or painted vermilion with a black upper lintel. The function of a torii is to mark the entrance to a sacred space. For this reason, the road leading to a Shinto shrine is almost always straddled by one or more torii, which are the easiest way to distinguish a shrine from a Buddhist temple.

Code of the Order of Isshin-Ryu

Figure 40: 1972, Puerto Rico. Master Cooling's first trip to Puerto Rico to teach.

Organizations provide their members various "codes" or "creeds" by which to conduct themselves or provide thoughts to reflect upon from time to time… to serve as a guiding point of reference throughout the development of the members. For those of Christian faith, the Ten Commandments serve as the principles upon which to live as provided directly by God to Moses. All military branches have their codes. Martial arts are no different. Isshin-Ryu karate has a Code of Karate. Each one has specific meaning to the on-going development of the student. Those 'codes' have been written about by many other authors on Isshin-Ryu karate and will not be presented here.

Upon the formulation of the Order of Isshin-Ryu, Master Cooling developed the Code of the Order of Isshin-Ryu, additional standards upon which students in the OI can look to and reflect upon in their ongoing training. On the 46th anniversary of the founding of the OI, Denshi prepared email correspondence to all OI members that provide his thoughts on the founding of the OI as well as his thoughts on the OI codes and from where they came. Here are his words to the members of the Order of Isshin-Ryu:

> January 15, 2017
> To All OI Members:
> On this 46th anniversary of the Order of Isshin-Ryu, I would like to share the answers to some questions that I have been asked over the years.
>
> ### *Why did you start the Order of Isshin-Ryu?*
> When I was first coming up in karate, I observed individuals getting promoted and advanced in Isshin-Ryu karate because they were friends, bought someone a beer, won a fight, or the instructor needed money. Isshin-Ryu ended up with some high-ranking people that did not have qualifications for the rank they wore around their waist. I did not want either myself or my students to have that reputation. Everyone should meet the same standards for a given rank. I also wanted to belong to an organization, a family, that existed and functioned as professionals, did what they said they were going to do, kept their word, made things happen instead of watching things happen, and treated everyone with the exact same standard.
>
> Unfortunately, I was born without any patience. I wanted to live in a world that is black and white without any gray. I wanted to be surrounded with people who have conviction about what they believe…even if it does not match my personal view. These are people who answer the question that is asked (not the question they want to answer) with a "yes" or "no," not a "I will let you know" or "I will get back to you" and never do. In karate, you either block/slip/redirect the punch, or you get hit - there is no gray area.
>
> I was born a warrior and wanted to be with fellow warriors. I wanted to be the sheep dog, not the sheep and not the wolf. So, I set out to create that warrior family and surround myself with people who felt the same way. If someone in that family said that they had your back, you knew it was absolute and they were trained to handle any trouble that might come your way…that was loyal to each other, right or wrong…where everyone was treated equally and could excel in what they did best.

What is the origin of the Code of the Order of Isshin-Ryu?

These are maxims that I have collected over the years. Some are my thoughts, others I picked up from someone who used the saying frequently or from my reading.

No.	Code	Origin
1	A karate-ka is fierce in battle and gentle in life.	Sensei Malachi Lee
2	Things aren't always as they seem.	From a Garfield cartoon and re-worded it.
3	Do not always act in the expected manner.	Mine
4	Do not reach a conclusion without all the facts.	Mine. At age 15, I was tired of someone gossiping without facts. Meaning: trust, but verify.
5	Everything is relative.	Mine
6	Opposites appear the same.	From Barry Murphy, Cambridge, MD. Only friend I had as an adult who was never a martial artist.
7	Do not block an offensive move until necessary.	Mine
8	Separate important from unimportant.	Mine
9	Nothing is, until it is.	Master Isham Latimer
10	I cannot prevent the wind from blowing, but I can adjust my sails to make it work for me.	From Jimmy Dean, country singer. I took the original quote and reworded.
11	Do what you say you're going to do, when you say you're going to do it.	Mine

12	If it's not yours, don't touch it. If it's not true, don't say it. If it's not right, don't do it.	The Cowboy Code – author unknown.

"You can't choose your relatives, but you can choose your family."

Toby Cooling

Sho-Dan Ho

When brown belts are on the verge of becoming a black belt, their respective sensei will elevate them to Sho-Dan Ho. The word means "half step" and recognizes a level of achievement without formal promotion or status to black belt ranking. Sho-Dan-Ho is not a rank but rather a status that is announced at the OI shiai. This announcement makes it known to all black belts the students will be going up for their black belt test at the next shiai. The instructors are put on notice to watch these students closely as they are on the verge of joining the black belt ranks.

The students are expected to make the rounds and visit as many sensei as possible to have their kata and techniques evaluated prior to their test. It becomes a two-way street. The students ramp up their work and effort, the black belts step in and provide comments, corrections, support, and encouragement to make sure the students become a quality member of the black belt ranks.

Master Cooling created the Sho-Dan Ho status in 1979. At that time, a sensei was holding back one of his students from testing for his black belt. Therefore, Denshi awarded the Sho-Dan Ho rank and stated the sensei will have to put them up for black belt sooner or later. According to an October 18, 1979 newsletter to his OI black belts, the Sho-Dan Ho must demonstrate his ability to teach the entire class, know and be able to explain all meanings of the eight hand-kata, have the correct attitude, and proven his trust, loyalty, and devotion to the sensei, the OI, and Isshin-Ryu karate.

For testing at the black belt level, Master Cooling noted the following standards back in the early 1980s:

- To show existing black belts you are of black belt quality.
- To see if a person is good enough to be a black belt in the OI.

- To examine the student's kata, to conform to the guidelines of the performance by other black belts in the OI – this helps preserve the way kata is expected to be performed.
- To complete the student's kata by filling in everything missed by black belts who prepared the student for the test.

Junior Black Belt

Figure 41: 2000 – Ema Bajlovic receiving promotion to junior black belt. L-R: Nikolina Slijepcevic-Novakovic, Bajlovic, Sensei Ron Tyree

Many Isshin-Ryu organizations recognize a junior black belt rank. Often, a very young student will move up through the ranks and will have learned the requirements of black belt at a very young age. They can demonstrate the kata and techniques of a black belt and have a good degree of skill with kumite or sparring. However, the aspect of maturity must also come under consideration prior to earning a black belt.

The Order of Isshin-Ryu has a junior black belt ranking; however, it took a long time to adopt it. Master Cooling never promoted anyone to black belt below the age of 16. Denshi recalls Ron Tyree (see figure on left) was a brown belt for several years due to being under 16 years old at the time. As far back as 1981, the OI considered a junior rank, but only up to Ik-kyu or 1st degree brown belt. The junior black belt rank formally came into existence when Sensei Karen Bronson and her various dojos in Michigan joined the Order of Isshin-ryu in 1995.

Sensei Bronson had a young black belt in her dojo prior to joining the OI. She made the argument that she was losing kids from her dojo since it was not possible for them to become recognized as a black belt until they were 16 years of age. She noted that many times, the kids work as hard and as long as the adults and some form of rank promotion was warranted if they could perform the requirements as instructed. Denshi made the concession to adopt a junior black belt ranking to recognize efforts of qualified students below the age of 16.

As of this writing, there have been only four junior black belts conferred in the Order of Isshin-Ryu.

Using the Title of "Master"

Currently, the Order of Isshin-Ryu assigns the title of 'Master' at the hachi-dan, or 8th degree black belt level. However, there was a time when this was not always the case. An early student pamphlet from the mid-70s shows the Master title bestowed as early as the Roku-dan, or 6th degree black belt level. This is consistent with many other karate styles and organizations in America today, including other Isshin-Ryu karate organizations. Other styles of martial arts, such as Tae Kwon Do, go as low as 4th or 5th degree black belt when the term Master is used to address someone in the martial arts school.

There is much debate, often heated, regarding the use of titles at specific levels of rank within the martial arts. The OI tries very hard to stay above the fray in this regard. The ranking system common today and conferred in martial arts comes from Jigoro Kano, the founder of Judo. Dave Lowry writes in *The Karate Way*, "Belts in black or any other color were not a part of martial arts practice before the twilight of the feudal period in Japan, which ended in 1867. Kano awarded the first black belts around the turn of the last century." There are a multitude of possible titles you may come across within martial arts nomenclature, all representing a variation in rank or level of achievement. Without a detailed description, some of these are the following: sensei, master, grandmaster, renshi, kyoshi, hanshi, kaicho, soke, shihan, etc. Within the OI, there are two in use… sensei and master.

According to Wikipedia[18], *sensei* (先生) is a Japanese honorific term that is literally translated as "person born before another." The proper usage of the word in written form is after a person's name, such as Tyree Sensei, and means "teacher." However, in Japan, the word is also used as a title to refer to or address other professionals or persons of authority including accountants, lawyers, physicians, and politicians. In the Orient, the word sensei is also used to show respect to someone who has achieved a certain level of mastery in an art form such as musicians and artists as well as martial artists.

---

[18] https://en.wikipedia.org/wiki/Sensei

Figure 42: 1979 – Elkton High School – Elkton, MD

1st row (L-R): Bailey Russell, John McDonald, Eduardo Gonzalez, Charlie Deitterick, Buster Hash, Tom Miller, Barry Smith, John Judway, Maria Melendez, Toby Cooling

2nd row (L-R): Juan F. "Paco" Lopez, Bob Whited, Larry Jackson, Isham Latimer, Tom Sanson, Bud Ewing, Jose Diaz

3rd row (L-R): Juan D. Lopez, Tom Campfield, Duane Dieter, Ed Cabrera, Frankie Hastings, Bill Spence, Aston Hugh, Milledge Murphey

The title of *sensei* is used to represent someone who is a black belt instructor; however, within the OI you are not automatically given the title of sensei upon earning your black belt. You must have authorization to open and run your own dojo. As stated previously, master is the title used in the OI beginning with an 8th degree black belt level and up. All other possible terms used to denote a high ranking black belt are avoided in the OI. This is the preference of Master Cooling and, obviously, other organizations can choose the methodology that works for them.

As a higher level black belt and called 'sensei' where otherwise the title 'master' is used commonly throughout the martial arts, I am perfectly content and relieved the OI defers to the prior term up to and including 7th degree black belt. My former Kendo sensei had studied and trained for well over 50 years of his life in Kendo and held the rank of ku-dan (9th degree black belt). Yet, students always referred to him or addressed him as 'sensei.' I asked him one day at his apartment with just the two of us present, "Sensei, I'm sure you have long ago earned the right to be called 'master.' So why do you want us to only call you 'sensei'?" He replied, "Popp-san, the word 'sensei' have many weights. Many responsibilities." He meant, by using the term sensei, which means **one who has gone before**, carries all the honor you will ever need to be recognized by others.

Being a true sensei requires a constant, endless effort to uphold the values and ideals of what the title stands for – a teacher of martial arts. Master Cooling is my teacher, and if I ever refer to him as 'sensei' he wouldn't take offense. For that is what he is, my sensei – my teacher in the martial arts.

At the black belt level, people often refer to the 'polishing' of one's techniques and character, which is why it is often stated that black belt is only the beginning. The beginning of such polishing that takes the rest of your life. And this is a primary role or function of the sensei… to mold and refine this character in students. Dave Lowry makes this point in his book *Clouds in the West* where he states, "The sensei must always bear in mind the tremendous responsibility he has for shaping character. Fundamental to that is the willingness to see his students go further than he himself has gone." To debate about a title other than 'sensei' tends to overlook the importance of the effort behind what is required upon becoming a sensei. It is a heavy burden to serve as a teacher and carry out that function well.

In August 2000, Master Cooling left the following thoughts with respect to what senseis within the Order of Isshin-Ryu must keep in mind:

1. An ability to demonstrate, on request, precisely what they are teaching;
2. A strong need to share their knowledge of martial arts;
3. Inspiring respect as an instructor, thereby leaving the impression of a professional;
4. Remember what it was like to be a white belt;
5. Behave in and out of the dojo in a manner that reflects integrity and excellent moral character; and
6. Continues to add to their knowledge of Isshin-Ryu and martial arts.

With respect to number six, many of Master Cooling's students have delved into other forms of martial arts with a high degree of success and accomplishment. This is presented in Chapter 10 – Budo of the Order of Isshin-Ryu, as well as information provided within the Senior Dan Bios section of this book.

Denshi has always imparted this basic philosophy: You are the rank and position that others recognize and accept you as. You don't make yourself a master, others recognize you as a master. Adding in a recent interview, "I think the best title is *sensei*. You can't go wrong."

One Family

Master Cooling continually refers to the Order of Isshin-Ryu as his family. On the surface, this appears to be something you take at face value as part of the karate organization to which you belong. It sounds straightforward. But the term 'family' in this case and the meaning behind it go much deeper than simple words. Time and time again, the OI family has stepped up for one another in time of need, on every level. When one of us hurts, we all hurt. When one of us succeeds, we all succeed.

One of the truest summaries of the 'family' concept came from Sensei Karen Bronson. Sensei Bronson petitioned to join the Order of Isshin-Ryu and was accepted in 1995. She fell ill with cancer and eventually passed away on January 9, 2002. She was posthumously inducted into the Isshin-Ryu Hall of Fame in 2006. She expressed her gratitude for her OI family in *The Gateway* (the OI newsletter) in June 1999 with the following letter:

To My Family, by Karen Bronson

As you, my OI family, are aware, I have been going through a very tough physical and emotional time recently and will be in this so-called battle for some time yet. Since the prognosis, all of you have pulled together, collected funds for transplant and medical expenses, and supported me in any and all ways possible. I cannot even begin to know how to thank you all for this, but most importantly, you have shown me that we are truly a family. The one most important facet of the OI is that we always come to each other's aid and champion each other's causes and necessities, and in the matters of life and death (that some of us are dealing with) we take no prisoners!

I hate to be redundant, but it bears repeating: Those of us who have spent time searching for the place we belong, and not giving up until we could get the very best martial arts available, and who have been fortunate enough to be accepted in the Order of Isshin-Ryu, are much more emotional about our OI family because we had to fight to get here.

In the Arts, it is always a fight. For you all to have gotten where you are; to continually bring us the very best karate that is out there. The fact that you all are patient enough to accept us newcomers, teach us everything we can learn, travel to help us, and always have a kind word, lots of patience, more understanding than most people are capable of, yet at the same time make us feel as though we have always been with you and are as important to you as anyone else, is incredible!

I guess what I am trying to convey to you is that even though I am in the midst of the biggest and most difficult battle I have ever faced, I feel that I can only win because I have the most supportive, helpful, and strong family next to me... all the way... that anyone could ever hope for! The past few months have put it into perspective for me... we are together, forever.

Thank you all, again. As Master Cooling says, you cannot pick your relatives, but you can pick your family! God bless you all.

Sensei Larry Jackson summed up Sensei Bronson in this manner, "Karen Bronson was a warrior. I saw her fight pain and sickness while she trained in her art, knowing that death was not far away. And her students still came first. She showed more spirit for the OI than a lot of members that came up through the ranks. Karen Bronson will be missed, but her spirit will continue."

This is what the OI family is truly about. Always be there for one another, and never give up.

One Dojo

As of the publication of this book, there are 14 dojos within the Order of Isshin-Ryu as listed on www.OIKarate.org. The distance between them is great. From Afghanistan to Puerto Rico. From New York to Florida. However, the approach has always been that we are one dojo under the direction of Master Cooling.

Figure 43: 1993 – Pigeon Forge, TN. Order of Isshin-Ryu attending the Isshin-Ryu Hall of Fame tournament. L-R: Larry Jackson, Bill Sullivan

Sensei Jesús M. Jiménez once asked a class at Hombu dojo, "How many dojos does the OI have at this time?" The students attempted several times to recall from memory the total number. The numbers were varied, and, after several tries, Sensei Jiménez finally responded, "We are one dojo. We have many schools and sensei, yes. But we are the Order of Isshin-Ryu. One dojo."

Regardless of which dojo you belong in the OI, you are encouraged to travel to other dojos and work with the sensei and students there. This develops well-rounded karate-ka and formulates bonds not found in many other life pursuits.

Chapter 3
BLACK GI: HISTORY AND EVOLUTION

"Be constantly mindful, diligent, and resourceful in your pursuit of the Way."[19]

Gichin Funakoshi

It may seem trivial or unimportant, but students of karate should have knowledge of all aspects of their art, including the reason the uniform was created and why it is still in use today. As Gichin Funakoshi wrote down for his students, the guiding principles of karate helped to serve as reminders to karate-ka on the focus of training beyond merely learning and mastering physical technique. Number 20 is the last principle and tells us we must be continually mindful and diligent in our pursuit of the martial arts. This requires understanding the uniform of the martial artist from those styles originating in Okinawa and Japan – called the *gi*. While many students focus on hard training, which is a good thing, students should also pause, reflect, and appreciate the formulation of the gi in order to be considered a true student of budo, or way of the martial arts.

---

[19] *The Twenty Guiding Principles of Karate,* by Gichin Funakoshi and Genwa Nakasone, ©2003 Japan Karate-do Shotokai, published by Kodansha International, Ltd.

General History of the Gi

Cotton was introduced to Japan from Korea and China during the fifteenth century, known as the Warring States period. From there, the Japanese took full advantage of what cotton has to offer in the form of casual clothing, especially considering easier processing than of silk. The introduction of cotton into Japan was the beginning of the formulation of the cotton karate gi as we know it today.

Figure 44: Jigoro Kano, founder of Judo.

The earliest proponent of the cotton gi was Jigoro Kano, the founder of Judo. Pictures from as far back as the 1910s and 1920s show Kano and his students wearing a crude version of the *judogi*, or the name of the gi used in Judo. Due to exchanges of ideas and training methods between Kano and the founder of Shotokan and modern karate, Gichin Funakoshi, the usage of the gi in training extended to karate in both Japan and Okinawa. As noted in the book *Shotokan's Secret*, "Funakoshi received a special welcome from respected Judo master Jigoro Kano at the Kodokan. Kano asked Funakoshi to teach some karate moves to the senior judo instructors, and Judo's advanced *atemi waza* (striking techniques) is the result. Funakoshi, in turn, adopted Kano's color-belt ranking system and had lightweight Judo uniforms made for his karate students. This system was the origin of the white cotton gi and colorful belts we wear today." However, during the early days of karate training students typically wore street clothes as this was more comfortable at that time.

Dave Lowry writes in his book *In the Dojo*, "Karate, introduced to Japan about the same time the judo uniform was assuming its present cut and shape, was originally practiced in everyday clothes or, in the humid heat of the Okinawan islands, in loincloths." This is evident in pictures of master instructors teaching their students around that time. General searches on the internet will yield various examples.

The color of the gi is another area of significance. The traditional color is white. The reason comes from both economic and cultural values. White is easier to manufacture and does not require dyeing the material, thus eliminating that expense. This was important in the early days of both Judo and Karate as both arts were available to the masses as well as being taught within universities, so not everyone in those days could afford expensive clothing.

From a spiritual value perspective, Lowry says, "…white…is reflective of a certain spirit of simplicity and naturalness that is consonant with the values of the budo." Simplicity is imperative to traditional martial arts training. No flashy colors. The dojo floor must not be cluttered and messy. Everything about the process of training and learning must have an almost "Zen-like" quality. Very simple. White is an essential quality of this type of simplicity.

Another aspect of the karate gi is that it helps practitioners understand they are about to participate in something different, something unique. In his book, *In the Dojo*, Dave Lowry notes, "The wearing of a [gi] is a physical way of establishing that this activity is not like others. New students may look and feel awkward. Part of any budo training is coming face-to-face with this awkwardness, acknowledging it, and then attempting to overcome it."

In truth, any activity that is to be taken seriously generally has some type of uniform that sets the activity apart. This gives practitioners continual awareness that they are doing something outside of normal day-to-day activities. Martial arts require a very high degree of focus and awareness. Wearing the karate gi helps students "flip the switch" mentally prior to walking onto the dojo floor. The gi tells them that it's time to remove all frustrations, worries, and problems, get down to business, and train hard.

Red Trim and Hachimaki

The red trim on the bottom of gi pants and the *hachimaki* (sweatband) tied to a student's *obi* (belt) is a tradition that goes back to Master Cooling's early years in karate training. As a green belt, he often traveled to the dojo of Don Nagle in Jersey City, New Jersey to train and learn. In Master Nagle's dojo, a student earned the privilege of wearing red trim on their gi pants from green through brown belt as a symbol of achievement. As Denshi recalls, "It was our identification that we came from Don Nagle's fighting dojo."

The *hachimaki* is a headband in Okinawan and Japanese cultures, usually made of red or white cloth and is worn as a symbol of perseverance or effort. They are worn on many occasions, i.e., women giving birth, students studying hard to prepare for exams, office workers, or expert tradesmen. The *hachimaki* is discussed in Peter Urban's book *The Karate Dojo* where he explains, "…it is a symbol of one's dedication to the hard work necessary to train correctly. The *hachimaki* is a constant reminder that one must never train half-heartedly." It must be noted that Peter Urban and Don Nagle were good friends and training partners in the early days of karate in the United States. The exchange of training ideas and dojo customs are evident between these two martial arts pioneers.

Figure 45: Elkton, MD. Brown belts at Hombu dojo. L-R: Bailey Russell (black gi), Samuel Sposato, Alan Jenkins, Jeanette McCarl, Sandy Evans, Dan Lorden, Glenn Fanning. Note the hachimaki hanging from the obi of several students.

For students training in the OI, the hachimaki is not worn on the head but instead is tied to the obi, or belt, for all green and brown belts. Tying the hachimaki equals the Western gesture of rolling up one's sleeves — getting serious and beginning to do the work. In the OI, it is awarded at green belt to signify that students have begun the serious work necessary to become a black belt.

Figure 46: 1985 - Bill Sullivan, as a brown belt, preparing to compete in kata division at annual OI shiai. He was promoted to sho-dan at the end of the day.

Black Gi Used in the Order of Isshin-Ryu

All the original Isshin-Ryu pioneers to bring the system stateside – Long, Nagle, Armstrong, Mitchum – all wore white gi. Grandmaser Long often wore black in later years; however, Denshi recalls of those early days, "They wore white. That was it. No questions; it was white."

In 1977, Master Cooling simply wanted to be different than everyone else and have something to set the OI apart; hence, at black belt level everyone wears black instead of white. Although black belts in the Order of Isshin-Ryu wear black and students wear white, there is a degree of flexibility in this rule. While training within a dojo of the Order of Isshin-Ryu, black belts do have the choice of color they wish to wear. However, whenever attending a formal event such as an Order of Isshin-Ryu shiai, a tournament sponsored by another organization, or a demonstration to the public, the black belt is instructed by Master Cooling to wear all black. This mandate is due to military influences.

Figure 47: June 28, 2009 - Chesapeake City, MD. David Ginn receiving promotion to black belt, upon which time OI students are allowed to wear the black gi.

L-R: *Toby Cooling, Bud Ewing, Bill Sullivan, Mike Magill, Jo Bramble, David Ginn*

Almost exclusively, military personnel returning from service in the East are responsible for spreading martial arts in the United States. These men followed strict dress codes with their uniforms; therefore, it makes logical sense to apply the same level of discipline to the uniform worn during martial arts training. Denshi makes the point in this manner, "Does the Army let you wear what you want when Class A uniforms are required? The purpose of the Order of Isshin-Ryu wearing the same uniform is the same reason the Army does it. To show uniformity and that we are one unit instead of a bunch of stragglers."

The 'Dress' Gi

Master Cooling recalls, at one point in time, Master Steve Armstrong had a custom uniform made. This served as an inspiration to do likewise in the OI. In the early years of the OI, several black belts were coming to the dojo and to the shiai donning a variety of colors on their gi. In response, Denshi formulated a 'dress' style uniform in 1972 to be worn by black belts for special functions, including the OI shiai (dojo competition), black belt evaluations, public demonstrations, and the like. This gi was designed by Master Cooling.

From there, the gi was made by Charlie Deitterick's wife, Deanie, using black belt member Malachi Lee's gi as the pattern. Deanie made each one by hand. As shown below, the gi was black with wide pinstripes of white and red along both sleeves and along the outside of the pants, which flared out at the bottom.

Figure 48: 1972 - Ocean City, MD. Charlie Deitterick performing tuifa kata wearing the OI 'dress' gi from the early 70s.

Figure 49: 1972 - Elkton, MD. Kneeling L-R: Juan Lopez, Tom Miller, Charlie Deitterick, Toby Cooling, Maria Melendez, Bob Whited, John Nickle, Barry Smith. 2nd Row Kneeling L-R: John Remick, John Judway, Tom Sanson. Standing L-R: Bud Ewing, Paco Lopez, Dale Stanton, Bob Burns, Bailey Russell, John King, Jose Diaz, Bill Spence. Note the 'dress' gi worn by most in this photo.

As shown in *figure 49* above, the dress gi was worn by many, but not all black belts. There was no requirement to wear it, and some felt more comfortable in their traditional plain white or black gi.

An Exception to the Black Gi - Showing Respect to Others

In April 2013, several members of the Order of Isshin-Ryu attended the Isshin-Ryu World Karate Association (IWKA) tournament in Akron, Ohio. The guest of honor for the event was the son of the founder of Isshin-Ryu karate, Grandmaster Kichiro Shimabuku who serves as President of the IWKA.

Host of the event, Sensei Heidi Gauntner, made a special request to all attendees to wear a traditional white gi as well as a plain black belt for all black belts, regardless of rank. Knowing various Isshin-Ryu organizations often wear black gi, Sensei Gauntner reached out to Master Cooling to request lifting our standard and wear white gi as they do on Okinawa.

Master Cooling agreed to the request; however, the members of the Order of Isshin-Ryu in attendance kept the patch signifying our affiliation with the Order of Isshin-Ryu. Some standards cannot and should not be compromised.

The Order of Isshin-Ryu is flexible to support our friends in Isshin-Ryu karate and other martial arts. For the IWKA event, Master Cooling was willing to change in support of Sensei Gauntner and her guest, Grandmaster Shimabuku, to show respect and honor the founder's son on his visit to the United States.

Figure 50: April, 2013 - Akron, OH. The Isshinryu World Karate Assoc. (IWKA) tournament. L-R: Author, Master Toby Cooling, Master Bud Ewing, and Master Diane Ortenzio-Cooling.

Chapter 4
FAMILY

"The patience and dedication that a sensei puts in his students are a reflection of his love for them."

Sensei Jesús M. Jiménez

In Japanese, the word for family is *kazoku* (家族). Merriam-Webster provides no less than eight different definitions for the word *family*. Several of these pertain to the Order of Isshin-Ryu family very well. With respect to a **household**, *a group of individuals living under one roof and usually under one head*. Although there are many dojos within the Order of Isshin-Ryu (fifteen active dojos as of this writing), Sensei Jesús M. Jiménez of the Puerto Rico dojo says it best, "We are one dojo. The Order of Isshin-Ryu." In a manner of thought, the various dojos live under one roof and all under the guidance of Master Toby Cooling. This means any member from any dojo can visit another OI dojo and feel like a welcomed family member.

Figure 51: 2012, Chesapeake City, MD. L-R: Ronnie Cimorosi, Jesús M. Jiménez, Toby Cooling, Barry Smith, Kurt Kline

Regarding a **clan**, *a group of persons of common ancestry*. All of us within the OI stem from the lineage of Master Cooling within the art of Isshin-Ryu karate. Pertaining to **race**, *a people or group of peoples regarded as deriving from a common stock*. Our common stock goes beyond what brings us together, which is the practice and study of Isshin-Ryu karate. We work to improve ourselves and others within the OI family. To be a member of this family means having a 'never give up' attitude. With respect to **affiliation**, *a group of people united by certain convictions or a common affiliation*. Our convictions define who we are and what we do. Lowering our standards is not an option. Rather, for those who are struggling, we put in the work to bring them up to the standard. Quality should never be sacrificed.

Figure 52: July 1996, Pigeon Forge, TN. OI awards at the Isshinryu Hall of Fame. L-R: Barry Smith (Induction into Hall of Fame), Isham Latimer (Spirit of Isshinryu), Ronnie Cimorosi, Jr. (Male Instructor of the Year)

Martial arts are more than technique or rank. It is about people. Grandmaster Shimabuku imparted more than his style of martial arts. He infused his spirit, personality, and dedication to training within his students. This is an underlying goal of any family – karate or otherwise, to develop relationships that last a lifetime. Legendary Shotokan karate master Hirokazu Kanazawa wrote the foreword to the book *The Essence of Karate* and sums up this relationship well in regard to the training under Shotokan founder Gichin Funakoshi where he states, "The senior students looked after the juniors while the junior students respected their seniors. Through such vertical connections, along with the horizontal connection of friends learning from one another, Sensei Funakoshi demonstrated how such wonderful relationships could lead to the weaving of a rich human community." This is what the Order of Isshin-Ryu family feels like. Knowing you have a karate 'family' is invaluable beyond the walls of the dojo as many can attest. Master Cooling stated during interviews for this book, "You don't belong to the Order of Isshin-Ryu. You ARE the Order of Isshin-Ryu. And it goes both ways. You don't just represent me wherever you go with the OI patch. I also represent you wherever I go with the OI patch on my arm."

I can attest to this with my relationship with my Kendo sensei, Reiun Kim. Sensei Kim did more than teach Kendo. He took time to get to know his students beyond the dojo environment. Although he commanded respect in the dojo, he was humble and respectful to everyone. He maintained this even keel when you could tell he was upset that you didn't perform the techniques properly. You wanted to do well for him, you wanted to make him proud of you. This is what family is all about. The instructors in the family want to experience the learning of students through their eyes. Dave Lowry frames this well in his book *In the Dojo* where he writes, "The sensei has gone ahead a little further – or maybe a lot – and has come back to be a guide for his student. As he walks the same path once again, not as a first-time traveler but now as one who leads another, he sees a different journey, or at least he sees it through different eyes. Both teacher and student are enriched in the process." This is how it felt training under Sensei Kim. You could tell he enjoyed watching things "click" in the dojo, when students had glimpses of improvement. This is not much different than a father and son dynamic. The same occurs in the Order of Isshin-Ryu. When students progress, it is a reflection on everyone, and the family grows even closer together.

Master Cooling constantly puts people first. He has a very good understanding that everything meaningful in life stems from relationships. Time and time again, I've seen Master Cooling first and foremost connect with his karate family on a personal level. He makes it a point to take the time to get to know everyone and continually ask how life is going, how your relatives are doing, and if there's anything you need or want to discuss. He makes every attempt to keep his family 'connected.' In September 2017, I visited my sensei at his home in Nevada. Hurricane Irma had just passed through Puerto Rico and was hitting the Florida Keys. At breakfast, Sensei Jesús M. Jiménez called from his home in Puerto Rico to let Denshi know that although there was property damage, his family was safe and doing fine. Being relieved to overhearing the news, I thought that would be the end of the conversation. To my surprise, Denshi made a point to hand over his cell phone to every OI member at the table including his wife, myself, and Joe Ragan who was also visiting. It was important to Master Cooling to make sure each OI family member there had the opportunity to speak with Sensei Jiménez and offer our prayers and support. Regardless of what is going on in our lives, Denshi leads by example… showing us that 'we are family first.'

Figure 53: 2017 - The OI family tradition continues. L-R: Black belt Nikolina Novakovic with daughters Vesna (san-kyu, age 11), Maja (san-kyu, age 10) and Ivana (roku-kyu, age 7).

Denshi is most concerned about everyone in the Order of Isshin-Ryu – his family. Those of us with children know how wonderful it is when they succeed in their endeavors. The same holds true for your martial arts students. When someone in the Order of Isshin-Ryu succeeds, Denshi couldn't be any happier. This compassion for those in his organization is his lifeline.

Anyone who dives headfirst into martial arts training should be saluted for making the effort to participate in something that is not easy to do. Denshi appreciates this type of commitment. How many people today go outside of their comfort zone and try something new? Or even try anything? Everyone seems to want to sit back and remain comfortable. This is not the expectation if you want to be a member of the Order of Isshin-Ryu.

The OI accepts and protects our family and treasures those who try to improve themselves, all for the sake of becoming a better martial artist and a contributing member of their community. And if you stumble and fall along the way? No problem. At least as a member of the OI, you are putting yourself on the line every day, working to improve. And for that reason, the word 'family' means that much more to the Order of Isshin-Ryu.

When we think in terms of improvement or process, there tends to be a global perspective first and then filtering down to local. For example, the implementation of various laws or regulations. They are passed for the common good globally, but then those laws filter down locally for enforcement. But when we think in terms of taking care of one another, the focus or primary attention should be geared toward the family first, and then expanded outward to neighbors and community and the like.

This is the mindset of the Order of Isshin-Ryu. We make sure we take care of one another first and foremost, and everything else tends to fall into place. This, in turn, develops a sense of synergy among the members. Denshi has expressed an "open door policy" among the OI dojo to facilitate the continual development of bonds not just within the precepts of martial arts training, but also as brothers and sisters among one another. It is quite common to hear someone in the OI state they expect a fellow OI member to assist them in times of trouble or strife before a blood relative would help.

Coming Back Home

For a variety of reasons, personal or professional, people often fall out of regular training. However, time and again those people can rely on the OI family to be there for them whenever needed. One example of someone returning to the OI family to fulfill his goals is Bob Foard. Bob started training in the OI when he was 12 years old but had to quit at one point. Many years later, he returned to the family when his daughter started to train. He couldn't stand being on the sidelines, so he joined the classes and started over from the beginning as a white belt.

Shortly after starting back in the OI in 2005, Bob wrote a letter to Master Cooling during a 10-hour flight to Hawaii. Below is that letter.

> March 16, 2005
> Denshi,
>
> It was good to see you at the last shiai. Some of my thoughts I would like to share with you. They say your kids will keep you young. Whitney, my 12-year-old came home from school one day and said she wanted to learn karate. I kind of let it go for a couple of weeks thinking she just wanted to hang out with her friends but she kept bringing it up, so I said, "If you really want to learn karate, you have to understand this is a lifelong commitment." I then shared with her some of my experiences. She kept it up with the "I want to, I want to." So, I said, "Tell you what, you can start in karate class, but I pick the dojo." She agreed so I called Bud Ewing (my sensei the second time I started back). He said a shiai was coming up, so I took Whitney and the rest of the family to watch. She wanted to start right away.
>
> As I watched her in the kids' class for a couple of nights, I thought *'I need to get back into this.'* After asking Sensei Tyree if he would take me on as a

student, I started back in the Tuesday/Thursday night adult class. Whitney is now working out with us in the adult class and we both love it. This is something we can do together, working through the ranks.

Since I had my children late in life, both Whitney (12) and Madison (6) have always seen me at the top. In their eyes, I have always been the boss of our businesses (a funeral director). They weren't around when I was struggling and going through the building process. So, Whitney seeing me start as a white belt the same as her, is good for her to understand we all start at the same place.

At the last shiai, I watched the black belt promotion. I started thinking, "Man, me sitting in front of yourself, Master Ewing and Sensei Tyree would be an incredible, meaningful experience for me since you were my first sensei, then Master Ewing, and now Sensei Tyree." What a lucky guy. If my health stays good, I WILL DO IT! My heart and desires are there, and they always have been. I just took a 20-year break! As you said to me two shiai ago, my kid's enthusiasm will grow through me. In business, I have learned not to dwell on looking back, but to focus on looking forward. I have a very talented sensei, and I am sure you will agree. So, it is all up to me. I remember Ronnie Tyree as a skinny, uncoordinated young kid and WOW! Look at him now!

When I was 14, you brought karate to Chesapeake City. I remember the first demonstration you did was in the schoolyard of the elementary school. One of the baddest guys in town was there, Ronnie Biggs. You were demonstrating board breaking and he just kept breaking boards, just as you were, as if to show you up. I remember you said to him, "Yeah, but your hands will hurt in the morning and mine won't." After seeing that demonstration, I was infatuated with karate.

The first time I quit was because my mother made me give it up as a disciplinary action. My school grades were bad, and she knew I loved going to karate class so she made me give it up. I remember my dad was not in agreement with her, but she won out. At that point, I lost the heart. Seeing my fellow students advance when I wasn't. Then, after college and some work experience in Baltimore, when I moved back to Cecil County (MD), I started back to class. I was around 29 or 30 years old, and Master Ewing was my sensei. He promoted me to blue belt and that summer, I started playing fastpitch softball with my buddies and gave up karate for the summer. I can't explain it, but I guess that summer never ended until now. I can only imagine where I would be if I had just stuck with your teachings through the OI.

Not being able to change the past, I can only look forward to the future, and I can thank my daughter for bringing me back.

You should be proud of what you have done with the OI and through your teachings, the positive effects that you and your organization has had on many people who stuck with it. Maybe it is not too late for me, and the opportunity is still there for my two girls at such a young age.

Rock (Mr. Foard)

Master Cooling relays a funny story while at the Isshin-Ryu Hall of Fame tournament in 2015. During one conversation, someone mentioned the stringent requirements of Isshin-Ryu. Just then Bob Foard happened to be walking by. Denshi said, "You're not kidding." He stopped Mr. Foard and said, "Bob, how old were you when you first started with me?" Bob replied, "Twelve." Then Denshi asked, "How old when you earned your black belt?" Bob smiled and said, "Fifty-eight." Everyone just stared at both Denshi and Bob. Of course, this length of time was the result of interruptions such as career, family, and such. But as this goes to show, you never really leave the OI family. You just take long breaks from the training. Once the OI family gets into your heart, it never goes away.

Figure 54: 2017 - Chesapeake City, MD: L-R: Grandmaster Toby Cooling and one of his orginal five students, Bob Foard.

Eye Opener

I attended the 2001 Isshin-Ryu Hall of Fame tournament along with my student, Jerry Robinette, primarily to support the Order of Isshin-Ryu and to witness Master Bill Sullivan receive the Hall of Fame's Instructor of the Year award.

The morning after the tournament, Jerry and I wanted to grab a quick breakfast before the long drive home. We noticed Master Sullivan already enjoying his morning meal and he signaled us to join him. Somehow, the topic of conversation moved to Grandmaster Harold Long, one of Isshin-Ryu karate's pioneers who brought the system over to the United States in the late 1950s. I had a fair degree of the historical perspective of Grandmaster Long based upon the books I had already read on Isshin-Ryu karate. I even had the opportunity to meet him a few times in the past both at the Order of Isshin-Ryu shiai (tournament), which he attended from time to time, and also at the annual Isshin-Ryu Hall of Fame event.

Figure 55: 1994 – Cecil Community College - Elkton, MD. Grandmaster Harold Long serving as center referee for black belt kumite at annual OI shiai. L-R: Mark Wallace, Long, Bud Ewing.

Master Sullivan noted how each year on October 12, the anniversary of Grandmaster Long's passing, he raises the flag of the U.S. Marines on his front yard. Being a U.S. Marine himself and a veteran of the Vietnam War, he said this flag was presented to him by Grandmaster Long many years ago. I noted that is really a respectful thing to do. Master Sullivan stated, "Well, it's more than that. Do you know the story about the Chosen 13?" My ignorance prevailed, and I was stumped. I said, "No. What is the Chosen 13?" He explained the Battle of the Chosin Reservoir during the Korean War. Harold Long played an integral part in this battle. In 1950, the battle of the Chosin Reservoir was fought against the Chinese Army, where temperatures ranged between four degrees below zero to thirty-five degrees below zero.

On November 27 the Chinese 9th Army surprised the US X Corps commanded by Major General Edward Almond at the Chosin Reservoir area. A brutal 17-day battle in freezing weather soon followed. In the period between November 27 and December 13, 1950, 30,000 United Nations troops under the field command of Major General Oliver P. Smith were encircled and attacked by approximately 120,000 Chinese troops under the command of Song Shi-Lun, who had been ordered by Mao Zedong to destroy the UN forces. The UN forces were nonetheless able to make a fighting withdrawal and broke out of the encirclement while inflicting crippling losses on the Chinese[20].

This battle has been termed "the most savage fighting in modern warfare" by today's historians. The marines who survived became known as the "Chosen Few." Today, this group is referred to as the "Eternal Band of Brothers." Master Harold Long was one of those survivors.

I was fascinated by Master Sullivan's account of this battle and Harold Long's involvement and survival. This information brought a much clearer perspective and appreciation for his raising of the U.S. Marine flag presented to him by Grandmaster Long. It made perfect sense to me and brought much more respect and admiration for Master Sullivan and his dedication to the United States.

I would never have known any of this unless I had the chance to sit down with Master Sullivan and talk openly about a variety of topics like all family members should do. The lesson: always look for opportunities to sit down with your dojo family members and talk. Learn their backgrounds. Find out their experiences from the past. You never know what you'll come away with and be enriched for the better.

What Does Black Belt Mean?

For those without direct experience in martial arts training, the black belt signifies those who have attained an expert level in self-defense methods from the Orient. This is simply not true. The black belt rank symbolizes students' achievements as those who are ready to truly study, research, and train as serious students of their chosen system of martial arts. According to Master Cooling, "You are now ready to learn."

Students realize how much effort they put in to attain black belt but at the same time, they realize there is so much more yet to learn. In his book, *Sword and Brush*, author Dave Lowry discusses this realization at the black belt achievement where he states, "…the [student] is suddenly confronted with the fact that what he thought

---

[20] wikipedia.org/wiki/Battle_of_Chosin_Reservoir

was the perfection of the technique was merely the introduction to it. An entirely new vista has opened up for him. What had been his destination has been revealed as a pass through the mountains, one that gives way to another broad view waiting to be explored."

I posed this question to as many of my OI family as I could in the process of writing this book. There are people of quite diverse backgrounds and experiences who begin their study of Isshin-Ryu karate, and the Order of Isshin-Ryu is no different. You must understand there are varying goals and intentions for those who begin their karate training.

One concept that black belt signifies… salvation. Not so much in the sense of saving your soul, but from the aspect of proving to yourself you *CAN* accomplish something difficult, something that requires an immense amount of self-determination and effort. Being a long-distance runner myself, I can compare this to the sport of running. When you begin running, the thought of completing a marathon simply doesn't register in your mind. You think to yourself either 'why?' or 'no way!' when posed with the question of whether such a run is in your future. But, over time, it becomes evident that you are able to go longer distances, and the thought of 26.2 miles is a real possibility. Dean Karnazes is an ultramarathon runner. He describes in his book *The Road to Sparta* the underlying concept of the marathon as follows:

> ….the marathon is not about running; it is about salvation. You see, we spend so much of our lives doubting ourselves, thinking that we're not good enough, not strong enough, not made of the right stuff. The marathon offers an opportunity for redemption. Opportunity, I say, because the outcome is uncertain. Opportunity, I say, because it is up to you, and only you, to make it happen. The ingredients required to tackle this formidable challenge are straightforward: commitment, sacrifice, grit, and raw determination.

These thoughts easily crossover to those required of martial arts training and what is required to earn a black belt. There are those who clearly have natural abilities and seemingly move their way up the ranks without effort. But the majority do not possess such qualities and gifts. They are normal, everyday people who see something appealing to the martial arts and wish to partake of the training and take away the valuable lessons and life-serving concepts that karate can provide. They must work harder, much harder, than the average person. In a sense, their training is like a marathon. It is painful and not easy for them. These are the type of people that reflect the true meaning of what a black belt means… *never giving up.*

Family

This is the essence of the Order of Isshin-Ryu family. When you see others working so hard to accomplish a goal such as black belt even though they don't possess natural talent, you respect them and their efforts. You grow closer to those people and bonds develop on a 'family' level. You make it a point to be there for them, to continually encourage and help them whenever you can. There is no sign at the door that states: ONLY NATURAL ATHLETES MAY ENTER. Karate really can be for anyone who is willing to put in the time and effort. Those are the ones who truly learn what family is all about and appreciate what this family offers.

Figure 56: 1988. Front row L-R: Toby Cooling, Bill Sullivan, Barry Smith. Back row L-R: Harold Long, Bud Ewing, Phil McIlroy, Butch Hill.

Chapter 5
SHIAI AND DAI SEMPAI

"It's all about the willingness to outwork and outlearn everyone."

Mark Cuban

The word Shiai (試合) has several translations from Japanese: match or game, tournament, or round (as in 'round' of golf). Shiai are the annual gathering of members of the Order of Isshin-Ryu to compete in *kata* (forms) and *kumite* (sparring). This is a tradition going back to the earliest days in 1971 when the OI was still small in numbers and members were closer in proximity to one another. Currently, the OI holds three shiai per year and often hosts visitors from other Isshin-Ryu organizations as well as various other martial arts disciplines. This helps to develop and strengthen bonds that can benefit everyone both within and outside of the dojo and competitive environment.

The purpose of the OI shiai is multi-faceted. Beyond the competition aspect, students who are eligible for their next rank and where their sensei has provided approval have the opportunity to evaluate in front of a panel of black belts. In a 1982 interview with *Cecil Whig* newspaper, Master Cooling said, "For many, karate has become a way to pattern their life's direction using its teaching in awareness, confidence, and comradeship." Therefore, to advance in rank students must demonstrate their improvement in the skills required for such rank at the OI shiai. For kyu ranks, this begins when evaluating for yon-kyu, or green belt. Each subsequent rank advancement requires testing in front of a panel at the shiai. When the time comes for evaluation for sho-dan, or first degree black belt, the testing occurs at Hombu dojo in Elkton, Maryland the Friday night before the shiai. These evaluations, as one might expect, take longer to cover all the requirements and ensure the candidate has a firm grasp of not only the physical skill but also the meaning behind the techniques, kata (forms), and the history of the art.

The evaluations for rank are far from automatic, even if the candidate's sensei feels they are ready to test. Students must demonstrate their understanding and abilities, often in front of black belts they have never met or only see infrequently. The stress and anxiety of the evaluation is a critical factor that students must deal with to show confidence in their skills and their desire to attain rank. Sometimes, those factors overwhelm students, and they have trouble performing well during an evaluation at the shiai, even though within their own dojo, they are well-prepared for their test.

Figure 57: March 1982 - North East, Maryland. Isham Latimer promoting his student, Willie Davis, to black belt at annual OI shiai. To the right of Latimer is Master Toby Cooling, then a nana-dan (7th degree black belt).

When students do not pass their tests, they should not view it as a failure. They should perceive it as a process in the development of their martial arts skills and personal character. When adversities such as not passing rank examinations are dealt with successfully, students' characters are improved tremendously. This development also applies to sensei. They may take their students' evaluations quite hard as they put in tremendous time and effort with each student over time. However, the sensei shouldn't take it personally, as they are only the guides. They cannot perform on behalf of their students… it is completely up to each student to perform up to the required level. The sensei will go back to the dojo and work with their students not only on the physical aspects but the mental aspects as well. The students improve throughout this process, and the sensei increase their skills as teachers.

Location

The current location of the shiai is Bohemia Manor High School in Chesapeake City, Maryland. This is where several early members of the Order of Isshin-Ryu attended high school, including Master Cooling. The earliest shiai were often held outdoors in the Spring and Summer instead of inside a *dojo*. *Jo* means "a place" and *Do* means "way." As such, dojo means a "place to practice the way" of the respective karate system. However, dojos were not always held inside as Dave Lowry points out in his book *In the Dojo* where he writes, "It is pertinent to note that this "place" did not, in the long history of Japan's martial arts, necessarily refer to a building. Practice and teaching more typically went on in open spaces such as fields left fallow, courtyards, or perhaps on the wide *engawa*, or verandas, that surrounded more sumptuous homes." This was certainly the case in the days of *Te* (systems of martial arts on Okinawa that pre-date the formulation of karate) and the early days of formalized karate systems on Okinawa.

The Order of Isshin-Ryu made full use of this tradition of training outdoors as shiai were often held in the backyards at various locations including that of Master Cooling's parents. Keeping in mind Okinawans often trained outdoors due to the climate of the region, and Denshi just got back from training there, the outdoor sessions of early shiai during the summer months in Maryland made perfect sense.

Trophies

The Order of Isshin-Ryu does not award trophies at the annual shiai. Winners in the various divisions are simply called forward by name to be recognized for their performance on that day. However, there was a time when awards were presented. The early years of the OI awarded a medallion type award.

There was a shiai held in 1973 at the dojo of Sensei John Remick in Glen Burnie, Maryland. Master Cooling recalls two sensei had begun arguing over placings in a particular division. Due to the chaos that followed between OI family members, it was determined with the consensus of the black belts at the time to never award trophies again. Denshi remembers asking those involved, "You're going to give up a friendship over a piece of plastic and imitation marble?"

The objective of the shiai is for members to gather and compete in a traditional martial arts competition, at a reasonable price, without concern over trying to win a trophy. This way, the intent is to keep the competition pure and for everyone to develop their skills and further friendships and bonds every time they attend a shiai. Black belt Aaron Walker put it this way when he attended his first shiai as a white belt beginner, "Here was a group of people - of all ages, body types, ethnicities, socio-economic backgrounds, and professions - avidly and earnestly working, learning and growing together in their efforts to become better martial artists and better people." This is the underlying purpose of the shiai – not just to compete, but to help one another improve their martial arts.

Dai Sempai

Dai Sempai (大先輩) is a 'role' served by someone in the Order of Isshin-Ryu upon the direction of Master Cooling. When the time comes for the role to be assumed by someone new, Denshi will make the announcement at the annual shiai for everyone to hear.

According to Peter Urban in his book *The Karate Dojo*, Dai Sempai is used upon attainment of san-dan or third degree black belt. Urban writes, "Karatemen on this level are highly respected and are referred to in their dojos as 'dai sempai,' or 'number one older brothers.'" In the Order of Isshin-Ryu, the Dai Sempai is a position held by someone getting ready for their grade testing for red and white belt, which is for roku-dan or 6th degree black belt. *Dai* means "big" or "great." Sempai refers to anyone who precedes you in the dojo. Therefore, Dai Sempai is someone who is far senior to you in the martial arts. As Sensei Kurt Kline recalls, "As we grew up in the OI, we came to understand it to mean 'second in command.'" He goes on to say, "The role should be viewed as a training ground for leadership. Someone who is able to stand on their own and run the organization. Therefore, when I served as Dai Sempai it was an honor and a privilege."

The Dai Sempai position was enacted by Master Cooling in 1980. Bud Ewing was the first Dai Sempai in the Order of Isshin-Ryu. Denshi explains, "For red and white belt promotion, I wanted the candidate to be able to do all the various functions within the OI. It evolved into requiring the person to being named Dai Sempai and running the shiai effectively and efficiently prior to evaluation to 6th degree black belt."

In the early days of the OI, the Dai Sempai was always Bud Ewing as he was Denshi's right-hand man. But eventually the role was passed to Juan Lopez, and as Sensei Kurt Kline remembers, "It was an emotional, painful moment for Sensei Ewing as he always served the Dai Sempai role. However, that was softened a bit as he was also promoted to roku-dan at the same time." Currently, it is effectively the person who runs the shiai.

Shiai and Dai Sempai

Figure 58: 1999 - Order of Isshin-Ryu shiai. L-R: Toby Cooling, Bud Ewing, Isham Latimer, Juan D. Lopez, Barry Smith, Jesus Jimenez

Essentially, the Dai Sempai is in charge of running the shiai, or competition, for the Order of Isshin-Ryu. There are three shiai held every year in the Spring, Summer, and the Fall. The shiai brings together all members of the OI for friendly competition in kata (forms) and kumite (fighting or sparring). The Dai Sempai is responsible for running the event and ensuring everything goes well.

The role has changed somewhat over the years. In the 80s, there were quite a few black belts attending the shiai. If someone wasn't good at running the events, then the shiai would last forever. This was because invariably the black belts serving as judges would often take breaks, go for a quick food break, or just catch up with old friends outside the arena. As Sensei Kline puts it, "It was almost like herding cats. It was definitely a challenge to keep things moving along."

The role of Dai Sempai is a thankless job as well. During my tenure as Dai Sempai, I can recall hearing a 'thank you' only one time, from Sensei Ronnie Cimorosi, after a shiai was over and everyone was leaving the gymnasium.

Recent Dai Sempai, Sensei Adam Knox, notes "Part of the process of Dai Sempai, for me, was learning the ability to 'manage up.' When I started as Dai Sempai, half of the black belts at the shiai were red and white belts who outranked me. I started by trying to run the shiai with the black belts who were lower in rank than me, and it failed miserably. I did a terrible job. I had to learn how to be more comfortable approaching higher ranking black belts, both personally and professionally for help getting the shiai events completed." To a large degree, that serves as part of the maturation process as a go-dan: learning how to deal with all levels of black belts and getting to know the red and white belts better. Everyone at the shiai wants the day to go well, and they want to help. The Dai Sempai must learn how to make that process work effectively.

Figure 59: April, 1994. Sensei Mike Goodyear, on left, serving his turn as Dai Sempai at the annual OI shiai. With him is Sensei Ronnie Cimorosi.

Running a shiai consists of assigning judges to each division of competition, assigning a panel of black belts for student rank evaluations, and shifting things up, as needed, throughout the day. The complexity and effort needed to serve as Dai Sempai for a shiai is largely depending on the turnout on that particular day. No two shiai are exactly the same. As a result, the role of Dai Sempai is generally not a "once and done" function. Denshi prefers the Dai Sempai to serve in this role over a period of time, so the other senior-ranking black belts can have a chance to see this person perform in varying situations. This enables a better perspective on the candidate getting ready to take their 6th dan black belt evaluation.

The Dai Sempai must also be aware of honored guests. The guests could be Isshin-Ryu karate-ka who are close friends of the Order of Isshin-Ryu or martial artists of other backgrounds invited by Denshi to attend the shiai. These guests are typically invited to assist with judging the competition and the Dai Sempai must be aware of them to ensure they are getting these opportunities. In the budo, it is desired to show respect and appreciation to other martial artists. The OI always makes every effort to show this respect, and it is a critical function of the Dai Sempai at every OI function.

Chapter 6
SEMPAI – KOHAI: THE TEACHER-STUDENT RELATIONSHIP

"The poor teacher stands where he is and beckons the pupil to come to him. The good teacher goes to where the pupil is, takes him, and leads him to where he ought to go."

Saint Thomas Aquinas

A relationship exists within the Japanese culture known as *Sempai-Kohai*, which means seniors and juniors. This relationship is integral to the sound practice of martial arts of all styles and systems. Each martial art has its own customs and traditions in its teachings and practices from Chinese and Okinawan, to Japanese and Filipino, and so on. The Sempai-Kohai dynamic goes beyond these customs. It isn't necessarily written down or verbalized formally; however, after some time has transpired in training, students notice something going on beyond merely demonstrating techniques or proficiency in the dojo. Something else tangible is happening that may not necessarily be discussed in a structured setting.

Sempai-Kohai has been written about by many others, both in published books as well as in internet chat rooms, some of which are presented here. As stated, Sempai-Kohai is crucial in the ongoing development of the martial artist – both for students and teachers alike. This relationship exists in all facets of the culture, from shop workers to skilled tradesmen. The relationship is interdependent, as a *sempai* requires a *kōhai* and vice versa, and establishes a bond determined by the date of entry to an organization[21]. For karate training, Sempai-Kohai pertains to experiences both inside and outside the dojo.

When you become part of a dojo, those already training there are your seniors, your *sempai*. Those who come after you are your *kohai*, your juniors. This is regardless of rank, age, or experience. Since everyone has a relationship to those above or below them, this system keeps things moving in an orderly manner.

It employs a method called *on-giri*. On-giri refers to debt, duty, or obligation to others. The junior has a certain debt that he owes his seniors by virtue of their willingness to pass on what they have learned. The senior in turn has a duty to his sensei and dojo to bring his junior up through the ranks as a big brother would a little brother. For modern karate, 'brother' is either male or female.

By being your senior, by helping you, by kicking you when you are lazy, by acting as an advisor, coach, and confidante, the sempai assumes a tremendous responsibility. This responsibility stems from the days of the samurai. Author Dave Lowry brings the following perspective from his book *In the Dojo*, "...a ryu or dojo are seen to be only as strong as their weakest link. The attention, then, must always be on developing to the fullest those members whose skills are most lacking. In the dojo, that will be the beginners. It is only through the close attention of the seniors that these links are strengthened." The kohai who has been tutored and taken care of by his sempai becomes an *onjin*, a person under obligation, and as an old Japanese adage goes, "Life and death are light as a feather, but obligation, obligation is heavy as a mountain."

The master instructor or system head is responsible for teaching the sensei (even though his students may also receive instruction during seminars and clinics). The sensei is responsible for disseminating information to the seniors of the dojo, even though many juniors profit from their instruction. However, it is the seniors' responsibility to tutor the juniors and help them along whenever possible. This help goes beyond simply teaching the techniques of Isshin-Ryu. Master Cooling explained in a March 1982 newspaper interview with *Cecil Whig*, "Teaching is important because black belts must instruct to advance and, of course, the lower ranks must learn. But teaching is mostly instilling the art and stimulating questions from the student." He goes on to state, "There's no such thing as a karate teacher. He's a guide. You (the student or kohai) teach yourself."

Often, the instruction is not as formal as the sensei's; rather it is given by example. Just as every sensei has his/her specific method of passing on a style, every senior student unconsciously develops a favored method for helping sensei do so.

---

[21] https://en.wikipedia.org/wiki/Senpai_and_k%C5%8Dhai

These methods become like a dojo sub-style. When a visitor from another dojo settles in, he may have a few lessons to teach himself or he may have a few to receive, depending on where he falls in the sempai-kohai relationship.

Based upon the deep respect for loyalty and obligation that characterized old Japan, the sempai-kohai relationship often extends throughout the lives of those involved in it. It is a convention that allows a kohai to develop the attitudes of helpfulness and leadership that are necessary for mastery, and so in a reciprocal way, the lives of the sempai and kohai are bettered. The sempai understands fully what the kohai is going through in their training and how difficult the process may be, on all levels. Because of this, the concepts of mutual respect, compassion, and loyalty are generally developed

Figure 60: Hombu Dojo - Elkton, MD. L-R: Sensei Sotiere Nicholson of the Florida dojo and Master Toby Cooling.

over time. Author and Goju-Ryu stylist Roy Kenneth Kamen states this well in his book *Karate: Beneath the Surface* as, "The rigorous training martial artists suffer through, as we learn to fight by mastering the kata, elevates our character as we overcome our physical, emotional and spiritual limitations. The lessons we learn through training increase our compassion as we teach our juniors, who are themselves suffering through the training."

The sempai is always guiding, leading the student to what they need to do so they can be on their own someday. This involves gradually and deliberately directing the kohai regarding what to practice and review on their own to suggested reading material for further research and also the state of mind regarding various stages of the kohai's development.

At times, the sempai-kohai system may seem difficult. For the junior, it may seem that at times his movements are heavily criticized. Even outside the dojo he finds his behavior under the watchful eye and close scrutiny of a senior who is quick to correct mistakes or poor decisions. The sempai has a very good idea of the training needed from beginning to more advanced levels (i.e. from beginner to sho-dan or 1st degree black belt). He knows what you, the kohai, are capable of doing and being. The sempai has been through the tough times as a student in the past. He understands what is needed to push through the difficult moments of training and pushes you because he cares. He wants the kohai to improve, to overcome challenges, to become better each and every training session. The sempai knows that if you cannot overcome his criticism and tough times in the dojo, how will you ever be able to handle difficult times on your own or outside the dojo? How will you ever be able to answer the challenges of real life when they arise?

This approach to teaching is not by accident. It has evolved over many, many years and is attributed to the cultures of the Orient such as China, Okinawa, and Japan. The martial arts were often practiced in secret and mainly passed down within the family structure. To become a student of a highly regarded master of martial arts was no easy matter. You couldn't simply ask to learn, pay your monthly fee, and begin your training. This is noted in the book *Steal My Art*, where author Stuart Olson describes how he learned T'ai Chi from renowned master T.T. Liang. Olson writes, "Traditional teachers in Asia could not be approached as they are in present times. Money was secondary; trusting a student was of utmost importance. In some cases, Liang had to just follow other students performing the form, and he could not even speak to the teacher until he had learned the entire form by assimilation."

Essentially, the student would have to work extremely hard to learn the sensei's art – to try to steal it – since the sensei, himself, worked beyond the point of exhaustion and frustration to learn. Why would, or should, the sensei freely give away complete knowledge and skills to just anyone? The teacher, or sempai, places a very high value on their skills, knowledge, and abilities – and rightfully so. Therefore, students need to understand they are being tested and pushed hard to see if they are willing to put in the work to learn what the sempai had to endure in order for them to attain their knowledge and skills from their instructors.

Only the highest levels of work and effort will garner the opportunity for the student to learn the art being studied in its truest form. This is summarized well by Olson again where Liang explains to him, "A student's money means nothing, smiles and compliments mean nothing, promises and favors mean nothing. All that matters is the knowledge that they (students) will cherish their bounty (what they've learned), and the harder they work to steal your art, the more you ensure their success and skills. It is every teacher's duty to ensure that their students become better than he is, and this can only be accomplished if they are made to work really hard for it."

Sempai – Kohai: The Teacher-Student Relationship

Figure 61: Easton Dojo Members. L-R: Mike Magill, Bill Sullivan, Jo Bramble.

If you are a beginner in the martial arts, remember that and listen carefully to the advice of your sempai. Their experience is hard-won. At times, the kohai may think it's too much to deal with. The seemingly endless criticisms, the hard training, all the history and terminology you need to absorb. It is at precisely those times where you need to trust your sempai and yourself that you will pull through. Granted, this is not easy to do and not everyone will be able to persevere. For those that do, it will be well worth the time and effort. If you are a more advanced student, keep in mind that training is only a part of your purpose in the dojo. There are kohai in need of your guidance, and it is up to you to set the example.

We learn through observation, listening, or imitation. A good student will utilize all three of these learning styles to become a well-rounded martial artist. Sometimes, it seems the student wants all the answers immediately. You must try to avoid this type of thinking or approach. Often, sensei will not provide the answers freely. He will only impart a morsel of knowledge and then see where the student takes it from there. This provides for independent thinking and research in order to discover what works for the student.

An aspect of the Sempai-Kohai relationship that is sometimes overlooked is that it goes both ways. It's a two-way street. Very often, the sempai is learning from the kohai, and they don't even realize it. Charlie Deitterick, a black belt from the early days of the OI, states, "One thing I learned…you owe as much to your worst student as your best student. And you'll learn as much from your worst student as your best student." He was referring to a specific example of a time when he learned one of his best kumite, or sparring, techniques from one of his more challenging students.

Figure 62: October 10, 2015 - Chesapeake City, MD. L-R: Author, Adam Knox after his promotion to Roku-dan.

Challenging, in that this student was not very good at sparring; however, his beginning student was able to cover up his openings extremely well. Sensei Deitterick needed to really put in a lot of time and effort to figure out how to get around this student's defenses to make his techniques work. In this example, the kohai presented challenges, and the sempai had to figure out, or learn, how to overcome something in the sempai's training process. This happens all the time in the martial arts and is one of the elements that makes karate training work so well for the growth of everyone involved.

There is another way to look at it. At each new rank level, think about wiping the slate clean and re-learn everything. The memory wants to be used. This is how we learn. Go back and see what you probably missed along the way. The sempai can instill this mindset into kohai and as the kohai reviews all that has been learned, the sempai, in turn, benefits from this review as well. It's a two-way street.

Social media such as Facebook and YouTube have truly opened a window of opportunity that has never been seen before. A good student will use these resources to further their knowledge of other arts and other approaches to Isshin-Ryu; however, the most important aspect of social media should be the growth of overall understanding of what others use as their approach to training. When we *understand* more fully what others are doing, we respect them more than before, and we can be more comfortable and confident in what we are doing ourselves.

As adult learners, we tend to worry too much about being a perfect student. There is no perfection. It simply doesn't exist. The mind tends to get in the way too much during the learning and training process. Simply trust your heart. If your heart is in the right place, everything will take care of itself.

In the book *The Sword of No-Sword*, John Stevens provides a Japanese calligraphy example by swordsman Yamaoka Tesshu. The shodo example by Yamaoka Tesshu states, "If the mind is correct, the brush will be correct." (*see figure 63*) In essence, Tesshu is saying when a calligrapher is brushing the characters "no-mindedly," or without distracted thought, the brush strokes will be alive and vibrant. However, if you are distracted or worrying about other things, the characters will appear lifeless and forced no matter how well they are constructed and brushed on paper.

The same holds true with martial arts performance. If your mind is preoccupied with thoughts of performing with perfect execution, you will look stiff and rigid. You must let go of these thoughts and simply perform naturally without worry about what others are thinking. Be yourself and move freely. This is different than self-observation where you break down your movements and technique and analyze and self-critique everything to improve the movement. But when you switch into performing a specific kata, you must 'let go' and trust your training and not 'think' about it. Watch a professional athlete or an Olympic competitor. All the work and obsessing over performing correctly has been done already. On the field of competition, they will remove the thoughts, worry, and doubt and simply execute.

You could expand or modify Tesshu's lesson to say, "If the heart is correct, the karate will be correct." Could this be something the founder alluded to with his naming of Isshin-Ryu? Perhaps, but that would be pure speculation at this point since we can no longer ask the founder himself. I like to think that the aspect of the heart within the name of Isshin-Ryu goes beyond just "one heart." It is well-documented that when asked why he chose the name of Isshin-Ryu, Shimabuku replied, "Because everything begins with one." That may be what he said, but to me, the words fall a bit short of what Shimabuku and

Figure 63: "Kokoro tadashikereba sunawachi fude tadashi" (If the mind is correct, the brush will be correct). Calligraphy of Yamaoka Tesshu (1836-1888), founder of Muto Ryu School of Swordsmanship. This piece was painted by the author - August 2012.

his system actually focuses on or attempts to acknowledge as critically important. When you look at the life of Tatsuo Shimabuku, the types of students he developed, and the types of karate-ka his black belts eventually turned out, it is quite evident they all share a common denominator: a pure heart devoted to the development of strong Isshin-Ryu karate.

As sempai, you have a choice. You can either draw out the best or the worst in people. Sempai should work to draw out the best in the kohai. You have a duty to those who have gone before you by passing on the system being taught in the correct manner and developing kohai who, in turn, one day will become a sempai. As the teacher, you owe it to your sensei as well as the founder of Isshin-Ryu, Master Shimabuku, to take this role very seriously. If you bring out the best in others, you are fulfilling the concept of Sempai – Kohai as it was intended.

Sometimes, it simply takes a kind, encouraging word to help a student work through some difficult spots in their training. Other times, it takes leading by example. Unless you can demonstrate what you are asking, the request of the student will likely fall on deaf ears. Other times, the sempai role may require some 'tough love' or a kick in the butt to get the student moving in the right direction.

Generally, all it takes is putting the student in a position to succeed instead of predicting they will fail. Listen to the kohai's goals, dreams, and aspirations in the martial arts; determine what the student is good at and give it additional attention, and encourage them to be the best they can be. It may sound simple, but it takes time and devotion to the Sempai – Kohai dynamic.

Part of this concept involves understanding there is no special formula or playbook involved. All students bring different variables to the table, both physically and mentally. The sempai must approach each student differently. The concepts of the art being taught are the same; however, each student will react differently and learn at a different pace. It's simply human nature that if not recognized and dealt with by the sempai, it will certainly create a problem in the learning experience.

These differences should be accepted. Why? In the long-term, figuring out the teaching method for each student can, in turn, help the sempai improve as a teacher and mentor. Learning to make small adjustments in the teaching process based upon what students require at a given time is a way to improve your overall character as a martial artist. I've heard students in the past tell me, "Thank you for being so patient. Sometimes I feel like I'm going in reverse instead of improving." The bottom line is this: if I can finally help a student overcome a hurdle in their training process, I've also overcome a hurdle of my own, and I've become a better teacher because of it.

Sensei Jesús M. Jiménez of the Puerto Rico dojo discusses two primary factors involved in the Sempai-Kohai dynamic: aptitude and attitude[22] as follows:

> The aptitude is the natural ability, talent, and capacity of learning. This quality on the karate-ka will take him to accept and understand why he must refrain from interfering with the sensei. Showing concern to another karate-ka who is his or her brother or sister. This concern will take him or her to follow the commands or guidance of the sensei, in gratitude for the time he spends with him or her showing the inner meanings of the martial arts. The student must learn that to be a leader, first know how to obey. By all the time the sensei, the sempai, and the kohai pass together, they will develop a strong affection or warm attachment that will create an unselfish loyalty.
>
> The attitude is the mental position or feeling about a fact or state. This is the way the sempai and kohai manifest themselves to each other and the way to show respect, obedience, and love.

Master Cooling has stated many times over the years "Teach all that you know. Don't hold back any knowledge from your students. Provide them everything you can. Only then will you be able to free up space in your mind to learn more." Only when you work with and teach students, especially beginners, do you learn how to reinforce your own knowledge.

Beginners offer challenges that more advanced students, or those of your same rank, do not. It becomes imperative to explain the concepts and techniques that a beginner doesn't understand. This is not easy. Someone of higher rank or the same rank as you already understand many of the concepts. If you only work with higher level students or people of your own rank, you will have a difficult time improving your own knowledge as you are then working at a level of assumption… the other people already have similar knowledge. At this point, there is less mental involvement and more physical training. You are no longer pushing yourself with respect to passing on knowledge and figuring out how to improve lower ranks. Development of the sempai relies heavily on the sempai-kohai dynamic. Traditional martial arts rely heavily on this relationship for the betterment of all those involved in the system.

This mindset is very similar among those in leadership positions, including high-level coaches. Dean Smith, the legendary late coach of the University of North Carolina basketball program, was a proponent to this concept of passing along

---

[22] The Isshin-Ryu Lighthouse, Vol. 1, Issue 1 – July 1998 (newsletter).

instruction. David Chadwick, a former player of Smith, in his book *It's How You Play the Game* devoted an entire chapter to this principle. A true leader is constantly looking to take every opportunity to teach whatever they can in a given situation. This forces you to search continuously for more information and experiences to expand your knowledge base. It's a never-ending cycle the sempai must strive to follow: teach everything and continue seeking more knowledge yourself. Always remain a student of the martial arts.

In her book *The Writing Warrior*, Laraine Herring touches upon this point. She states, "And I learned that unless I remain a constant student, not just of the craft of writing, but of its process and of myself, I will quickly become a fraud. I will turn into the didactic, rigid writer who speaks more than she listens, who rants more than she questions. I didn't want to be that writer. I didn't want to be that teacher." The sempai must always consider themselves a student and continually look to improve not only their martial arts skills but also seek character development. This is a process that must start at the top and filter down. Master Cooling provides such an example. He continuously encourages everyone, even the senior dans, to go out and learn new styles and techniques.

The sempai must have the ability to provide feedback in a positive, constructive manner. This fosters an attitude and spirit within the kohai that he or she can overcome any obstacle. Providing words of encouragement should never be underestimated. Often, this sort of reinforcement only takes a few seconds. For example, saying something like, "Mr. Jones your kata are really improving these past few months. I can see the effort you're putting out in the dojo. Just make sure you continue to work on those blocks!" The acknowledgment of someone's efforts is often the difference in the student remaining or quitting before their full potential is realized. This goes for not only children but adults as well.

Sempai need to keep the kohai focused. They will get discouraged. The training will get repetitive and monotonous. They may not advance as quickly as they want to. Students will not pass a rank test from time to time due to inadequate preparation, having a bad testing day, or possibly the sensei's miscalculation of the student's readiness to take the exam. In every case, kohai must learn the important thing is to keep working and the sempai bears the responsibility to get the message across to them. One example of the learning process and the Sempai – Kohai structure comes from black belt Aaron Walker where he summarizes the following:

> The general self-development accruing from training was the pleasant and deepening surprise of being involved in the OI. One trains under his or her sensei, but also gets reviewed and trained - as part of a feedback and

checks-and-balances structure - by other sensei in the OI. And it is in these circumstances that the body and ego take the most bruising. These were usually "tough love" workouts when one was pushed to the limits, but in the assurance that all the trainers were guiding one's development. Simultaneously, they were honing their own skills, and refining and advancing the art of karate. Even the belt evaluations - while ostensibly testing a candidate for rank promotion - were occasions for all to learn and grow.

Regardless of whether the student has a good test, a bad test, or is not testing as frequently as they wish, the reason you are studying martial arts is to research and train. Nothing is more important. The sempai should work every day to demonstrate and show the kohai the truth of this reality. If you are not putting training above all else, then your reasons for being a part of the martial arts is likely falling short of the mark. It's not about the color of the belt you wear, the number of kata you know, or how many trophies you've won over the years. What matters is simply the work you put in day in and day out in the dojo.

Another aspect of the Sempai-Kohai relationship is getting across the idea of forgetting about status or rank. I've often expressed that upon each rank promotion I felt unworthy, that I had to prove I earned the rank. I've always made it a point to think *I'm starting over* from scratch to demonstrate my worthiness of the rank promotion. This probably contradicts the general mindset where the student may think, "Yeah, I earned this rank. I worked hard to get this." This thinking is certainly true – to a point. But keep in mind there is so much more to your martial arts training than attaining rank. What could that be? Improving yourself and continually helping others. This is the only way the ryu, or style to which you are a part will continue for the benefit of future generations of students.

The sempai must ensure the kohai understands this concept. Instead of thinking of your rank, think about how blessed you are to have the ability to train in the art you love. God provided all the blessings you need to train, so always stay humble and be thankful for those blessings. It will be increasingly more difficult to improve and learn when you think you already know everything there is to know. Humility must remain regardless of the level or rank you attain. In his book *The Last Lesson*, Master J.C. Burris provides this perspective, "Only the process toward the real goal, the life-long progression toward understanding, patience, wisdom, and perfection of character provides the ultimate contentment and pleasure."

You must remember that you are part of something bigger, something interconnected, but you cannot see everything involved. As just one link in the entire chain, everything you do should be about the work you put into your training and

Figure 64: 2012 Dobbs Ferry, NY. Author training with the founding members of Chi Ryu Jujitsu. L-R: Author, Master Isham Latimer, Sensei John McDonald, Master John Costanzo.

never about you or your rank. As Ryan Holiday puts it in his book *Ego is the Enemy*, "It takes a special kind of humility to grasp that you know less, even as you know and grasp more and more." This is one of the major goals of the Sempai-Kohai relationship. Help the kohai develop the ability to humble themselves. Why? Because that is when true learning and value to the organization comes from. What is the barometer for true humility? When the individual consistently listens and then goes to work. Over time, the individual begins to understand and appreciate whatever little skill is attained, this is just a drop in the bucket compared to the totality of what could be learned, what can be displayed by following the proper path to the martial arts. And in due time, when the kohai develops proper humility, he or she can enjoy the process of learning, which requires being challenged and uncomfortable. When humility is present, these challenging and uncomfortable situations are not a concern. In fact, they are sought after as the kohai now understands this is needed to further their knowledge, to improve confidence.

When this level is attained, the kohai now can become a sempai in turn, and the ryu becomes stronger because of the devoted time to the proper traditions of budo. A long-time budo practitioner and author Walther von Krenner writes in his book *Following the Martial Path*, "The true purpose of all modern forms of Budo is to better oneself, and to develop a mindset that will enable practitioners to defend themselves no matter where they are or what they are doing." Therefore, the Sempai-Kohai relationship is central to the concept of true martial arts training. Each are dependent upon one another for the budo to thrive for generations to come.

Chapter 7
THREE ARROWS OF ISSHIN-RYU

"Conquer yourself and the world lies at your feet."

Saint Augustine

"Where we decide to put our energy decides what we'll ultimately accomplish."

Ryan Holiday

Watching a professional athlete perform at the highest level is enjoyable. They seem to be in complete control of their bodies and minds. The names and examples are virtually endless. How about a professional ballerina? A world-class musician? A motivational speaker? Or even a coach who seems to produce a winning team year after year? Surely, it can be captivating and inspirational watching someone who is at the top of their craft. Look into their eyes. They seem to project an attitude of "I got this." In the back of your mind, you just know they put in a great deal of time, trial, and error into becoming adept in their profession. What do they all have in common, regardless of their chosen endeavor or path?

Without question, they all share a common ability to combine the best elements of mind, body, and spirit. Interviews with them will demonstrate not just a command of their sport on a physical level, but also an understanding and devotion to the mental side of the ledger as well as an appreciation of growing the spirit. These concepts are not exclusive to martial arts. They go as far back as ancient Greece. Dean Karnazes discusses the Greek way of thinking regarding sport in his book *The Road to Sparta*, where he says sport should be a preparation for life. He states, "Athenians viewed intellectual education and physical education as inseparable equals…

(they) came to believe that only when mind, body, and spirit were aligned in perfect harmony could true human potential be realized and *arête* (excellence and virtue) be achieved."

From ancient Greece to the samurai of Japan to the early Okinawan karate-ka to present-day martial artists from all styles including mixed martial arts, the objective and goal is to develop a strong blend of physical, mental, and spiritual being– to which Isshin-Ryu refers as the "three arrows." In his book *The Last Lesson*, Master J.C. Burris sums up the three arrows as follows, "We act (the physical) and take care of our bodies; we learn and analyze and create (the mental), and we aspire toward fulfillment and maturity of the psyche (the spiritual)."

Isshin-Ryu karate provides a couple of ways to present the symbolism of the three arrows or to remind the student of Isshin-Ryu karate that these three 'arrows' exist and must be developed over time. One is through the three stars depicted on the Isshin-Ryu patch as presented in Chapter 1. These stars can also refer to the three main instructors of the founder: Chojun Miyagi, Chotoku Kyan, and Choki Motobu. Students of Isshin-Ryu are generally taught both concepts regarding the meaning of the three stars on the patch.

The other way is through the practice of kata (or fighting forms). Kata are sets of prearranged karate techniques used to train students in the art being studied as developed by the founder of the system. The goal or objective is to demonstrate the three arrows of physical, mental, and spiritual throughout all kata learned. Sensei Ronnie Cimorosi stated it this way in 1999[23] as a yon-dan (4th degree black belt):

> All three stars must be present when performing kata in order to grasp the true meaning of kata. All the stars must be of equal size and value; too much of one will upset the balance of the others. It takes all three ingredients to achieve victory in a fight, a fight that is against yourself… Karate is not complete without kata. Kata not only teaches how to put basic combinations in a fighting sequence but also teaches how to control aggression. It helps us to use our energy in a more productive manner to the point that we can turn it 'off' or 'on' like a light switch.

Sanchin kata is one of the eight empty-hand forms that Tatsuo Shimabuku selected for his Isshin-Ryu system, which comes from the Goju Ryu system of karate. Sanchin is a dynamic form that incorporates strong breathing, muscle tension coupled with relaxation, and a strongly rooted stance. Although the form does not

---
[23] The Three Stars, by Ronnie Cimorosi. The Gateway – March 15, 1999.

utilize many techniques in number, the sound performance of the kata requires many years of practice.

The meaning of the word Sanchin varies. Wikipedia[24] and author Joe Swift[25] utilize the translation as "three battles." The battle to unify the mind, body, and spirit. However, the interpretation of Sanchin as "three conflicts" is also presented in an article in Black Belt magazine by authors David M. Kahn and Richard Baptista[26]. They indicate the conflicts occur between the eyes, breathing, and posture. Both interpretations are interchangeable. Considering the form is traced back over 1,400 years ago to Daruma (see Chapter 1) and interpretation changes are inevitable, narrowing the meaning of Sanchin to "three battles" or "three conflicts" appears reasonable.

In terms of your training in martial arts, however, there should be a focus on development and not conflict from within. The thought of *harmony* of the three arrows would appear to be a better approach. In other words, a blending of the physical, mental, and spiritual instead of the three principles *battling* or *conflicting* with one another. Words matter. Therefore, you may wish to consider the three arrows in terms of the proper combination for the betterment of your overall development as a martial artist, both within and outside of the dojo. Keep in mind, based on various factors such as age, the growth and demonstration of each of the respective 'arrows' will vary. Without change, there is no growth.

Physical

Most likely, the first and easiest of the three arrows to notice is physical. When you begin training, you quickly realize there is quite a bit involved. Endurance, flexibility, proper breathing, balance, and increased strength. All of these physical attributes quickly come into play when you begin learning any form of martial art. Even pain comes into play. As black belt Aaron Walker notes, "Karate training is particularly focused on physical development and self-defense skills, but the lessons and benefits go much deeper and broader across all areas of life, if one acknowledges and allows it. First, one learns that physical pain and trauma won't defeat or dispirit you if you don't permit it. The body feels pain, but the strength and disposition of one's mind and spirit can overcome it."

---

[24] https://en.wikipedia.org/wiki/Sanchin
[25] http://www.msIsshin-Ryu.com/articles/swift/kata.shtml
[26] Uechi-Ryu Karate's Secret Weapon, by David M. Kahn and Richard Baptista. Black Belt: May 1990, Vol. 28, No. 5

You must quickly learn to be fluid and not rigid. This is easier said than done as the student generally wants to get all the movements and techniques correctly as quickly as possible in order to progress rapidly. However, when thinking and worrying too much about progressing quickly happens early on, it becomes more difficult to remain fluid. As Laraine Herring writes in *The Writing Warrior*, "Anything that doesn't have fluidity will freeze, and being frozen is the last thing you want – in your writing or in your body." She is expressing the essential quality of just continually moving and not staying too focused on one area of thought. It is interesting how this concept from writing carries over into martial arts. If a writer simply sits and stares at the paper or computer screen, they are literally frozen in thought. Rather, the writer should simply begin the process of getting thoughts out onto paper. Let the mind and body stay fluid, otherwise, nothing will happen.

Figure 65 - July, 1975: Public Demonstration. L-R: Dale Stanton kicking, Bud Ewing, and Larry Jackson.

From a physical perspective in martial arts training, this is exactly what happens quite often. The student sometimes gets overwhelmed with the thought of performing perfectly every time or the embarrassment of not performing correctly. Subsequently, this causes the student to freeze and be unable to perform as required. Instead, remove thoughts of performance and simply remain fluid.

The only thing that will improve performance is relentless practice over a long period of time. Such practice is useless unless the body remains fluid and simply performs the techniques without regard or worry on what the performance looks like compared to others. From the physical perspective, the student needs to find that place of self-observation and self-reflection without judgment. This clearly crosses over into the mental arrow discussed next; however, simply train and perform without getting caught up in making mistakes. Mistakes WILL happen, repeatedly. If you worry about those mistakes, then the physical arrow will quickly go nowhere, and you'll be imprisoned physically without hope of improvement.

The physical arrow of martial arts training requires sound habits. You must develop a habit of training for your body to understand, over time, exactly what your mind calls for in a given situation. The better athlete follows specific habits in their craft: time of day they practice, amount of time devoted to their training, etc. However, you will quickly develop a resistance to these habits. Your mind will come up with excuse after excuse to keep up your physical activities to attain your goals. You must push through these barriers and resistance factors to improve.

Matthew Kelly writes in *Resisting Happiness*, "The guy who wakes up every morning and goes for a run, and has been doing so for ten years, rarely experiences resistance in the morning when it is time to go for that run. He has forged a powerful positive habit and it is now effortlessly more powerful than resistance." The same holds true in martial arts, which is an important aspect of the physical arrow. Develop habits in your training from kata to kumite drills, and the physical arrow will grow strong.

Mental

The mental arrow requires a razor-sharp focus on what is being done at a given point in training. There can be absolutely no distraction in your training in order to hone this concept of the three arrows of Isshin-Ryu. This requires a strong sense of discipline and the will to make improvements. This will tie-in to the physical aspect of your training. Walther von Krenner makes this point well in *Following the Martial Path* when he states, "If practitioners train in the correct manner, this mental discipline should be developed just as the body is developed. This takes much more than just showing up to the dojo, working out mindlessly, and then going back to day-to-day life with no thought whatsoever of Budo."

Pick any job you can think of – doctor, lawyer, accountant, professional athlete, chef, whatever you wish to analyze. If you only put in the required hours, you will only improve so much. It takes a level of mental effort beyond the physical activity to have any hope of further improvement, which should be your goal not only in martial arts but anything in which you wish to participate.

Mastering the mind; however, is a challenging prospect and takes a continuous effort to stay on course. As noted in *The Road to Sparta*, author Dean Karnazes writes, "Mastering the mind requires an intimate awareness of one's weaknesses and shortcomings as well as the mindfulness to mitigate and overcome such vulnerabilities. A warrior is humble and unassuming, knowing that despite possessing great strength and discipline, triumph must be earned each and every day." Training the mind is an endless struggle of proper levels of thought between confidence, tenacity, humility, attention to detail, strategic training, and critical awareness of where one stands on the path of improvement.

With respect to the mental arrow, Master Cooling adds another layer to this development: **Keep your word**. Master Cooling summarizes this quite well when he talks about what is required in the mindset of a member of the Order of Isshin-Ryu. You need to keep your word. If you say you will do something, do it. You are part of a family – one that relies on each other in many ways. In an article from a 1996 newsletter to the OI[27], he writes:

> I recently returned from a visit to the Glen Lakes Dojo in Michigan. While there, Sensei Bronson had arranged for some "question-and-answer" time for her students. Each student wrote down ten questions for me, and the questions ranged from "On what day was Master Shimabuku born?" to "What can I do to improve my kata?"
>
> By far the most interesting question was, "What can I do to better serve my sensei, and the Order of Isshin-Ryu?" I would like to share with you my answer, because I think it's a point of view we sometimes overlook… Be true to yourself. Be true to your sensei. If you give your word, keep it. If you can't keep it, don't give it. A person is only as good as their word. If you take care of those things, everything else will fall into place."
>
> I went on to remind them that even though they are far away, they are still an important part of the O.I. It's also important that everyone understand that the OI is not some big organization that forces policy on everyone. It is a lot of small organizations (dojo) that contribute to make the larger group a success. It is a perfect example of the sum of the parts being greater than the whole. You, the individual, are the OI — you are the one that makes it work.
>
> Another important point about being in the OI. is tenacity. If nothing else is instilled in our members, it should be: If you get knocked down, you

---

[27] http://www.Isshin-Ryu.net/2011/12/master-cooling%e2%80%99s-1996-editorial/

> get back up. Even if someone tells you that you aren't capable, you tell them you can — you don't quit.

Mental improvement, like kata, requires structure. This is an essential element of martial arts training. Kata provides an excellent example of such mental training. These forms, which become progressively more advanced and difficult to perform, are required for advancement. Through the repetitive nature of karate training, and kata in general, there is the development of the structured focus needed to improve the mental 'arrow' of karate.

The mind must enjoy this type of repetitive movement for this development to occur. You need to become consumed in the task at hand. Author Dan Goleman in his book *Focus* describes the concept of 'flow' and explains, "Full absorption in what we do feels good, and pleasure is the emotional marker for flow. In this state, ideally, the circuits (in the brain) needed for the task at hand are highly active while those irrelevant are quiescent, with the brain precisely attuned to the demands of the moment. When our brains are in this zone, we are more likely to perform at our personal best, whatever our pursuit." So, a key concept is to block out thoughts that are not directly relational to your current task at hand – your training.

This is not always easy to do. We are overwhelmed with our problems from day-to-day living. These thoughts and emotions tend to follow us into the dojo, making it quite challenging to focus the mind where it needs to be for effective performance and development of our karate techniques. Then, add the distractions of all the technology at our fingertips, all the social media connectivity that didn't exist before, and the challenge of controlling our mental arrow grows exponentially. We must learn to remove these emotional and sensory distractions during our karate training in hopes for any level of improvement. This is clearly an ongoing battle; however, if you are aware of these negative influences then there is the chance to manage them accordingly.

Students often get caught up in results and cannot have any hope of enjoying the experience of their training. When improvement becomes difficult, when the student is having trouble getting over the next hurdle, they begin to make excuses. They start to talk more than actually doing something, because talking about it is much easier than working at the problem. Ryan Holiday puts it well in his book *Ego is the Enemy* while discussing the process of writing, "Writing, like so many creative acts, is hard. Sitting there, staring, mad at yourself, mad at the material because it doesn't seem good enough and you don't seem good enough. In fact, many valuable endeavors we undertake are painfully difficult, whether it's coding a new startup or mastering a craft. But talking, talking is always easy."

I'm sure every one of us can relate to this at some point in our training experiences. Rather than ignore the idea that you will have difficulty at some point in your training, that you will struggle, that you will hear criticism from your instructor(s), it is much better to talk about it and complain than it is to simply trust in yourself and just train hard. Holiday goes on to say, "The only relationship between work and chatter is that one kills the other." When you're talking, you're not working. When you complain about your struggles, you simply cannot improve but instead you stagnate or even regress. Master J.C. Burris sums this up well in his book *The Last Lesson* where he states, "Training for understanding of the art is the training that takes place after the others have gone – not training for show, not training for competition, but training for no reason except for self-knowledge and self-fulfillment." Rather than talk, just work – people will notice.

Figure 66: 1975 - Sensei Maria Melendez of the New York dojo, East 28th Street and Madison Avenue, New York, NY.

Another important aspect is to consider incorporating other activities to stimulate the mental facets of your learning to complement your physical training... something to slow down your thinking, to reflect on other aspects or endeavors. The samurai of ancient Japan took up various subjects of study to facilitate this "slowing down" such as the tea ceremony, flower arrangement, and calligraphy. In terms of current times, any type of artistic endeavor can serve the same purpose: painting, music, writing, poetry, etc. Shodo, or Japanese brush writing, is one example.

Shodo means "Way of the Brush" and is like training in karate. Learning the art of Shodo and improving oneself takes a very long time. At first attempt, brushing the various kanji of the Japanese language is a humbling experience, to say the least. The characters appear no better than if a toddler had made the effort. The brush and ink seem to mock your every action and effort. It comes down to continuous practice to unify all the essential elements of Shodo: calm spirit, confidence, spatial understanding, proper flow of energy from within out through the arm and brush and then onto the paper. This takes a substantial amount of time. Martial arts training is the same.

In karate training, everyone wants to attain rank quickly. This is just not possible, and you have to slow down your thinking and expectations and learn to use to the mind to your advantage. This fact was presented concisely by Sensei Maria Melendez in the student manual of Malachi Lee's School of Karate.

> ....we classify this by way of the "Five Finger Analogy." For every digit on the human hand, there is a fact of karate that you will learn (self-defense/sport/self-confidence/physical fitness/philosophy). You will benefit in each of these areas. But it will **not** come quickly. This is a serious study. Your mind and body are being positively affected and these are serious considerations.

Figure 67: "Yume Satori" (dream awakening). Calligraphy of Kosen (1633-1695)[28]. Painted by the author - May 2012.

---

[28] *Sacred Calligraphy of the East*, 3rd Ed. By John Stevens. Shambhala Publications, Inc.

Just like karate training, Shodo contains so many nuances in the practice that if you don't slow down and pay attention, you will miss them, and your art will appear lifeless and dull. The same holds true for your karate training. Learn to slow down and block out the distractions.

We are losing creativity and relying almost exclusively on technology. Computers, iPads, iPhones, digital pictures, movies, etc. There is no thought, no creativity, no personal expression of aesthetic values, no more slowing down and taking time to reflect and contemplate over anything artistic. Shodo is a personal experience that cannot be rushed. If executed or painted only after considerable thought, the work will seem 'alive' forever. This holds true for your karate performance. If you take the time to reflect on the techniques and how to improve them, then your performance will appear more 'alive' and spirited. Slow down the mind in your training and thrive within the process.

When you train your mind, you will have all sorts of wasted thoughts and it will be difficult to simply just train and enjoy the process. Worry, doubt, fear, anxiety – all will creep into your thinking from time-to-time. The goal is to remove these thoughts and simply experience the training. You must remove too much thinking and just train hard in order to persevere. Aaron Walker, student of the author, recalls this lesson when he states, "The training to persevere and not succumb to despair or defeat works - as I later learned - on relational, emotional, and psychological levels as well. It's better, but harder, to be the fighter rather than the victim. Just as in kumite, the opponent is not in front of you. He is within you." When you can calm the mind and remove excess negative thoughts, then movement, reaction, and even learning itself become natural and spontaneous.

This is why martial artists from ancient Japan turned to other aspects of their culture such as Zen, calligraphy, and the tea ceremony. These helped to concentrate the mind of the martial artist, which allowed for better training and learning within the martial arts themselves. As noted in *Following the Martial Path*, author Walther von Krenner writes, "It is for this reason that warriors in medieval Japan trained in Zen not to become spiritually enlightened, but to become better fighters." This emptying of the mind of negative thinking will help in the progression of the martial artist as his mind is not concerned with trivial things such as rank, how he or she compares to someone else, or the degree of success found in the competitive arena.

Remove the overwhelming desire to sprint to the next rank and enjoy the time in grade at each level. If you move along too fast, you'll miss out on some great details along the way. Removing the urge to only focus on the results allows you to be open and experience the quality of the teaching. An open mind has the ability to grasp the little things and 'connect the dots' in a more thorough manner than someone who rushes to the goal. The goal may be met but if you went quickly, you may not recall the important stuff needed to pass along to others.

My journey from white belt to black belt in the early 1980s only took one year and ten months. Looking back on it, I realize this was much too fast to truly appreciate the finer points of my training. However, when you're 15 years old and you can't get enough of training, you tend to go fast. Not until I joined the Order of Isshin-Ryu some 16 years later did I appreciate the fine points of Isshin-Ryu karate. I was required to go back and re-learn the bunkai (interpretations) of the kata to meet standards set forth by the OI. There was no longer a driving focus on attaining something. I simply just enjoyed the training and working with other outstanding martial artists in the OI family.

When you take off the blinders in your training; remove expectations; keep your mind open to whatever comes your way; remain a sponge for all the instruction before you… especially from the mental aspect, then you will be surprised how far you can go. My father, Frank Popp, started his Isshin-Ryu karate training at 43 years of age. He commented years later that when he started training, he had no expectations on how often or how far he wanted to progress in rank. He simply enjoyed the hard training sessions and the structured format of the classes. His mental arrow was in alignment with the physical arrow of his training. It served him well as he eventually progressed all the way to roku-dan, or 6th degree black belt.

Spiritual

The spiritual aspect of the martial arts seems to be losing importance or is often overlooked completely. This is a disappointing trend. In the foreword section of the book *Kodo: Ancient Ways*, Bishop Kenko Yamashita writes, "Although we have advanced the physical aspects and comforts of our existences, we have made little progress in our spiritual lives. If we only consider the physical aspects of martial arts, it is quickly outdated and useless in light of the type of weapons we have developed today to destroy our fellow man. By considering the wealth of wisdom and knowledge that has been handed down to us from the masters of the past, we can preserve a way to enrich and fulfill our lives."

Over time, the physical and mental aspects tend to deteriorate. However, the physical and mental provide the means to enhance the spirit and those two ingredients must not be rushed to develop the spiritual aspect of your martial arts development. Walther von Krenner points this out in his book *Following the Martial Path* where he quotes Kyudo (Japanese archery) teacher Onuma Hideharu[29], "Technique is the stairway to the spiritual level. To learn technique, you must carefully control the workings of your mind and body. Controlling the mind and body does not stifle the spirit; it sets it free." However, the spiritual aspect can continue growing, continue to evolve. So even those who cannot keep up physically as they did 20 or 30 years ago or due to a big injury or from the natural aging process can still contribute quite a bit from the spiritual aspect of martial arts training.

Students should never assume that because they cannot train as hard as they used to physically, that they are no longer able to pass on some level of knowledge to younger students. Nothing could be further from the truth. Budo practitioner and author Dave Lowry points this out in his book *The Karate Way* where he writes, "As one loses muscle mass, strength, and speed, if one is training correctly, one gains in the more subtle aspects of combat. There is no way for a human to avoid losing youth and all the advantages that go with it. If one's practice is solid, however, one can offset those losses considerably by polishing the more subtle particulars of the art." One of greatest qualities of martial arts training is that even though it is not possible to keep up with the younger generation from a physical standpoint, odds are very high, you can still provide many gifts in the form of mental and spiritual example. And more times than not, those gifts are highly sought after and treasured within the dojo.

True art is simply the expression of the artists' spirit. In Zen calligraphy art, it is the spirit of the artist that truly matters and comes through in a powerful expression of calligraphy. When watching an experienced martial artist perform, the spirit that comes from within is the essence of what matters. This spirit comes forth through the focus of the eyes, the controlled breath, and the kiai or shout at precise moments of controlled effort.

Pick any form of artistic expression: dance, painting, writing, photography, poetry, acting, etc. What is it the artist most wants to accomplish? I believe it is the transfer of their spirit into the resulting work. Someone who has fully grasped the essence of art, in general, can go outside of the "norms" of their chosen art form and project their spirit fully. This is the highest level of art. It requires a relentless pursuit of your art, a state of mind where you are devoid of negative thoughts such as worry, expectation, failure, stress, acceptance, and competitiveness. It takes time; however, you are already equipped with spirituality.

---

[29] Illuminated Spirit: Conversations with a Kyudo Master, by Dan Deprospero and Jackie Deprospero. Kodansha International, Jan. 1997

In his book *Resisting Happiness*, Matthew Kelly writes, "God wants to bless you with spiritual vitality. We all have an inner life. This consists of our thoughts and feelings, our hopes and dreams, our character and our relationship with God. We tend to focus on the outer life (physical aspects), but it is only a fraction of our life. Much more takes place as part of the inner life." We can, and should, explore this inner aspect of the martial arts to its fullest. Only then will our training have a heightened level of meaning and satisfaction, even when the physical and mental 'arrows' begin to deteriorate, which is only a matter of time.

The spiritual arrow is no different than the physical and mental arrows, from a learning and growth perspective. Continuous learning about your faith or religious background is essential to becoming a more well-rounded person. Regardless of your faith, get your hands on various books to explore in more detail the lessons to be learned. I tend to be partial to books written by Max Lucado regarding the Christian faith. These books have opened a whole new world to stories and lessons regarding being a Catholic. The bottom line is to treat your spirituality no different than building yourself up physically or mentally. Continuous exploration, research, and learning is key to being better today than yesterday.

Part of the process of the 'spirit' arrow is finding freedom in your practice and skills. This takes a substantial amount of time as it requires a complete understanding of your capabilities. The practitioner must accept the truth of where they are at a given time of their training. You must be willing to fight for this freedom, which goes beyond physical. The fight must creep into the mind and spirit of the martial artist. The legendary swordsman Miyamoto Musashi understood this freedom once he used a sword in both hands. At that point, he became freer in his motion and practice. All martial artists, to fully appreciate the spiritual aspect of their training, must break through into this freedom in their practice. Then, there is a high level of understanding and confidence in your study and teaching.

Within our training, we need to determine how we fit in and can serve others to pass along what we have learned in our training and experiences. Master Cooling always says to teach everything you know as only then more learning will come your way. God has given each of us the ability to serve others. "The Spirit has given each of us a special way of serving others" (I Cor. 12:7 CEV). Each of us can do this, not just a select few or the so-called elite, but everyone. We each have a special way: natural abilities, certain tendencies, specific inclinations. Maybe we lean towards the enjoyment of kata practice. Maybe we find satisfaction in development of kumite drills. For this, we can impart to others that which we feel a confidence in our training. Not one person possesses every imaginable skill at the highest level.

The spiritual arrow of Isshin-Ryu can, and will, last a lifetime. It takes a lot of commitment to the martial art you are practicing and studying. You must bear total responsibility to not only your training, but also to cultivating the style in others. You should honor your sensei with your best efforts and keep and preserve good, sound Isshin-Ryu above our own interests.

I've never met the founder of Isshin-Ryu, Tatsuo Shimabuku. As of this writing, the number of students who have either trained with or met the founder of Isshin-Ryu karate is getting dangerously low. However, we must all train to the degree that would make Shimabuku proud. Why? Well, when I hear others talk about Master Shimabuku and how he commanded the best out of those he trained, that makes me want to follow in that same tone. To practice, teach, and conduct myself in Isshin-Ryu to do justice to Isshin-Ryu karate and Tatsuo Shimabuku.

A big part of the spiritual arrow revolves around *faith*. Faith can carry you through the difficult times of your training, both in and out of the dojo. When we think in terms of faith, it is imperative to trust your sensei. You shouldn't be concerned with whether or not you are meeting some sort of invisible standard or level of performance. It is up to the sensei to make that determination and guide you in your training. You simply need to have faith in your sensei and train hard, and you will surely make improvements.

Your martial arts journey, just like the journey of life itself, is a journey navigated by faith. In life, wherever God leads you, He will provide the way for you to reach your destination. You simply need to trust in God and have faith that He will provide what you need. Not always an easy thing to do, but those who do have faith will be far ahead of those without any faith at all.

Having strong faith develops the endurance you will need in your training (and life). As described in James 1:3-4, "For... when your faith is tested, your endurance has a chance to grow. So, let it grow, for when your endurance is fully developed, you will be perfect and complete, needing nothing." In other words, never give up. Continue having faith in what you are doing, having faith that God will see you through the difficult times. This is the same with your martial arts training. Have faith in your sensei that he will guide you appropriately. This is often quite difficult. We are human, and we tend to think we have complete control over our improvement in our martial arts training. So, when we struggle or have difficulty at certain points in our journey, we tend to get down on ourselves. Rather, trust in your sensei and have faith that he or she will provide what you need to keep you moving forward. This will help strengthen your spiritual arrow considerably.

In his book *Wabi Sabi - The Japanese Art of Impermanence*, Andrew Juniper writes, "The quality of any piece of art is said to be decided before the pen or brush has been lifted, for it lies within each person, and the art that is produced is only as good as the spirit of the artist at the time it is made." This point is interesting and clearly is relevant to the performance of any martial art. What is the state of the practitioner's spirit? Has he or she invested time in the development of a proper state of mind and respect not only of the art itself, but also of those around him or her?

This 'spirit' is visible in any field: sports, culture, politics, entertainment, etc. For your martial arts to have true value, the spirit must be forged and developed. This calls for a multitude of factors to be recognized and honed over a long period of time. Respect. History. Awareness. Compassion. Dedication. Tradition. As Juniper goes on to state, "Zen monks were well aware that artistic expression is a carbon copy of the awareness of the artist, and if anything of worth is to be made then the spirit of the artist must be the criteria to be satisfied."

After closely observing a martial artist perform, whether it is kata, kumite, or simply teaching others, the observer with a proper level of spiritual development will clearly know whether such criteria has been met or not. This is like the concept of the artist's presence being strong; otherwise, the art being produced (or performed) will lack any life. Kazuaki Tanahashi writes in his book *The Heart of the Brush*, "Although [calligraphy] requires skills, aesthetics, and creativity, what is most appreciated is beyond these elements of art. Brush lines in calligraphy honestly reveal the artist's personality, level of accomplishment, and presence of heart and mind. This is a higher criterion for appreciating and valuing the work of art than aesthetic and technical excellence alone." The key point being, what is the intent of the heart and mind? When you watch a martial artist perform, you will notice if there is any 'presence' or 'spirit' behind the movements. You will know if the karate-ka has devoted any time to pursuing the spiritual aspects of his or her development. As Dave Lowry concludes in his book *Persimmon Wind*, "While one might master the technical range that comprises a martial koryu [system of martial arts], there is always more to learn, more broadly and deeply to go. There is for the bugeisha, only more practice, and a steady refining of the spirit."

Which of the three arrows is your strength? Mental, physical, or spiritual? The exact combination of the three arrows is a bit different for everyone. I cannot, and *should not*, try to project the three arrows the same way as someone else. Everyone is different. As they say, you should be you and nobody else. You can admire others such as your parents, grandparents, your sensei, highly-skilled athletes or artists; however, you are not them. Avoid comparison to others. "Stir up the gift of God that's in you" (2 Tim. I:6). Each of us has specific gifts regarding our martial arts abilities. Find it, develop it, and then pass it along to others for their benefit and growth.

To fully develop all three arrows, you must ensure ego is removed from the equation. This is extremely difficult to do, especially when a certain degree of accomplishment or skill is acquired in your training. This is different than confidence. Confidence is knowing you have a certain degree of ability, but not letting others know. Ego is when confidence turns into arrogance and you make it a point to let others know, vocally or by your actions. Even after skill is developed, you must continually work and strive to remove your ego, for it can be your downfall.

You need to continually work on the three arrows without an end in sight. What amount of work is needed? Ryan Holiday writes in *Ego is the Enemy*, "Is it ten thousand hours or twenty thousand hours to mastery? The answer is that it doesn't matter. There is no end zone. To think of a number is to live in a conditional future. We're simply talking about a lot of hours – that to get where we want to go isn't about brilliance, but continual effort." You cannot think of developing and blending the three arrows of Isshin-Ryu in terms of time. You cannot expect to have all three honed after so many years of training. The blending and development of the physical, mental, and spiritual aspects of your Isshin-Ryu training will take a full lifetime of awareness, work, and effort. Nothing less.

Progression with the three arrows of Isshin-Ryu karate must blend together at some point. Early in the process; however, it makes more sense to separate the concepts and consider one at a time. It is very difficult to think about the proper performance of a specific technique, believe that you understand it and then experience it first-hand. Likewise, it is a challenge to absorb the essence of various spiritual writings and concepts without first experiencing various physical and mental tribulations along the way.

Over time, students of martial arts learn the three arrows are interdependent upon one another, yet each arrow will adapt and change according to the needs of the person at a given point in time. Remove expectations or what you perceive how things should be and train hard to improve yourself and help others along the way through both word and deed.

Chapter 8
OVERCOMING OBSTACLES

"Crisis brings us face to face with our inadequacy, and our inadequacy, in turn, leads us to the inexhaustible sufficiency of God."

Catherine Marshall

"The rubber of faith meets the road of reality under hardship."

Max Lucado

*"Look straight ahead. What's there?
If you see it as it is, you will never err."*

Bassui Tokusho

Warrior. What image does the word create in your mind? The book *The Writing Warrior*, by Laraine Herring, presents a lot of concepts regarding the process of writing that relates perfectly to the martial arts. When I type into an Amazon to search the title of the book, I find various martial arts books including *The Unfettered Mind*, by Takuan Soho, *The Age of the Warrior*, by Robert Fisk, and *Ideals of the Samurai: Writings of Japanese Warriors*, by William Scott Wilson. This brings up the question: Is there martial arts training in Herring's background? I searched Google and reviewed Herring's website. There is no connotation or reference to any martial arts. She does cite yoga often in her book. Maybe there's some crossover there. Either way, the mindset of a warrior can be applied to a multitude of disciplines.

You need a warrior mindset, regardless if you are involved in martial arts or not, to improve yourself. Even someone who is studying to become a chef, for example, can very easily adopt a warrior mindset in their study and training. This 'warrior' attitude is essentially just a disciplined approach to whatever path you wish to follow or goals you want to accomplish.

Figure 68 - 1974, Elkton, MD. Public demonstration during Elkton Days Fesitval.

L-R: Bailey Russell, Robert McKewen, Toby Cooling (on platform), Bud Ewing (breaking), Alan Webb.

Similarities of the usage of warrior are found in the book *Wabi Sabi*, by Andrew Juniper. There is no trace of martial arts in Juniper's information on the internet, yet his book uses Zen concepts to explain the aesthetics of wabi sabi and Japanese culture. Wabi sabi itself means many things. Juniper notes, "It is an expression of the beauty that lies in the brief transition between the coming and going of life, both the joy and melancholy that make up our lot as humans." The concepts of wabi sabi have inspired the tea ceremony, flower arranging, haiku (Japanese poetry), garden design, and Japanese Noh theatre. One can logically extend wabi sabi thought to the traditions of martial arts as well – from the concept of samurai calming the mind in battle, to the highly frayed belt of the advanced black belt.

One does not necessarily need to be a martial artist to understand the warrior mindset. Authors Laraine Herring and Andrew Juniper have a good grasp of the warrior ideals, yet they do not have a martial arts background. Probably the most famous example would be the Zen monk Takuan Soho (1573 – 1645). Takuan was a priest of the Rinzai branch of Zen with no martial arts training in his background. Yet the samurai warriors of this period leaned heavily upon the guidance Takuan provided with respect to the development of the mind, which, at that time, not only meant the difference between winning and losing but also life and death. Takuan authored several famous texts during his lifetime such as the *Mysterious Record of*

Immovable Wisdom and the *Clear Sound of Jewels*. These books serve as invaluable guidance pertaining to the warrior lifestyle and demonstrate that the thinking of a warrior can stem from almost anywhere and apply to nearly any endeavor.

A warrior mindset can not only help you on your journey in life with attaining goals, it can also get you through those difficult times when you need to overcome problems or difficulties. These problems are not always the challenges or problems you face in the dojo. They most likely occur in various situations throughout your lifetime.

Everyone faces tough times or deals with difficult problems. However, not everyone sees problems in the same way. Often, people are overcome by their problems and have difficulty reacting while others seem to always find a way to overcome the problems that enter their lives. Many are left bitter or angry while others come out better. People either face their challenges and problems with fear or faith. Problems can either be faced alone or with the love and support of those around you, especially your family. The Order of Isshin-Ryu is such a family.

One of the main tenets of martial arts training is to develop students who are resilient in all facets of their lives. This is not always preached directly during training sessions though, and the students need to be aware of the potential to develop this resiliency in order for this to become a reality. Master Cooling has written within the OI student manual, "Karate is what you are willing to make of it for yourself, as we make no pretense of trying to make you into someone you are not." This means instructors do not mold students into what they envision them to be. Either students will see the benefits of hard training and seek that improvement on their own, or they will completely miss the point, drop off in their training, and eventually stop training altogether. This is unfortunate. Training hard in the martial arts is not easy and is often quite uncomfortable.

For those who can overcome this difficulty in the dojo, they are more able to take this mindset into their daily lives. Master Cooling confirms this ability as stated in an OI student manual from the mid-1980s, "In the dojo, individuals see the need for self-improvement, which carries over to other phases of everyday life outside the school environment." The manual goes on to state, "The ultimate goal of karate is the attainment of a strong moral character built through hard and diligent training." As such, students who do train hard and see the results of such training quickly understand that if they can accomplish certain goals within the dojo, then nearly anything outside of the dojo can be handled by the proper level of mental focus. Many within the Order of Isshin-Ryu have faced very difficult problems. The OI family always steps up to support the one facing difficult times and hurting.

Many times, obstacles come in the form of failure. Famous women's U.S. soccer player Mia Hamm notes, "Failure happens all the time. It happens every day in practice. What makes you better is how you react to it." In sports, there are far more failures than successes. In baseball, a .300 hitter is considered very good. This means, seven times out of ten the hitter makes an out – a failing result.

In karate, it takes years of serious, consistent study and training just to perform the techniques and kata in a manner considered to be competent. Still, there are small errors or flaws that the novice may not notice at first glance. This is not necessarily a bad thing. Accepting imperfections in performance can help you grow as a martial artist and a person.

With respect to the art of shodo, or Japanese calligraphy, Kazuaki Tanahashi notes in his book *Heart of the Brush*, "Everyone's goal should be to reduce problems, not eliminate them. The brush teaches you how to live with imperfections and, furthermore, realize that they are an essential part of beauty. You must be able to deal with these failures. Accept them and use them to your advantage."

Failures can serve as the motivation to improve. The founder of Honda Motor Company, Soichiro Honda, once stated, "Success can only be achieved through repeated failure and introspection. In fact, success represents the one percent of your work that results from only 99 percent that is called failure." Failure, or struggles with a specific technique you are learning, can help define a game plan or strategy in your training to continue your progress. This leads to using intelligence to assist in overcoming your obstacle or problem or prior failure. When you can combine intelligence, hard work, and sound preparation, this will most likely lead to success and overcoming your obstacle. Therefore, you must continually seek opportunities to learn and grow intelligence in all facets of life.

An intelligent mind can look at failures in a way that can lead to improvement in other ways. Master Cooling is well-versed in many areas of knowledge. He often recalls during casual conversation various historical accounts and explains them in fine detail. His conversations do not always focus on martial arts. Without fail, I've seen him ask questions to various people regarding the history of where they come from to enhance his understanding of that history.

While he served on the board of directors of a local bank, his area of responsibility centered around information technology and security of information. As such, he reached out to me several times due to my background and work in the information security field with my job as an information systems auditor. He asked me various questions in an effort to improve his understanding of his role on the board of directors and the types of questions he needed to ask of management from the bank to hold them accountable. This is a sound example of continually striving to improve your intelligence, which strongly benefits your mental capacity and abilities in the dojo as well as problems and obstacles that may surface in any area of your life.

****

Almost everyone goes through some type of obstacle, hardship, or negative situation. It simply is *a part* of life; it doesn't have to control or direct your life. There are many examples within the Order of Isshin-Ryu regarding members who have overcome major hurdles or setbacks. Below is a sampling of such stories.

Denshi

Master Cooling says he should have died numerous times. He has overcome an assortment of issues including bacterial pneumonia, kidney failure, and two urinary tract infections, among other ailments. As he states, "I qualified for the last rights five times. I think I'm alive for a reason, and it could be to stay around for those I have affected in the martial arts world. I feel I was meant to be a martial artist and leader, as I was terrible at everything else."

John McDonald

The year was 2000 and Sensei John McDonald heard the doctor's words regarding the diagnosis… colon cancer. Before this crisis, Sensei McDonald was as active and healthy as anyone could be. Sensei John Costanzo recalls, "I remember being with Sensei McDonald during this time and although he was forthright in sharing his condition with Master Latimer and myself, not once did we hear a discouraging word. He maintained a positive attitude while he went through a series of operations to remove the cancer before it spread."

He underwent a procedure resulting in wearing an ostomy bag for four months until his intestines healed to the point that they could be reconnected, and the ostomy bag could be removed. During this time, Sensei McDonald continued his martial arts workouts with Master Latimer. Costanzo notes, "To say the least, I was taken aback by his courage and diligence toward his training along with his desire to lead a normal life."

Just when it seems that things were back to normal, another shock occurred when he was told that his cancer had spread to his lungs and was now at stage four. The doctors informed John he had a three percent chance of survival. Subsequently, with Sensei McDonald's indelible will to survive, he tackled this second crisis head-on, despite these back-to-back setbacks.

Sensei McDonald went through a long series of chemotherapy sessions, sapping his strength, his endurance, and oddly, only the black hairs on this head. He never lost his gray hair! John Costanzo recalls a specific day at the dojo, "I remember when his wife, Cagle, brought him to see his dojo brothers at the Dobbs Ferry dojo fresh from the hospital. It was a bit of a shock to see how frail he looked, but even more of a shock was when, to our horror, he grabbed a *bo* and started doing a kata. Cagle swiftly put an end to this sort of nonsense and carted him home."

In the many years and months that followed, he courageously battled the effects of the chemo along with the tests that finally led up to his being declared cancer-free years later. Again, he went to practice and continued his training whenever he had the strength to do so. In addition, during the chemo period, he did a feature on the *Today Show* with Katie Couric who was focusing on how cancer patients can lead normal lives, despite their struggles. It showed action sequences of him leading his, then, dojo students online techniques and a section of him knocking me around with defensive techniques. I was proud to be a part of it. Obviously, Sensei McDonald beat the odds and is with us today. But it took years of dedication and life changes to make himself well. If anything, it increased his overall health regimen and dedication to his martial arts training.

Barry Smith

In the mid-90s, Master Barry Smith was diagnosed with throat cancer. Even after going through the procedure to have as much of it removed as possible, his karate training has never stopped. The location of the cancer made any surgery a high-risk endeavor for his doctors. Master Smith simply told the doctors, "I expect my quality of life will not change from this operation. I will be able to talk as if nothing happened." His belief system was as solid as steel and mentally, he would not be defeated.

He came through the operation and made a full recovery. Very few people can face seemingly insurmountable odds with the same warrior mentality they bring to the dojo. Barry Smith is clearly one of those people.

Bud Ewing

Master Bud Ewing overcame a detached retina during his training in the dojo. Yet, he continued to train through the healing period following surgery. As he explains,

"I simply informed everyone to be cautious around me, so accidents could be avoided. I wore special headgear during sparring, even though the face region, for me, was off limits. This was just an abundance of caution, but it allowed me to participate."

Most would be content with observing their students train until fully recovered. Not Bud Ewing. When asked why he would even consider training as if nothing ever happened, he replied, "I don't know. I just didn't really give it much thought (not training). I'm used to being in the dojo and working with students. I figured 'why not.' If I was smart about what I was doing, I didn't really see any reason to back away from working out." As Master Ewing demonstrated, there is no reason to use recovery as an excuse to make every effort to continue to train and not only improve yourself but to help others.

Doug Rogers

Doug Rogres is a black belt student of Sensei Ronnie Cimorosi. At the 2014 Isshin-ryu Hall of Fame tournament, Doug was in serious pain. I pulled him aside and had a long talk with him. I explained that he simply needs to keep going in whatever capacity that he is able. It may not necessarily be in a strong, physical way anymore. However, his knowledge and spirit would continue to serve as critical assets to the Order of Isshin-Ryu. We also discussed some various ways to deal with his back problems.

The very next year, he came back to the Hall of Fame tournament in Tennessee and was not only named the 2015 Male Karate-ka of the Year, he competed in the tournament the next day and won first place in senior division hand kata and competed for the grand championship. This demonstrates when one is committed to an endeavor, obstacles are just that, something that can be worked around and dealt with.

Although still having issues, Doug is still actively working in the dojo and helping students reach their full potential. As he explains it, "I'm going keep going. Karate is in my heart, and it's what I do. It doesn't matter if my back is hurting or sometimes holds me back. I know I can make a difference with others, and that's what I'll do, however I can do it."

Summary

What obstacles do you face? There are many for all of us. Age, injury, commitments to personal issues, etc. Everything you must face and deal with are there for a reason.

They are there because everything is as it should be. All obstacles are provided to improve our character and our commitment to our chosen path.

God is continuously working to improve us. He presents us with challenges and obstacles to hone our faith and resolve, and everyone is on a different path. Laraine Herring writes in her book *The Writing Warrior*, "…missing from many people's thinking is the awareness that nothing is the same as anything else. No two people's writing journeys are the same. No two people's abilities are the same, and no two versions of the story are the same. Don't compare one to the other. Examine the gifts that each one presents."

Whether it's following a writing journey or following a martial arts journey. The same is true. No two are the same. Obstacles are different for everyone. God provides different obstacles and challenges to everyone, so each can learn the lessons needed to overcome them according to His plan. This way, the rest of us can observe how those obstacles are overcome and put them in perspective.

A key to overcoming obstacles is to be in harmony with what is and not fight the fact that it isn't what you hope it to be. In *The Writing Warrior*, Laraine Herring explains, "Acceptance – a surrendering to what is – will make space for you to constructively problem solve. Accept the current reality of the situation and use that energy you would have used to fight to examine other ways of changing the scene." Leo Tolstoy wrote, "The two most powerful warriors are patience and time." Great words to live by; however, in today's culture, these are concepts difficult to apply all the time.

We want to overcome problems or fix things immediately. I am certainly guilty with regards to lacking patience. When I set a goal, I will work incessantly to meet it. The work ethic is one thing, but you must also learn to mix in a proper amount of patience. Setbacks will occur. Without patience, you will have a very difficult time accepting those setbacks, which, at the end of the day, maybe what you need to help you attain your goal in the long run. It comes down to trusting yourself because what will be will be, as God will steer you and provide what you need to overcome the obstacles you will undoubtedly face.

Chapter 9
PHILOSOPHY AND TRAINING

*"And if anyone thinks that he knows anything,
he knows nothing yet as he ought to know."*

1 Corinthians 8:2

*"Nothing in the world can take the place of persistence.
Talent will not; nothing is more common than unsuccessful men with talent.
Genius will not; unrewarded genius is almost a proverb.
Education alone will not; the world is full of educated derelicts.
Persistence and determination alone are omnipotent."*

Calvin Coolidge

Martial arts training is nothing short of a lifetime endeavor. For your training to mean something, you must commit your entire being into the art. Things will change over time. It is inevitable. All things are impermanent. All things are incomplete. If you train in martial arts for quick results or some form of ego-driven goal, you are clearly missing the mark in your aspirations. You will quickly discover that your martial arts study is long-term, and the lessons you learn will change, as well as your body and mind.

There must be a sense of joy in practice, not in accomplishment. We will always have tough days and difficult times. Do we stop practicing? Do we let those tough times slow us down, negate all our efforts? We should rejoice in our practice. Be thankful that we have the ability and the opportunity to practice. Not everyone has that chance. If you *can* practice, then you are blessed by the Lord, and you should give thanks each and every day that you have the opportunity and ability to train.

You must keep in mind various principles and concepts during your training. Students of martial arts training should be aware of these principles and reflect on them to apply them in a sound manner. Some of these topics will stand out more than others, depending on the situations you are going through or experiencing. At some point, everyone will come up against these during their training.

Repetition

The Japanese character for endure is *Nen*. Nen means to endure. In order to endure and persevere, you must take notice of what your mind is doing. Are you concerned with minor discomforts? Are there distractions happening that is taking you away from your goal or whatever you happen to be involved with at the moment? You must put your mind on something else or move away from that which is bothering you and causing discomfort so you can recalibrate your focus and energy. When you can do this, the activity at hand becomes much easier to accomplish.

Running on a treadmill is a good example. To me, this is a dreadful experience. It must be one of the most boring activities known to man. However, when I'm working out of town, there aren't many alternatives to getting in my daily run. Good running trails are sometimes hard to find, and there is no other choice but the treadmill. To make matters even worse, I'm a number watcher when I'm on the treadmill. I can't help it. How far did I go in the last couple of minutes? What is my speed set at, again? Do I need to bump up the pace a bit? And, every so often when you think you've covered a lot of distance, you look down and notice you've only gone two-tenths of a mile. It's crushing to your will.

So, you must devise methods to keep the boredom at bay and remain focused on the task at hand. Some people listen to music as they run, either as a diversion or to motivate them. There are those who don't like music and would rather listen to the sounds of just being outdoors or the monotonous thump of their feet. Either way, you must get into a repetitive routine that you enjoy; otherwise, your practice will not remain consistent.

The key to proficiency in any type of activity is repetition. Fundamentally sound repetition and not something done just for the sake of completing the activity. So, while running on the treadmill, one trick I use to stave off the boredom is focusing on my running form and technique. Often, the hotel gym provides mirrors that make observation of my running stride very convenient. If not, then reliance on 'feel' takes precedent. Taking note of my stride length, breathing, and whether my hands are tensed into fists (believe it or not, this can sap your energy quickly).

Performing in a consistent, efficient manner can remove the boredom and keep your mind so focused that the run is completed before you know it. Whether you cover a mile or a marathon, a focused mind on the execution of consistent movement will put your mind at ease regarding the extent of the activity. While running, I try to pay attention to my stride. Are the steps getting too long or am I keeping my feet below my shoulders? Am I staying upright or am I beginning to lean forward too much? Are my shoulders swaying front and back too much? Are my hands clenched into fists or are they open and relaxed? These things may seem insignificant; however, they are crucial to whether or not you are unnecessarily sapping your energy.

Take notice of a baseball pitcher throwing a no-hitter. Watch his movements on the mound and you'll likely notice he is repeating the same exact motions every time, without fail. He knows he must repeat each and every nuance of his activity the same exact way. This is because he knows repetition leads to not only efficiency but also keeping his mind off the overwhelming thought of what he is trying to do.

The same holds true for golfers. If you cannot repeat the swing effectively, you will fail miserably time and time again. This can only be accomplished through grueling repetition. In fact, you should have the attitude of thoroughly enjoying the repetitive nature of practice. This is what led Ben Hogan to become one of the greatest golfers in history. In his prime in the 1950s, interrupted during a three-hour practice session that had begun only minutes after he had shot a tournament-leading 66, Hogan said: "When I'm not playing, I like to be practicing. I enjoy every minute of (either). To tell you the truth, I'd just as soon do this."[30]

The concept of repetition also applies to martial arts training. Students should a develop a clear vision of their goals. From there, they should craft a plan to train diligently to meet those goals. The preparation must be relentless, and students should be able to "see" their goals being met. David Chadwick notes in his book *It's How You Play the Game*, "Preparation exacerbates the power of positive words in pressure situations." When students find a good instructor (sempai) who imparts ongoing words of encouragement and couple that with relentless preparation, the results are definitive and sound. This, in turn, yields confidence that can help students not only in their martial arts training but all throughout the challenges that life can throw at them.

---

[30] http://articles.latimes.com/1988-06-19/sports/sp-7809_1_ben-hogan-s-career

Laraine Herring in her book *The Writing Warrior* notes this about the profession of being a writer, "Writing is both flow and discipline. Art and craft. Intuition and perspiration." If you didn't know the source of the quote, the experienced martial artist would think its topic was about martial arts. The parallels are very interesting.

The same can be said about any endeavor the practitioner takes seriously. My late Kendo sensei, Duk Yeong Kim, often told me to practice my sword cuts five thousand times every day. Back then, I thought to myself, "Is he serious?!" Years later, I realize that he was. If you truly wish to improve and become proficient, you must carve out the time it takes to perform those five thousand repetitive cutting motions... no excuses.

Training in martial arts requires you to go outside of your comfort zone. This is summarized extremely well in the book *Following the Martial Path,* by Walther von Krenner, where he writes, "Real training is difficult. It takes constant effort. It requires self-reflection and a selfless approach to training. One must train with no thought whatsoever of pain and suffering. Students have to push themselves to rise above such distractors." One of my goals is to run three miles every day of the year. This level of repetition will surely improve my overall running efficiency. I can take the experience of meeting this goal and apply it to anything else – kata practice, weight training, work goals, etc.

There needs to be an ongoing routine in your training. Herring refers to the concept of "unconscious competence" when discussing routines and becoming a better writer. When you have an ongoing, dedicated routine to what you are doing – writing, running, swimming, art, your work, martial arts – then you can improve at a pace that you may not even be aware of. Competence creeps into your activity almost in an unconscious manner. Then as you learn new things along the way; your 'routine' or your 'repetition' will reinforce what was learned to the point that it will be retained in long-term memory. This is key to the structure of martial arts training – consistent, repetitive practice leads to success.

Uniformity is key to reinforcement. Going out of your comfort zone is the key to growth. What does this mean? A skilled person can repeat an activity routinely. Take any profession, and it's the same. Even a skilled doctor. They approach their work in a focused manner. This leads to reinforcement of the proper execution of the task at hand. For example, you may set a running goal of three miles each and every day. However, if you only run the same three miles then your personal growth as a runner will likely stall. You will quickly become extremely consistent in running technique and so forth, but other areas of growth, such as endurance, as a runner will likely only go so far. Try to mix up the type of running from time to time. Run some hills. Extend the distance periodically to say four miles, ten miles, etc. Run during the mid-afternoon or evening instead of every morning. Try out the treadmill in lieu of outdoors. Give the trails a try. You continually challenge yourself by going out of your comfort zone to see how your body and mind react. Pay close attention to your breathing and so forth during these varying types of training runs to reflect afterward and see how you fared. This leads to growth. This same type of personal challenge holds true in the martial arts. You must have the ability to combine consistency and different training methods to become a well-rounded martial artist.

Inspiration

Whether you want to train or not, you must find something to drive you, to help you break through any barrier that you may face, including boredom, laziness, excuses, lack of a training partner, or your sensei not being around to help you. These situations can creep in at a moments notice. You must discipline your mind and spirit to overcome them.

I am not a runner. I didn't enjoy running at distances whatsoever when I was younger. Now that I'm older, I still don't enjoy it, and getting up at 5:00 am and preparing to go to the hotel gym when I'm working out of town is the last thing on my mind. I'd much rather hit the snooze button and enjoy the bliss of slumber. Yet, in the back of my mind, I tell myself, "life doesn't knock at the door, you have to go out and get it!" I trudge down to the treadmill and simply get moving. Afterward, I feel fantastic and ready to tackle the day's work.

What makes someone do this? Inspiration, which leads to motivation. Robert Cole, a Ni-dan from the Easton, Maryland dojo, is now 85 years old. Watching Mr. Cole perform is truly

Figure 69: 2017 - Elkton, MD. Robert Cole (ni-dan) practicing technique in the dojo of Sensei Ronnie Cimorosi.

amazing. You can just tell he's not worried who is watching, what others may think, or any challenge he is facing. He simply goes out and performs and gets the job done. Period. At the same time, he's one of the most humble people you will ever meet. He once told me at a shiai, "Sensei Popp I won't be able to hold a candle to you today." I replied, "Mr. Cole, all you have to do is be yourself and do the best you can; you'll have the highest possible level of respect from everyone in this gym today." Mr. Cole is an inspiration to everyone he meets.

Other examples of inspiration can come from activities outside of the dojo. I always tell my students… you must strive to be the best in everything you do… give one hundred percent of yourself and let the chips fall where they may. Only then will others respect you fully. Always work to challenge yourself. Consider another sport and work towards a goal. This will complement your martial arts training considerably. Challenging yourself in some type of manner such as running or weightlifting as an example, and then meeting that challenge cannot be overstated. It takes an incredible amount of fortitude and discipline, man or woman, to set some type of goal and have the drive to meet it. This is inspirational on all levels. The type of inspiration is what leads to motivation and the ability to get yourself out of bed every morning and deal with the training required to better yourself every day.

Cross Train

Cross training helps push you mentally since different activities of physical exertion results in varying degrees of discomfort. This experience can help you in your martial arts training and vice versa. Training in different sports leads to research of those disciplines, which leads to understanding and knowledge. This knowledge can then be applied to and blend with each activity in which you participate.

Going back to the running example, sometimes your body and breath simply does not want to cooperate with what you have in mind on a particular day. You will feel like stopping to gather yourself before continuing, which basically calls for a strong walking pace to keep moving, especially when it's cold outside. Instead, you should simply slow your pace and try to calm your mind. This is how to break through barriers since most barriers begin in the mind. When you can control your mind, which in essence means to remove negative thoughts or simply put your thoughts in another place, then the barriers tend to go away, and you can work through the pain or wall before you.

As a specific example, on one of my winter runs a few years ago, I needed to utilize my mind more than normal. The day was extremely cold, maybe around 20 degrees Fahrenheit. Why run when it's that cold outside? Well, my goal at that time was to run three miles every day for an entire year. So, I was focused on the goal and weather was not going to be a factor to deter me.

Shortly after starting the run, I felt horrible. My joints were aching, my breathing was difficult, and I couldn't get my mind off how cold it was. I thought to myself, how can I cope with the pain and discomfort for another 2.5 miles? I reverted to my thought process. I needed to put my mind beyond the cold, the wind, my fingers, my blurred vision, and my tightening quadriceps. I think about my pace. Am I pushing too hard, trying to go too fast? Am I landing mid-foot to ensure my knees and ankles are not absorbing too much shock from the pavement?

As I began to take inventory of what I was doing, listening to my body's reaction to pace and form, I slowly settled into a rhythm where I no longer was concerned with the cold and wind. At around the 1-mile mark, I began to enjoy what I was doing. The sound of my feet, my controlled breathing, feeling the perspiration all helped to add a degree of comfort. I took notice of the mountains off in the distance since the weather was clear without a cloud in the sky. I observed the landscapes along the neighborhood roads. I took note of when the breeze was blowing and when the air was calm. Putting my thoughts on these other diversions let to my body and breath get back to normal. My muscles became loose, and my knees and ankles began to feel much better. I didn't notice my running pace anymore, the pace felt natural

Figure 70: 1986, San Francisco. Sensei Tom Sanson running the 1986 San Francisco marathon.

and unforced. When my mind was centered and controlled, I became 'in the moment' of what I was doing with no anticipation or expectation.

Not everyone enjoys running and certainly may not have the desire to run a marathon, much less fathom they could deal with the painful experience of such a long-distance event. Yet, those who can complete a marathon will sign up and run these events time and time again. Why? They can get their mind around the enormity of the event, what is required physically, and actually look forward to running 26.2 miles. They know that during the process of running for that many miles, they will experience various feelings of adrenaline and a sense of accomplishment that cannot be experienced otherwise. They can put their mind somewhere else during the event and become 'one' with whatever is happening at the time.

Many years ago, I witnessed Tae Kwon Do pioneer Jhoon Rhee perform 100 push-ups in 60 seconds. He did this at the age of 70! When he finished, he stood up and had a smile on his face. He was actually smiling! How can someone at such an age perform such a physical feat requiring tremendous effort and appear to be enjoying himself? I think it comes down to the mind. You must set or calibrate your thinking prior to the activity and expect you will enjoy what you are about to do.

The mind plays such an important factor in being able to perform at a higher level. Whenever you see an athlete perform something that you think requires a high degree of skill, you can be assured that they have trained their mind just as much, and most likely even more so, than their physical skills.

The learning process is most likely to be successful when the individual is organized and motivated and maintains a healthy lifestyle that includes quality sleep and physical exercise. This was the order of the day in many ancient civilizations, and today's neurologists and psychologists also agree. It is highly encouraged to participate in physical exercise and events outside of the dojo. Running events, obstacle course runs, weightlifting, and other forms of exercise including golf, tennis, and swimming can contribute tremendously to the learning process and experience within the dojo itself. Many other forms of exercise have motions that crossover quite well into the dojo.

Research Other Arts

Students must be willing to put in the time and effort to learn as much as possible about their chosen art. At a certain point in time, they will logically wish to extend that knowledge outside of Isshin-Ryu circles and begin looking into other arts as well. Not knowing is bad, but not wishing to know is much worse and detrimental to development as a martial artist. This may sound like a simple truth, but many people often fall into learning traps where they reach a certain level and then have no further desire to expand their knowledge base. There is so much history in martial arts. The student, regardless of age or rank, should have a never-ending aspiration to learn as much history on the martial arts as possible.

Studying other martial arts provides perspective. You must learn your style isn't the only one out there that has all the answers of perfect self-defense. There is an entire universe of martial arts that offer much to those willing to open their minds and learn. The key here is to remain open to all forms of martial arts instead of having closed-minded thinking. Isshin-Ryu is an outstanding form of martial arts that has been proven repeatedly, not only on the street but also in the competitive arena. However, a martial artist seeks as much knowledge as possible to blend with their core system. Researching the backgrounds of the two main systems that comprise Isshin-Ryu (Shorin-Ryu and Goju-Ryu) is essential. A desire to learn more about the kata from those systems is crucial. Master Shimabuku brought into his system two kata from Goju-Ryu and five kata from Shorin-Ryu. What about the other kata from those two systems? Gaining knowledge and insight into the kata that Shimabuku didn't utilize can further your knowledge and understanding of Isshin-Ryu as well.

Figure 71: 2014 - Newark, DE. Author with Yoshihito Sakimukai Sensei, who is the head of Chintokan in Jacksonville, FL. This seminar presented Shorin-Ryu bo kata as well as Shindo Muso Ryu Jodo techniques.

The OI will always be my core system of training and learning; however, I need to go outside and train and research other arts such as Shorin-ryu karate, Kendo, Modern Arnis, Kombatan, Aikido, and Jodo. Training in other forms or styles of martial arts opens the window to see the relevance these other systems have with your core system. At the age of 50, Grandmaster Shimabuku began his study of Kobudo, the art of traditional Okinawan weaponry. He sought out the instruction of Shinken Taira and eventually incorporated many of the techniques of Kobudo into his system of Isshin-Ryu.

At 50 years of age, Shimabuku had been involved in martial arts for well over 30 years and had developed and formalized his own system. Yet, he still looked for more knowledge and explored other arts at his disposal in an effort to improve himself as a martial artist.

Jodo: the suriage strike, I can see how the execution of his strike (explain it in detail) is very similar to a thrusting strike to the mid-section with a six-foot bo (called kun). As such, training in Jodo can add to my experience and understanding of kobudo, or Okinawan weapons, training.

In the book *The Writing Warrior*, Laraine Herring writes, "While theory can help you find new ways to looking at problems and activities, and help you think more critically about your own choices and reactions, what matters most is your direct experience..." In other words, if you only practice and research one particular style or method of training, you will tend to only reflect those teachings in your performance, causing your growth to be limited. Go outside your normal routines and study other arts. Your craft (martial arts) should not be limited to your genre (Isshin-Ryu karate).

Of course, this should only happen after a good, solid foundation in your initial style is developed and after many years of practice. But at some point, you should go beyond your own dojo and style and expand your experiences to gain a fuller knowledge of other martial arts. This will, in turn, expand your skills and understanding of martial arts. Put yourself out there and train with as many different instructors as you can. Each one has something unique to offer. This is a principle that the Order of Isshin-Ryu pushes heavily.

Everyone we meet can help us on our life's journey. Some help a little, some a lot. It's all worth it. It doesn't matter who or what they help us with. They propel us along the path to become a better martial artist and a better person. All sensei within the OI have something different they bring to the table. Students should seek out these instructors and train with them for a new experience in their training, which leads to more growth.

Walther von Krenner makes this point in his book *Following the Martial Path* by stating, "Have you ever noticed how much of our practice focuses on studying? We are not members, adherents, patients, or clients. We are students. The emphasis is on learning, and to learn we must be open and ready to learn ourselves. Zen master Dogen reminds us that study is self-empowerment. No one can study for you, and you cannot bypass it and buy the result. You have to do it for yourself. This requires discipline. It requires constant reflection, because, without reflection, there can be no growth."

Figure 72: 2014 - Newark, DE. Shodo (Japanese calligraphy) brushed by the author being presented to Andy Rodriquez Sensei for his dojo. Shodo says "Iwa Dojo" (one harmony school). The author has trained with Sensei Rodriquez in Shindo Muso Ryu Jodo.

I had been a black belt for many years when I came across a book titled *Old School - Essays on Japanese Martial Traditions*, by Ellis Amdur. This book documents a style of kusarigama (Japanese chain and sickle) called Isshin-Ryu. I had never known another form of martial arts that shared the same name as the system Master Shimabuku developed. Apparently, a samurai of the seventeenth century, Tan Isshin, developed the system. The point: build your library on the martial arts. Get your hands on whatever you can regarding the history of not only Isshin-Ryu karate, but also many other styles of martial arts as well. This process of continuous learning must be a never-ending process to further enhance the value of your training.

Observation

This aspect of training is often overlooked. How much do you observe not only by watching others perform but also yourself? Are your intentions or expectations blocking your progress? Are they serving as a distraction during training? Good students do not become occupied with thoughts of rank or speed of learning. They simply enjoy the training so much they can't wait until the next class. They take the time to work what they've learned at home, on their own, without becoming overly worried if it meets some defined standard. Everyone is a bit different, so it doesn't make sense to try to compare your performance to others. Simply observe your instructor as closely as possible and try to pick up the little details.

Early pioneers such as Long and Nagle would tell how they demonstrated a technique and then leave the students to their own devices to figure out how to make the techniques work properly.

Part of the observation process requires the student to 'feel' the effects of a technique. Walther von Krenner notes this process in his book *Following the Martial Path* where he states, "Originally, martial arts were not taught using detailed explanations. Instead, instructors demonstrated techniques. They expected students to pay attention to what was occurring, and then to practice repeatedly until they could duplicate what their instructors had done." Part of this 'demonstration' was to make the student feel the technique in terms of speed and power, as well as the specific area of the body being targeted. This cannot be underestimated in terms of the true learning process. If you don't, on some level, understand the damage a technique can do then it becomes difficult to fully understand the technique, let alone to eventually teach the technique to students who come after you.

Do You Know Your Sensei?

Part of learning from your instructor goes beyond the techniques of whatever martial art you happen to be studying. Your learning experience improves dramatically when you get to know your sensei on a much deeper level.

Part of that may stem from the point of time in the student's life. Younger students, such as teenagers, are much more impressionable. Karate becomes their life, and they want to be around their instructors to learn lessons beyond the dojo.

As Sensei Kurt Kline puts it, "There are no walls to the dojo. Early in my training, I hung out with other students at Denshi's house, helping out here and there. Sitting around a table talking with your fellow martial artists is just as important as punching and kicking. If you don't take advantage of that time outside of the dojo, you are missing out on an important aspect of your training." Sensei Adam Knox follows up by saying, "I would continually hang around Ron Tyree and Bud Ewing and take the conversation beyond normal talk to martial arts topics and then back to normal conversation. Over time, this becomes a natural process and is imperative to your development as a martial artist. To this day, I do that because it adds ongoing perspective to my knowledge and experience."

Sitting down and discussing life on a variety of topics is an essential part of understanding your martial art, albeit on an indirect level. I feel this is a quality of

Isshin-Ryu (one heart) karate. What lies at the core of your sensei's heart? This is a concept that is not always spoken but somehow understood by many. How can anyone think they can garner the deeper instruction of their instructor unless they can truly understand and respect the person on an intellectual and emotional level? Your sensei is not perfect. As Dave Lowry states in his book *In the Dojo*, "The sensei is not always wizened (nor universally wise); not always patient (nor prescient); not always technically infallible (nor invincible)." Your sensei has strengths and weaknesses both within your chosen martial art as well as in their personal life. Get to know them… for everything that they are and have been through can teach you something about yourself.

Figure 73: L-R: Master Bud Ewing and student, Kurt Kline.

I have traveled to Nevada many times to visit Master Cooling at his home. I would estimate that 80 percent of the time spent with my sensei has nothing to do with martial arts technique. This is by design. You need to come to some level of trust with your instructors, and they, in turn, need to come to that same level with you. They are passing down an art to which they have devoted their entire life. The lessons they learned both in and out of the dojo in their experiences are invaluable. You cannot put a price tag on what they possess and how much those lessons, learned and cultivated from seriously hard work, can help you in your own martial arts training and in the obstacles that you face in life. After many extended conversations with Master Cooling, it is evident how hard he takes it when someone leaves the Order of Isshin-Ryu. This is understandable. It takes an immense amount of time and effort to pass down the martial arts in the intended manner. The OI is Master Cooling's family. When someone leaves, it is as if a family member is lost to him. This is because he truly cares for everyone in the OI, and he takes the time to get to know them beyond the walls of the dojo.

Martial arts are not a pursuit to be taken lightly. Serious damage can be inflicted not only on others but also to yourself if you do not learn and practice responsibly. This can also extend to damage of your instructor's reputation as well as the organization to which you belong. As such, good instructors do not freely give away all their knowledge – nor should they – just because you pay a monthly fee to train in their dojo. The sensei needs to have a very high degree of confidence that you will respect and preserve their teachings and not damage everything they've trained so hard to attain before ever meeting you, their student. This takes time. This takes an effort, on the student's part, beyond simply showing up and training with many others at the same time. You don't want to be just another number in the dojo, you want to seek out personal transmission of the sensei's art. You need to get to know your sensei beyond the walls of the dojo – on many levels. Again, Lowry sums this up as follows from his book *In the Dojo*:

> Like any intricate or complicated art, budo has so many subtleties, so many individualized manifestations, that there is no way it can be taught through books or video or through a teacher standing at the front of a big hall and counting movements like a drill sergeant. The relationship must be immediate, at least for those practitioners seeking to move further along the Way than just the first steps. There is no other satisfactory method by which to accomplish this arduous journey than by submitting oneself to a qualified sensei and then trusting him to lead.

Developing as strong a bond as possible with your sensei can be a life-changing experience. It is no different with a coach, a teacher, a friend, or a distant relative. When developed correctly, this mentorship experience can and will last a lifetime. And a good sensei will realize that this relationship will be as beneficial to them as it is to the student. When the sensei can see the student's heart better, when the sensei knows the dedication of the student is true, sensei will be apt to share more information and well-earned experiences to further the student's improvement.

Make Failure Your Friend

Who wants to fail? Nobody. But if your perspective is in the right place, failure can serve you incredibly well. Many athletes who have succeeded in their sport often cite the number of times they've failed. Michael Jordan, most likely the greatest basketball player of all time, is well-known for stating his accomplishments, but successes are just a fraction of the overall time he spent working on his craft. The public was not privy to the number of times he failed. Those failures helped to mold his eventual leadership on the basketball court and the resulting championships he won with the University of North Carolina and the Chicago Bulls.

In the political realm, Abraham Lincoln was the model of failure. He failed numerous times in bids for a seat in the Senate and lost the presidency before finally winning the presidential election at the age of 51. His failures helped him develop into one of the greatest leaders in U.S. history.

The same is true for your martial arts training. Failures can add to your abilities when you learn from them. A failure or setback provides the opportunity to learn and to look inward and seek what went wrong. Only then can you appreciate the efforts you put forth, to be proud of your commitment to your craft. Failures not only develop your physical abilities but also your patience and your mental toughness.

Successful performance or abilities in martial arts do not happen automatically. They can only occur after many attempts and failures. Unless you fail at some point, you cannot understand what it takes to be successful and appreciate the mindset needed to overcome obstacles.

Figure 74: 1994 - Elkton, MD. Annual OI shiai. L-R: John Costanzo, Shelley Bell, Ron Tyree, Carmen Grace, Ronnie Cimorosi, Kurt Kline, Diane Ortenzio-Cooling

There is no exact formula for success. If there were, everyone would be successful. The illusion of success and what it takes to be a successful martial artist needs to be removed from your mind. Success is a different formula and level for everyone. What I deem successful will surely be different from your concept of success. Therefore, what is most important is to not fear failure but to embrace it and use it to your advantage. Viewing failure as a critical component of your training can lead to your eventual improvement as a martial artist.

You must never stop training and moving. When there is movement, you will have growth. This movement applies to all three 'arrows' presented in Chapter 8. You must continue moving forward physically, mentally, and spiritually. You must consistently strive to seek new paths along the three arrows and move towards new goals. This will never happen by sitting still. Knowledge and growth don't come to you. You must continually seek it if you value it enough.

Therefore, you need to continuously seek out mentors in all areas of life. It's healthy to cross-train in many other areas to benefit your martial arts study. Consider activities outside of the dojo such as running, weightlifting, yoga, etc. And do not limit those other activities to purely physical. Consider expanding your horizons into mental areas like chess, reading, writing, and so forth. These additional activities will have various high-level people to which you can draw additional perspectives and incorporate into your training.

Nobody has all the answers to everything or is the definitive source of authority. But everyone has something to offer. Famous and innovative martial artist Bruce Lee stated, "Take what is useful, and make it your own." Laraine Herring puts it this way in her book *The Writing Warrior*, "Be an active participant in your learning and be open to all that's around you." This thought applies to everything you do, not just learning to be a better writer. In the martial arts, the sensei provides the framework for the student to learn the art. But the student is in full control of their progress. This progress can become much more meaningful and rounded if the student keeps an open mind and looks for learning opportunities everywhere, both inside and outside of the dojo from both a physical and mental perspective.

Ego

Undoubtedly, one of the most difficult aspects to control in your martial arts training will be the ego. However, this must be an essential obstacle to overcome to allow continual learning to occur. This topic was touched upon at the end of Chapter 7. Ryan Holiday writes in *Ego is the Enemy*, "When we remove ego, we're left with what is real. Ego is self-anointed; its swagger is artifice." Granted, it is difficult to quell the ego after a fair degree of skill is developed. You can perform and do something the average person cannot. However, ongoing improvement is dependent upon not thinking too highly of yourself. You're just a person trying to make yourself better each day, and in turn, helping others improve themselves. God is in complete control, so don't believe you have skills beyond what He has provided.

Ryan Holiday adds another layer of perspective in *Ego is the Enemy*. He writes, "Our cultural values almost try to make us dependent on validation, entitled, and ruled by our emotions. For a generation, parents and teachers have focused on building up everyone's self-esteem." This is interesting. Cultural aspects clearly play a part in a person's development. It seems all sports today provide participation trophies. We seem to want to reward everyone just for taking part in an activity. Without any level of hard work to improve yourself, you are given that trophy. How can this benefit someone in the long run, especially children? Does it make sense to reward a student just for showing up to the dojo? Of course not. It's refreshing to watch a student come back to the dojo and see that they've worked on their techniques, kata, Japanese terminology, etc. That level of work and effort, in turn, energizes the instructor. It goes both ways.

The martial artist must take away pride and seek humility. Money, status, rank; these things are fleeting and cannot change you for the better on the inside. What is the only thing that matters? The heart. Is it in the right place? When your soul leaves this earth, whose status really matters? Remaining humble is not easy. When you receive a specific rank and the belt you wear in the dojo changes color, humility tends to go out the window. We may say we are humble after a promotion, but often it's the other way around. After all, we are only human. Author Max Lucado writes, "Humility. The moment you think you have it, you don't." You need to work extremely hard to keep a level head, regardless of your rank or status. Remember, you were a white belt beginner once. And all white belts know it.

From the budo perspective, the Japanese culture addresses this 'self-esteem' problem with *shoshin*. Shoshin means 'beginner mind.' You must continually have the mindset of a beginner. Never fall into the trap of thinking you've arrived after reaching a specific goal or rank. When you continually think using a beginner's mindset, your mind remains open to new ideas. You remain diligent in learning new things and trying new paths to determine the best approach to progress.

The path to learning and improvement never ends. Pablo Casals is considered one of the greatest cellists of all time. At 95 years of age, a reporter asked him, "You're 95. The world considers you to be its greatest cellist; and still, at 95, you practice six hours a day. Why?" He responded, "Because I think I'm making some progress." This response is the concept of shoshin personified. You always think and feel there is room to improve, for that is simply the reason you participate in the martial arts. To gradually improve every year, month, day, etc. You must continually push yourself, try new things, stretch the limits of what you think is possible, and challenge yourself to learn more. This mindset is essential; otherwise, progress and growth will level off or stagnate, leading to frustration and possibly discontinuing

Figure 75: Shoshin (beginner mind). An essential quality for self-improvement.

your training. If ego remains, then shoshin is not possible.

Your toughest opponent in life that you will need to overcome is yourself. Competition is a fantastic outlet to determine where your skills lie at a specific point in time. However, the conflict within to become not only a better martial artist but a better person is a lifelong endeavor that will be your most difficult to face. William Faulkner stated, "Don't bother just to be better than your contemporaries or predecessors. Try to be better than yourself." For this, we need to assume total responsibility for our efforts.

If we are not improving or becoming a better person over time, we need to look inward and review if our efforts are up to par. Winston Churchill said, "The price of greatness is responsibility." Master Cooling is a big proponent of responsibility. This follows the concept of the Sempai-Kohai relationship as discussed in Chapter 7. If you are not willing to assume total responsibility in your training and dedication, and couple that with the philosophy of simply trying to become better than the day before, the road of your training will be laden with problems and setbacks. You will simply not have the proper mental toolset to overcome hurdles when your improvement stalls.

Remain Humble

An essential part of martial arts training is to always remain humble no matter how much you accomplish or what rank you are bestowed by your sensei. This is not always an easy thing to do. In our culture, it seems that attitudes change once a certain degree of success is achieved, regardless of the endeavor. It doesn't matter if it's work, sports, or a hobby. The inclination is to hold yourself in high esteem once you reach a goal. It becomes easy to attach a label to yourself and think you have 'arrived.'

Ryan Holiday makes this interesting point in his book *Ego is the Enemy*…"There is real danger in believing when people use the word "genius"…..or any label that comes along with a career: are we suddenly a "filmmaker," "writer," "investor," "entrepreneur," or "executive" because we've accomplished one thing? These labels put you at odds not just with reality, but with the real strategy that made you successful in the first place. From that place, we might think that success in the future is just the natural next part of the story – when really it's rooted in work, creativity, persistence, and luck."

How often have you seen someone rest on their laurels after they have achieved black belt? It's as if black belt is their goal and once they make it, now they have arrived and deserve the respect of everyone around them. It takes a dedicated effort to remain humble at this point and realize the hard work is just beginning. There is so much more to learn. Now, more than ever, is the time to humble yourself and set the example for students within the dojo to show them that once black belt is achieved, there is much more work yet to do.

The same is true for any level of black belt that you may achieve. I've always said that at each black belt promotion I felt I didn't quite deserve the recognition for that level. But since my sensei felt I deserved the promotion, I would make it a point to double down my effort and work even harder to, hopefully, demonstrate that I did deserve it. This takes conscious thought.

Recall the Japanese mindset of *shoshin*, or "beginner mind." This should never go away. Always remember there is no need to compete against anyone. Your only concern should be self-improvement no matter what you achieve in the martial arts as well as in life. There is always another level to reach, always more areas of your martial arts (and your life) where you can improve.

The process of continual self-improvement is next to impossible when you cannot remain humble with yourself and others. Ryan Holiday goes on to say, "On an individual level it's absolutely critical that you know *who* you're competing with and *why*, that you have a clear sense of the space you're in." When your sensei sees that you continually work to improve yourself – physically, mentally, and spiritually – all the while remaining humble in the process, then you become far more of an asset to your dojo than you realize.

The Dojo Atmosphere

Several authors have written about the traditional karate dojo and what generally constitutes a sound environment for learning budo properly. The bottom line regarding the dojo is that it is a place where we do our best to improve ourselves. It is the one place, for many people, where life can make some sense. Everyone starts at the bottom. You have the opportunity to eliminate negative thoughts going on your life and simply train as hard as you can. The objective of everyone there is to help one another along the difficult path of the martial arts. In short, it is a refreshing change of pace to the often-unfair realities of life. The dojo is often considered a sacred space and should be treated with complete respect and kept clean and immaculate.

As Goju-Ryu stylist Roy Kenneth Kamen writes in his book *Karate: Beneath the Surface*, "I consider the dojo floor to be a sacred space. It is where all the answers to karate can be found. It is like the canvas on which an artist paints. Upon entering and leaving, we bow to show our respect for all the dojo signifies and all of the knowledge we gain there." Showing this respect applies to any endeavor you follow or anything you use in your life journey. Go to a gym and watch how people treat the equipment. Do they slam around the weights without regard to who owns it? Do they clean the equipment after usage?

Think about a police officer and his firearm. That equipment is intended to keep the public safe and potentially could save the officer's life. Therefore, he or she treats the weapon with ultimate respect both in how the gun is handled and in keeping it clean and in perfect working condition. The same holds true for your karate weapons, your gi, and your obi, as well as keeping the dojo floor clean and in perfect condition. Treat the dojo with respect, and the dojo will serve you well in your martial arts training.

Walther von Krenner writes in his book *Following the Martial Path*, "The dojo truly is a spiritual place, and the entrance to the dojo serves to separate it from the outside world, just as a *torii* gate separates a Shinto shrine from the secular realm. However, the entrance must eventually cease to serve as a boundary. The outside world and the dojo must become one. This does not mean that the training space is no longer considered sacred and important. It is just the opposite. The sense of reverence that one develops in the dojo must transcend the location. It must be applied to the world at large. When this happens, training stops being something special. It becomes ordinary, yet it turns out to be a necessary part of life."

In other words, the dojo should not be thought of as a static location to learn or practice the lessons garnered from your training. You should take the mindset of dojo activity everywhere you go. I'm not talking about violence in this regard, but rather how to avoid conflict and treat everyone with respect and dignity.

The same attitude should hold true with respect to the church environment. God didn't intend the church to be the only place to learn and observe the principles of Christianity. You must also live those principles wherever you go. If you do not live the principles of the church beyond the walls of the church, then you are missing the point of even *going* to church. The objective is to make church and your daily living one and the same regarding the atmosphere or personality that you project onto others.

The same should be true with your dojo life and daily life. This means treating people with respect, even if their opinion does not mirror yours. Everyone is going through battles for which they have no knowledge or insight, at least initially.

Controlling your anger is another dojo principle you need to project in daily life. In the dojo, anger accomplishes nothing, and a good sensei will dissolve it before it takes hold. Even if someone you come across is having a bad day – if you respond back to them in the same way – it will only make matters worse. Everyone should be ready and willing to help others improve in all facets of training. Taking this principle outside of the dojo can lead to a much better life, as the help you provide may well come back around when you least expect it.

These are just a few examples of the type of atmosphere a good dojo will foster. The instructor bears the responsibility to his students to ensure this atmosphere is maintained in the dojo at all times and teaches that these principles should also project throughout the student's demeanor in his or her daily life.

Chapter 10
BUDO TREE OF THE ORDER OF ISSHIN-RYU

"As an artist, you must be ever-vigilant when it comes to pushing yourself forward in your craft. You must resist the call of the familiar and push yourself deeper into your own work."

Laraine Herring

There are a variety of martial arts under the umbrella of the Order of Isshin-Ryu, all of them with the purpose to complement the techniques, philosophies, and teachings of Master Cooling's method of Isshin-Ryu. As noted in Chapter 1, even the founder of Isshin-Ryu, Tatsuo Shimabuku, explored various styles and systems during his lifetime. Above all, he was a martial artist and as such, he continually researched other styles in his quest to become a more rounded and complete karate-ka. He was very much aware of the benefit of continuous research and exploration in the martial arts, as was every practitioner of Okinawan karate at that time. According to Master Cooling, Shimabuku stated until the day he died, "Isshin-Ryu is a living thing, constantly changing and always improving."

At a certain point in training, the individual must move from practicing a martial art to becoming a martial artist. Denshi makes the point, "Without changing the move of the kata, if you have a better bunkai (interpretation), then show it to me and I'll use it. I want to continue to learn." This drive to continue learning is not simply a statement. Denshi puts this philosophy into action, as should anyone serious about their training.

Figure 76: 2008 - Chesapeake City, MD. Order of Isshin-Ryu summer shiai. L-R: Jerry Robinette, John Costanzo, Matthew Herd, Dan Popp, Ronnie Cimorosi, Larry Waldridge, Mark Wallace, Chris Taggart, Chris Harris, Dan Lorden, Diane Ortenzio-Cooling

Master Cooling frequently attended seminars of other styles throughout his career, and he continues to do so today. Shortly after moving to Nevada, he and his wife Diane attended an Aikido seminar in Reno. As Diane notes, "I really wanted to go to this seminar in Reno as there were instructors of various backgrounds and styles. We attended to learn and gain some fresh perspectives." Being a ninth-degree black belt and going outside of your style, your comfort zone, and humbling oneself to once again become a beginner is not always easy. However, Master Cooling has always followed this mindset, and he encourages all of his black belts to do the same.

There comes a time in a karate-ka's training process where he or she will benefit greatly from the exploration into other martial arts styles or systems. This was commonplace on Okinawa during the time Isshin-Ryu was founded. The concept of 'cross training' in martial arts is beneficial to both the student and the instructor, and those who are confident in what they teach encourage this research. Author Matthew Apsokardu interviews various American karate pioneers in his book Tales from the Western Generation. One of those interviewed is Paul Durso, a Shorin-Ryu karate student of Grandmaster Eizo Shimabuku, where he was asked if Shimabuku ever had a problem with cross training in other styles. His response:

> "That sort of thing was never a problem with him. You have to understand that the Okinawans were already mixing things up. Mixed martial arts was not a new concept. Shimabuku's personal background was in Goju Ryu, Shorin Ryu, Isshin Ryu, and more (e.g. Kendo[31]). Developing and expanding

---

[31] Additional example provided by the author.

> experience causes growth. With growth comes change. With growth comes some movement away from classic purity. Growth can enhance or change things depending on the person growing."

This mindset remains the same to this day. There is no perfect system of martial arts, and there is no perfect martial artist from which to learn. Regardless of system or rank, every instructor has something to offer. The astute karate-ka will not only look to instructors for learning, they will also keep their minds open and receptive to contemporaries as well as students with the intent of picking up anything that might be of use in their own training. That is what a martial artist does – continually strives to better themselves in body, mind, and spirit. And this betterment can come from any source, at any time. The process of continual striving is intended to go beyond the boundaries of any particular style in order to gain a better understanding of yourself and what is possible.

Roy Kenneth Kamen states in *Karate: Beneath the Surface*, "My efforts have enabled me to see past boundaries that altered my martial arts practice. I no longer feel bound by "commonly" held beliefs about Goju-Ryu karate." Kamen documents his research beyond studying various martial arts where he also explored historical aspects of karate, meditation and proper breathing, the concepts of Yin and Yang, as well as concepts from the practice of Yoga. There are vast amounts of paths you can take and explore, both from the physical aspects of martial arts to areas outside of the budo that relate to improvement of mind and spirit. These paths ultimately assist you on your journey and, hopefully, lead to a similar conclusion: to further your understanding and improvement.

The additional budo taught and practiced within the Order of Isshin-Ryu in no way modifies the system of Tatsuo Shimabuku: Isshin-Ryu karate. Master J.C. Burris raises a good point in his book *The Last Lesson* where he writes, "It is important that I begin relaying these concepts now because of the close association of martial artists of different arts and styles, the cross-training, and the blending of arts that is taking place. I do not mean to imply that the blenders of the arts are violating a sacred trust, but I am saying that when we change Isshin-Ryu, we lose Isshin-Ryu." In other words, when the techniques of any system of martial arts are modified, then you begin to water down the founder's intentions. Therefore, the OI does not alter Isshin-Ryu in any way. Isshin-Ryu is a solid system of karate and self-defense. The budo presented in this chapter are additional areas of study to enhance the martial artists' abilities, which everyone readily agrees becomes a must at some point in the evolution of your learning process. Burris goes on to write, "Add those aspects of other arts that are necessary for your students to develop the self-confidence and tools to enable them to further develop character, which is our mission, after all."

Not all systems presented in the following pages come directly from Master Cooling. The systems offered or available within the Order of Isshin-Ryu umbrella either come directly from Master Cooling or there is a direct link to the system from one of the OI's higher ranking black belts. One of Master Cooling's basic principles is this: "Whatever you learn outside of the Order of Isshin-Ryu, bring it back to the family and teach it." This concern and commitment to the OI family is what facilitates ongoing growth within the organization.

There are times when members of the OI extend their training and research into other martial arts but do not have the opportunity to offer what they've learned within the OI curriculum. Black belt Sean McCann studied Aikido. I had the opportunity to also study Aikido for approximately six months before the instructor had to move to another state. Those six months were some of the most enjoyable workouts in my martial arts career. I had the responsibility to teach. I was the student, and it was refreshing to 'start over' and learn new techniques.

When the individual is given the opportunity to learn new styles and techniques and, in turn, teaches them to the rest of the family, this helps to help solidify their knowledge. A good example of this was when one of our black belts, Jerry Robinette, moved to Australia and married a student from the Australia dojo. Shortly after moving there, he started to study Krav Maga. Krav Maga, or "contact-combat," is a military self-defense system developed for the Israel Defense Forces and Israeli security forces (Shin Bet and Mossad) that consists of a combination of techniques sourced from Boxing, Wrestling, Muay Thai, Jujutsu, Aikido, Judo, along with realistic fight training[32]. During a visit back to the United States a few years later, Jerry was requested to lead a class at the OI Hombu dojo in Elkton, Maryland and show some of the techniques and self-defense philosophies of this art. Jerry was a bit hesitant at first, considering many of the higher ranking black belts would be taking part in the workout. However, he also understood that in order to enhance his own understanding of Krav Maga and to further his level of confidence as a martial artist, he knew that leading the class was an opportunity not to pass up.

When Denshi allows members of the OI to do this, it helps bring value and confidence to their contributions to the entire family. This also provides for spontaneous creativity within the training and ongoing improvement of the Order of Isshin-Ryu techniques. It all stems from Denshi's commitment to his family and providing the freedom to learn new things and bring them back into the OI fold.

---

[32] https://en.wikipedia.org/wiki/Krav_Maga

In the next chapter, when reading the biographies of the OI members at the red and white belt level (6th degree black belt and above), you will notice quite a bit of crossover of training into other styles and systems of martial arts. It is very common for martial artists to blend training into other styles with their 'core' system. Martial artists tend to seek out other systems to understand their own body in a more comprehensive fashion when it comes to balance, breathing, footwork, and the like. Or the individual may simply wish to study a more traditional budo to explore the historical aspects of what that system offers. Whatever the reasoning behind it, martial artists generally like to extend themselves by exploring what other arts have to offer and determine if they can include additional concepts and techniques into their own training programs. It is a commonly known principle: *without additional learning, there is no growth.* This principle should extend beyond martial arts; it should apply to your entire life.

The high-profile cases of those who have done this are extensive: Bruce Lee, Tatsuo Shimabuku, Remy and Ernesto Presas, and on and on. This crossover even extends to delving into arts from other countries or cultures. Ernesto Presas grew up in the Philippines but also achieved black belt ranking in Japanese Kendo. The same happened with Eizo Shimabuku, Tatsuo's younger brother. Highly advanced in Okinawan karate, he also achieved dan ranking in Japanese Kendo. As presented earlier in Chapter 1, training in other styles and pulling what the practitioner felt the best of each system was a common practice on Okinawa.

Chin Na

Chin Na are joint locking techniques used in Chinese martial arts. There are several different meanings of Chin Na: "seize and control," "press and grasp," "hold-grip," and "seize and break." Overall, the objective of applying Chin Na techniques is to control or lock an opponent's joints or muscles and tendons, or to divide muscles and tendons, to neutralize the opponent's fighting ability. For that is one of the main precepts of Chin Na: If the opponent is still able to strike back in any way after your technique is applied, your technique is wrong. Chin Na movements are found in nearly all systems of martial arts to some degree, and their application causes a very high degree of pain – yet they are intended to control and not to necessarily cause permanent damage.

The Southern Chinese martial arts have more developed Chin Na techniques than Northern Chinese systems. The Southern styles have a much more prevalent reliance on hand techniques that cause practitioners to be in closer range to their opponents[33]. There is no system categorized as Chin Na per se; however, several Kung Fu systems specialize in the use of these techniques including Eagle Claw, Tiger Claw, Praying Mantis, and Shuai Jiao. In all other systems of martial arts, practitioners use the application of Chin Na techniques to enhance their own art and provide for a deeper understanding of their techniques.

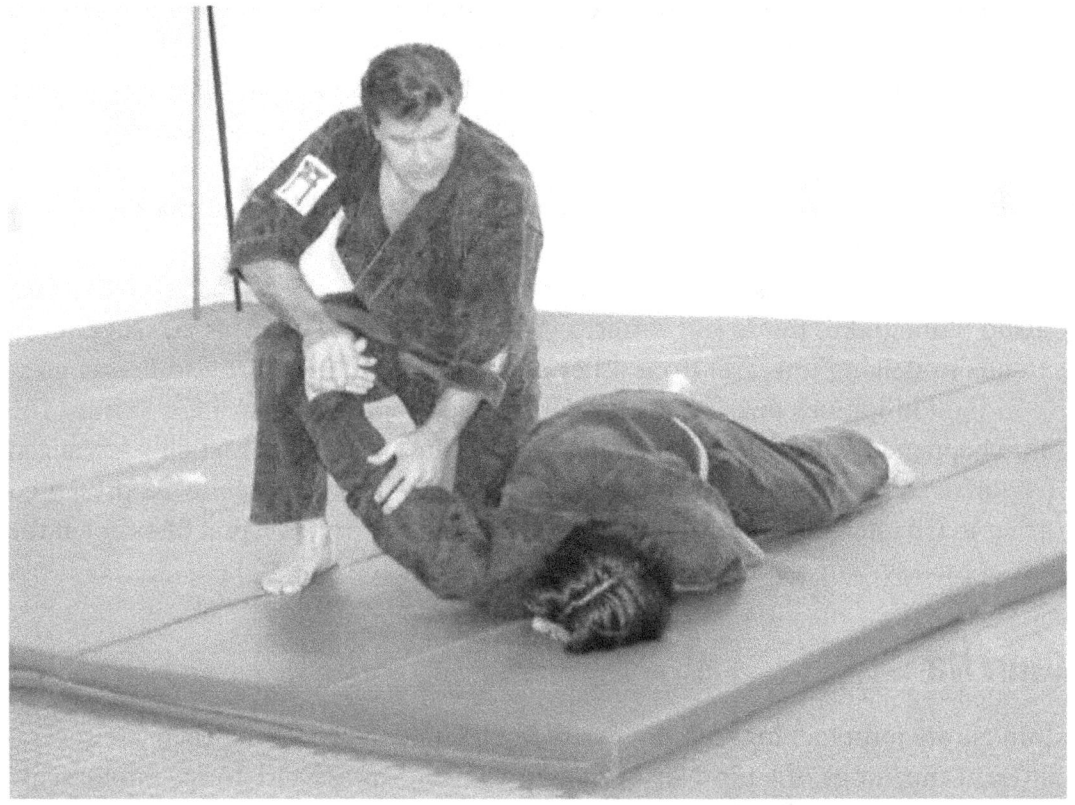

Figure 77: Master Cooling demonstrating Chin Na technique for seminar participants.

Chin Na teaches leverage, application of force, spatial orientation between you and an attacker, and how to read an opponent's intentions and body weaknesses[34]. There are somewhere around 700 different Chin Na techniques developed over the centuries. The Order of Isshin-Ryu has formally adopted over 30 of these techniques that are introduced at the advanced black belt levels. The intent is to make senior OI black belts aware of these movements and how to apply them in everyday situations.

---

[33] https://en.wikipedia.org/wiki/Chin_Na
[34] http://www.blackbeltmag.com/category/chin-na/

From there, students are encouraged to research and develop additional techniques. This concept is especially true in the Chi Ryu Jujitsu system developed by Master Isham Latimer. Chi Ryu Jujitsu applies techniques at close range with the opponent, which is highly suitable for Chin Na application.

Needless to say, Chin Na requires extensive time and effort to learn and apply correctly for effective use in a real situation. According to leading Chin Na exponent Dr. Yang, Jwing-Ming, "You must train first your Yi (mind in Chinese). You must put your mind where your technique is, then you can feel if the technique is right, and you will be able to direct your Qi (life force or life energy – ki in Japanese) to support the technique. You must train your sense of touch so that you know without looking whether your control is effective[35]." Dr. Yang notes that each technique is designed for a particular circumstance, and there are times where the technique would be ineffective. Couple this with the fact that the opponent could possibly counter your intended technique, and you will need to learn how to modify your Chin Na application. Dr. Yang cautions, "You have not mastered the art until you have learned these things."

Kyusho

Kyusho is the art of striking various points on the body, or a way of attacking the nervous system, to control an attacker. Kyusho utilizes striking and grabbing motions against pressure point targets that lead to control over your opponent. Knowledge of pressure points and the effects of these meridians comes from centuries of research by proponents of Chinese medicine. The martial arts of Okinawa and Japan have also contributed largely to the development of Kyusho. The concept of pressure points is present in the old school Japanese martial arts; in a 1942 article in *Shin Budo magazine*, Takuma Hisa asserted the existence of a tradition attributing the first development of pressure point attacks to Shinra Saburō Minamoto no Yoshimitsu (1045–1127).[36]

Denshi has stated, "Everyone can learn *how* to punch, but not everyone knows *where* to punch or strike." Without remembering where he heard this quote, he recalls, "It's not important to hit something, it's important to hit something important." Since it is more difficult to strike a moving target, one of the main objectives is to strike a pressure point that is not moving. Many times, this requires the Kyusho

---

[35] *Truly Learning Chin Na,* by Dr. Yang, Jwing-Ming. January 21, 2008. https://ymaa.com/articles/martial-arts/learning-qin-na
[36] https://en.wikipedia.org/wiki/Pressure_point

practitioner to 'set up' this objective by trapping or controlling a limb just prior to the striking technique against the pressure point. In other words, do something to make sure what you want to hit isn't moving; otherwise, you will have a much lower probability of your technique being effective. As an example, if you wish to strike the attacker's head, which can be highly mobile and difficult to strike, make sure you trap and control the attacker's arms, so the attacker's body and pressure points become immobile first.

Modern Arnis and Kombatan

Historical records dating back to the 8th century show Kali (kah-lee) as the martial art of the Philippines. Late in the 16th century, the Spanish began a 400-year occupation of the islands and promptly banned the practice of Kali; however, elements of the art were hidden in plain view in the form of native dance and folk plays known as *moro-moro*. Over time, the arts resurfaced and under Spanish rule, the arts became known as eskrima, estocada, arnis de mano or arnis. Historians indicate there are as many as 200 systems of Arnis, Eskrima, and Kali. Some of the more popular styles being Illustrisimo Kali, Doce Pares Eskrima, Balintawak, Cabales Serrada, Modern Arnis, and Kombatan[37].

Filipino martial arts are now extremely popular due to the effectiveness of the techniques and the training of the weapons involved, including sticks and knives. In contrast to traditional karate systems where the student first learns empty-handed techniques, the student of Filipino martial arts begins training with weapons in hand and then progresses to empty-handed techniques at the more advanced stages. Some of the methods of training deployed within Arnis include:

- *Espada y daga* (sword and dagger) – employs a long blade and a short dagger.
- *Solo baston* (single stick)
- *Sinawali* (to weave) – employs two sticks of equal length, twirled in a "weaving" fashion for blocking and striking.

The two arts from the Philippines utilized extensively within the Order of Isshin-Ryu are Modern Arnis and Kombatan. The Presas family is one of the main proponents of the martial arts of the Philippines in the United States. Remy Presas (1936 - 2001) is the founder of Modern Arnis. Ernesto Presas (1945 - 2010) is the

---

[37] http://www.presas.org/kombatan/arnishistory.htm

founder of Kombatan. The brothers had extensive training with numerous Arnis styles and blended those styles to form their own systems, as noted.

Remy Presas
(1936 – 2001)
Founder of Modern Arnis

Ernesto Presas
(1945 – 2010)
Founder of Kombatan

There are various members of the OI with backgrounds in these arts including Isham Latimer, John McDonald, Diane Ortenzio-Cooling, and Dan Popp. In 1977, Remy Presas was in New York providing seminars on Modern Arnis. The New York dojo, located at 28th street at this time, invited Presas to teach a week-long course at their dojo. Master Isham Latimer and Sensei John McDonald worked with Grandmaster Presas for eight hours each day during the week. As a result, they both earned teaching credentials in Modern Arnis.

It is interesting to note that the Filipino martial arts blend extremely well with other arts, including many forms of karate. In his book *Modern Arnis*, Remy Presas indicates this fusion of technique by stating, "Arnis makes many martial artists discover new things about their own style. They recognize the beauty of Arnis because it blends naturally the best movements from many arts. Most of my students continue to study their own styles – they just use Arnis to supplement their understanding." John McDonald discovered this "blending" experience first hand. During that week-long course at the New York dojo in 1977, they took the concept of "flow" being taught by Grandmaster Presas and, on their own, combined the movements of

Modern Arnis with the kata of Isshin-Ryu. At the end of the week, they demonstrated what they came up with to Grandmaster Presas. Sensei McDonald recalls, "He loved it! This is because his thing was, once you have it (flow) don't keep it separate. Bring it into what you do and make it a part of your movement." Soon after working with Grandmaster Presas, the New York dojo introduced Modern Arnis to the OI.

Figure 78: 2017 - Lake Tahoe, California. Grandmaster Rick Manglinong teaching techniques from Kombatan. Diane Ortenzio-Cooling is the training partner.

Modern Arnis fell off the radar, so to speak, over time; however, others have delved into the martial arts from the Philippines. Upon moving to Nevada, Master Diane Ortenzio-Cooling met Grandmaster Rick Manglinong in 2009 where Rick teaches Kombatan in Lake Tahoe, California. Grandmaster Manglinong is a direct student of both Remy and Ernesto Presas. In 2007, he was awarded Grandmaster (9th degree black belt) rank from Ernesto Presas. Diane continues to train with Grandmaster Manglinong to this day.

Sensei Popp trained in Modern Arnis for many years prior to joining the OI in 1996. He earned black belt ranking under Grandmaster Manglinong at the 2012 Order of Isshin-Ryu *gasshuku* (special training). Both Master Ortenzio-Cooling and Sensei Popp are affiliated with SMP[38] Arnis headed by Grandmaster Manglinong and Punong Guro Sal Todaro. This organization is focused on preserving the teachings of both Remy and Ernesto Presas.

Another example of how martial art styles and systems can blend together and add to the growth of the individual martial artist pertains to OI's founder, Grandmaster Cooling. In 2011, Master Cooling was observing his wife and her friend, Jo Traina, work a drill called "40 locks" taught in Kombatan. This drill entails various joint locking techniques combined into a flowing combination one after another. During a break in the training, Denshi asked to review some of the techniques. Jo made the comment that she likely wouldn't be able to show him much of anything new. Master Cooling replied, "Actually, I noticed you are performing several techniques I've never seen before, and I was wondering if you could show them to me again."

On the drive home from the workout, Denshi commented to his wife, Master Diane Ortenzio-Cooling, "Why do you need 40?" – referring to the 40 separate joint locking movements from the drill covered in the seminar. He told her, "I can consolidate the drill down to about half of the movements."

About a week after the seminar, Master Isham Latimer was visiting Denshi in Nevada, and the two of them solidified a new joint locking practice drill. Stemming from this effort was the birth of an extension to the OI curriculum, called "Denshi's 20" – a series of joint locking flowing movements named after Master Cooling. As this reflection indicates, you never know where you will pick up something new or different that may complement your skills and knowledge. Without an open mind to other systems and a respect for what others are doing in their training, you may very well miss out on some excellent opportunities to expand your knowledge and abilities.

Chi Ryu Jujitsu

In 2003, Master Isham Latimer spearheaded the development of a new system of martial arts – Chi Ryu jiu-jitsu. He collaborated with his students, Master John Costanzo (8th dan) and Sensei John McDonald (7th dan). Together, they developed an

---

[38] Sining Marsiyal ng Pilipinas. (www.SMPArnis.org)

eclectic style system that comprises the skills, philosophy, and principles from various sources, including:

- Order of Isshin-Ryu Karate
- Kodokan Jiu-Jitsu
- Sanuces-ryu Jiu-Jitsu
- Xin Yi Liuhebafa Chuan (Tai-Chi) and
- Modern Arnis.

Figure 80: 2014 – Dobbs Ferry, NY. L-R: John McDonald, Isham Latimer, John Costanzo. The author presented Shodo artwork which reads "Chi Ryu Jujitsu."

The system is comprised of seven forms – two developed by both Costanzo and McDonald, and three formed by Master Latimer.

A major contributor to Chi Ryu Ju-jitsu is Liuhebafa Chuan, also known as Six Harmonies Eight Methods Boxing[39] and Water Boxing. This form was developed in China by Chen Xi Yi, who was known as a pioneer of the internal forms of martial arts. He was a Taoist sage during the Song Dynasty (960-1279[40]). The actual name of the style is "Hua Yue Xi Yi Men," whereas Liu He Ba Fa is merely a description of the principles involved. Chen Xi Yi is known for his advanced theories on philosophical Taoism, Buddhism, and Confucianism. "Xi" is what cannot be heard; "Yi" is what cannot be seen[41].

Liuhebafa has core principles and training methods not found in other martial arts. One of the main tenets of the system is internal strength – not from muscles, but rather from tendons and bones (i.e. the structure of the body). This internal

---

[39] https://en.wikipedia.org/wiki/Liuhebafa
[40] https://en.wikipedia.org/wiki/Song_dynasty
[41] Liuhebafa Chuan – The 4th Internal Art, by Nomura Akihiko. Hiden Budo & Bujutsu Magazine (Japan)

strength is developed through its training methods such as 12 short drills, or movements, repeated continuously on both sides in the spirit of slower Tai Chi motion. There is also a form, called Zhu Ji, which consists of 66 movements. Zhu Ji contains no repeating movements and when performed correctly (i.e. proper speed of Tai Chi) can take up to 40 minutes to perform.

Ultimately, as Master Latimer expresses, "A skill or technique is simply physical movement." The technique is influenced by the formal study of a particular system over time. Regardless of the style; however, every skill or technique has one fundamental element at the genesis and that is *movement*. Therefore, the most efficient method of movement is essential to the effectiveness of any skill or technique. The most efficient and effective manner of movement is as natural as possible and is vital to the level of coordination between mind, body, and breath, as the movements are performed. There is a deceptive level of force in the skills when these three elements are present and in harmony. This seems to be perceived by many as being something automatic. However, it is perhaps this aspect of coordination that is most difficult to learn and harness because to accomplish it one must move slowly, without ego, intent, stopping, starting, or winning, and losing ideas.

Therefore, Master Latimer has incorporated the training in Liuhebafa Chuan, as the basis for all other skill set development in Chi Ryu jiu-jitsu. He and his collaborating black belts refer to the set movements as "forms" rather than "kata," because the term form notes greater possibilities within movement (limitless), rather than techniques that have clearly defined parameters, including stopping and starting points. Form is intended to devoid the body and mind of tense (muscle constrictions), during all movement. This allows for the improved chi, or qi (energy), circulation essential to achieving a higher level of oxygen throughout the circulatory system. It is also a method for achieving better overall health.

In 2007, I started training with Master Latimer in this martial art. I thought the T'ai Chi movements would blend quite well with my background in Isshin-Ryu, Arnis, and Kendo. I soon found out how deceptively complex the system is. The simple warm-up breathing exercises were extremely uncomfortable at first. I was constantly being told, "Relax. Don't tense your fingers. Let them relax and allow the energy to flow. Keep the knees slightly bent." All of this made sense and sounded easy enough, but at the end of 15 minutes of breathing exercises, my legs shook, and my feet hurt. I was used to moving around, so standing still, relaxing, breathing, and moving slowly and deliberately was something that took time to develop.

According to Master Latimer, his focus for the past 12 years has been that of health-related issues among martial artists today. He feels that as martial artists we may overlook the fact that there is more to maintaining good health than how hard we can punch, kick, perform kata, do kumite, and apply joint manipulation techniques, etc... Much of what we know and can physically perform is the result of our state of overall health including mental, physical, and emotional. We should not neglect things like good nutrition, proper rest, and positive thinking.

Grappling / Mixed Martial Arts

Figure 81: 1979 - Elkton, MD. Master Cooling applying arm bar technique to Barry Smith. L-R in background: Paco Lopez and Eduardo Gonzalez.

Mixed martial arts became part of the training offered within the Order of Isshin-Ryu around 2001 – 2002. Sensei Dan Cross was instrumental in getting the program off the ground. Black belts who were interested started to seek out Sensei Cross to cross train their Isshin-Ryu with grappling arts. But even before mixed martial arts began to take root in the OI, Sensei Juan Lopez initiated high-intensity full contact training in 1987. These classes were open to black belts only and were offered in addition to the regular class schedule and training. Most of the students were ni-dan (2nd degree black belt) or higher. Sensei Cross was a regular during those full-contact workouts and noted everyone quickly realized how much wasted movement they still had and how excited everyone would get mentally. As such, fatigue would quickly set it. However, this type of training led by Sensei Lopez quickly paid dividends. Sensei Cross explains, "Relaxation must be accomplished both physically, mentally, and emotionally. This is fully realized in full contact fighting."

Although the full contact training eventually faded, Sensei Cross is quick to point out that Sensei Lopez' leadership during this time would become a major stepping stone for the beginnings of mixed martial arts training within the OI some years later.

Several black belts approached Sensei Cross in 2001 to see if they could start up another group to enhance their fighting skills. Joe Zurolo discussed with Sensei Cross how frustrating he was when he fought other black belts. He had a difficult time figuring out how to match up against them. He asked about full contact training, along with another OI black belt, Shannon McGee. Sensei Cross agreed to train them along with other black belts in full contact and grappling. Each member of the group seemed to have a reason why they were there. Some wanted simply to get into better shape. Others just wanted to work out with friends and fellow OI members. Still others had goals within the full contact or mixed martial arts spectrum of competition.

Joe Zurolo and Shannon McGee were two who had specific goals regarding competitive fighting in mixed martial arts. Sensei Cross agreed to be their trainer. He had a good foundation to work with beyond both of their black belt credentials as Joe was a college football player and Shannon was a state champion wrestler in high school and was also involved in bodybuilding. Considering the athletic talents already in place for both men, they were putting in serious training hours for mixed martial arts.

After two years of training, they set up their first fight(s) in Fort Wayne, Indiana at a competition sponsored by early MMA star Dan Severn. Both Joe and Shannon came away with one win and one loss each, a very respectable showing. Sensei Cross recalls Shannon's loss came against a much smaller opponent than Shannon. Although Shannon had superior size and strength, his opponent had the better grappling skills. He allowed Shannon to take him to the ground where he then displayed those skills. Sensei Cross remembers the words of Master Cooling, "Don't play another man's game."

Figure 82: 2016, Chesapeake City, MD. Master Ron Tyree working grappling technique at OI annual shiai.

Both Joe and Shannon eventually retired from MMA competition due to injury. Shannon had a good degree of success in winning the Reality Fighting V light heavyweight title in November 2003 in Atlantic City, New Jersey. Sensei Cross recalls some of the obstacles they needed to overcome in their training, "We had to adjust to some things. We used the Isshin-Ryu straight punch; however, we adjusted slightly to keep people from shooting in under the straight punch and getting a takedown. You must train to stop the takedown and be able to transition from stand up to going down. If you do that, you will be very successful." At one-point, Shannon was being scouted by some of the top MMA camps. He was invited to California for a workout if he passed the physical. The exam showed ruptured vertebrae, which led to the end of his MMA career.

Master Ron Tyree is now carrying the torch and teaching grappling and mixed martial arts at the Hombu dojo of the Order of Isshin-Ryu. He has several consistent students who train with him and compete from time-to-time.

Matayoshi Kobudo

Kobudo stems from the early days of Okinawan martial arts when the farmers needed something to defend themselves from the samurai sword during the Japanese occupation of their island. Kobudo and Karate-do complement one another. As author Andrea Guarelli points out in his book *Okinawan Kobudo*, "Kobudo and Karatedo were two wheels of the same axle, each one very important for the other. For people who practice Karatedo today, the study of weapons represents an opportunity to analyze historic free-hand techniques and their applications from a modern perspective."

Matayoshi Kobudo is a general term referring to the style of Okinawan Kobudo, or weapons, that was developed by Matayoshi Shinpo (1921 – 1997) during the Twentieth Century. Martial arts were practiced by the Matayoshi family for over nine generations and drew heavy influence from Japanese, Chinese, and indigenous Okinawan martial arts styles[42]. Shinpo learned Kobudo from his father, Shinko Matayoshi (1888 – 1947), who was highly respected in the Okinawan martial arts community where he trained with renowned masters such as Go Kenki (Wu Xian Gui).

---

[42] https://en.wikipedia.org/wiki/Matayoshi_Kobudo

Figure 83: April 2017 - Puerto Rico. L-R: Sensei Luis Cuadrado (Kimo Wall's successor in Okinawa Kodokan) and Sensei Ronnie Cimorosi working Matayoshi bo technique. Standing in the background is Sensei Edgar 'Tato' Rivera.

Matayoshi Kobudo has connections to Isshin-Ryu karate in that Shinpo Matayoshi trained with both Chotoku Kyan and Chojun Miyagi. Furthermore, as Guarelli notes in his book, "He was one of the most advanced students of Higa [Seiko] sensei and he taught Kobudo in Higa's dojo, along with Shinken Taira and Kendo Nakaima." Master Tatsuo Shimabuku learned Kobudo from Shinken Taira as well, so the influence of Matayoshi Kobudo on Shinken Taira would be expected.

This system of Kobudo comes to the Order of Isshin-Ryu from Sensei Jesús M. Jiménez of the Puerto Rico dojo. Sensei Jiménez started to learn Matayoshi Kobudo from Kimo Wall. Sensei Wall studied Matayoshi Kobudo under Shinpo Matayoshi on Okinawa in the late 1960s and early 1970s while stationed there as a young Marine. Sensei Jiménez is currently a sho-dan in Matayoshi Kobudo.

Matayoshi Kobudo is complex and deploys a large number of weapons in the curriculum. Shinpo, who passed away September 7, 1997, had numerous students to which he imparted different aspects of the Matayoshi system. Guarelli notes in his book, "He decided to split his knowledge among different students, so he could transmit the most amount of specific information possible without overloading each student. Then, students would share with the others what they had learned."

Kobudo is an Okinawan weapons system teaching a variety of weapons including: bo, sai, kama, and eku. Sensei Wall was studying Goju-Ryu karate under Seiko

Higa when, one day while waiting at the dojo for his sensei to arrive, he met both Shinpo Matayoshi and Seikichi Odo, both highly sought after kobudo experts on Okinawa. From there he would become a student of Matayoshi. Eventually, Sensei Wall settled in Puerto Rico and founded his own organization, Okinawa Kodokan.

Figure 84: April 2017 - Puerto Rico. L-R: Ronnie Cimorosi, Mike Watson, Kimo Wall, Doug Rogers.

Over the years, various OI members have traveled to visit Sensei Jiménez in Puerto Rico. Most recently, Sensei Ronnie Cimorosi earned his sho-dan (1st degree black belt) in Matayoshi Kobudo in May 2017 awarded by both Sensei Kimo Wall and his top student, Luis Cuadrado. In 2017, Sensei Wall suffered a stroke and is no longer able to teach. He has passed the leadership of his Okinawa Kodokan to his student, Sensei Cuadrado.

The Matayoshi system employs a variety of classical Okinawan weaponry including: bo (6-foot staff), eku (oar), nunti (see figure 46 where a nunti is attached to the end of a staff), nunchaku, sai, tonfa, and many others. Training in pairs is a hallmark of Matayoshi Kobudo as author Andrea Guarelli explains, "One difference from other schools is that in the practice of Matayoshi Kobudo training in pairs is a fundamental part."

Kendo

Kendo, meaning "Way of the Sword," is descendent of the more military aspect of swordsmanship called Kenjutsu. The bushi, or classical warriors of Japan, used their swords in Kenjutsu to establish and maintain social order from the ninth to the middle of the seventeenth century. Thereafter, the role of the classical warriors as a ruling group became largely symbolic[43]. The need to modify the art into a "way" became rather apparent.

Kendo is the senior, most respected and popular of the modern budo disciplines[44]. The exact founding date of Kendo is unknown. The term *Kendo* was used as early as the seventeenth century, although popular usage began sometime after the Meiji Restoration (1868), the period signaling Japan's emergence as a modern state[45]. Modern Kendo is based on a legacy of classical Japanese swordsmanship that is at least as old as the history of the Japanese nation… although, the precise form was developed after the close of World War II[46].

During the mid-17th century, protective gear was developed to protect the practitioners from harm. Also, the invention of the bamboo *shinai* (sword) around the same time called for a change in the name of the sword arts being studied from Kenjutsu to Kendo.

Kendo training develops the mind and body much the same way as any other types of martial art. Its theory, techniques, and methods of training developed by the various schools, have been handed down through the centuries and today have been molded into an educative sport with all of the action and history of the past contained within its present training[47]. The main targets used in Kendo are the head, ribs, throat and the wrist of the right arm only. The wrist of the left arm may be a target only when the opponent has raised his shinai over his head in an attack posture. A point is called only when the top six inches of the shinai strikes the intended

---

[43] Modern Bujutsu & Budo – The Martial Arts and Ways of Japan, Vol. 3, by Donn F. Draeger. ©1996 By Donn Draeger. Weatherhill, Inc.
[44] See footnote #23.
[45] Kendo, by Minoru Kiyota. ©1995, 2002 by Minoru Kiyota. Shambhala Publications, Inc.
[46] See footnote #23.
[47] This is Kendo – The Art of Japanese Fencing, by Junzo Sasamori & Gordon Warner. ©1972 By Sasamori & Warner. Charles E. Tuttle Company

Figure 85: 1998 - Hershey, PA. The author (on left) practicing Kendo.

target. However, this is not an automatic point. There must also be a demonstration of proper movement, posture, and *kiai* (spirit shout) for a point to be awarded.

Many of the well-known karate-ka of Okinawa also included Kendo in their curriculum of study and research. As noted earlier, Eizo Shimabukuro (Tatsuo's younger brother) attained high dan ranking in Kendo. The founder of the Matsubayashi style of Shorin-Ryu karate, Shoshin Nagamine (1907 - 1997), also studied Kendo. Martial artist and author George Alexander writes of Nagamine in his book *Okinawa: Island of Karate*, "...he was ranked san-dan (3rd degree black belt) in Kendo after four years of study in that art. He studied Kendo intensely in order to more completely understand the similarities between Kendo and Karate."

Kendo has a high degree of etiquette and customs as it is the national sport of Japan. These courtesies must be followed at all times while the dojo for sound learning of this art. All the customs stem from the age of the samurai. In the following excerpt from the book *Japanese Swordsmanship - Technique and Practice*, authors Gordon Warner and Donn Draeger provide an explanation of the approach followed even today by modern Kendo-ka:

> To be seated while wearing the long sword was an irresponsible act, a gross insult to others present. But above all, the warrior sought to avoid becoming the victim of a surprise attack. If he placed his long sword in its scabbard on the floor at his right side, cutting edge facing him, this act was tantamount to declaring that he had no aggressive intentions and, furthermore, that he expected none on the part of his host. But if he turned the cutting edge of his sword away from him, this was an insult not likely to be ignored. Moreover, a sword allowed to rest in its scabbard on the floor at a warrior's left side was an ominous sign. It signified not only that its owner distrusted his host but also, perhaps, that he had aggressive intentions of his own.

Sensei Dan Popp brought Kendo to the Order of Isshin-Ryu shortly after being accepted as a member in 1996. Dan began studying Kendo in 1990 under Reiun Kim. Sensei Kim was born in South Korea in 1926 and eventually moved to Japan for military school. Sensei Kim's instructor in Japan was Hukuoka Gorozaemon, a 9th dan.

ORDER OF ISSHIN-RYU SENIOR DAN BIOS

"The budo sensei's creation is in the forging of a mature budoka who can, in turn, express his personality and unique creativity through his art."

Dave Lowry

Grandmaster Toby Cooling
Ju-dan - 10th degree black belt

Walter Cooling, nicknamed "Toby" by his family, began martial arts training in Judo at the age of sixteen. At 20, he began training in Isshin-Ryu Karate under Sensei Tom Lewis in Salisbury, MD. Some time later, while a green belt, Sensei Lewis asked him to attend a meeting with him in New Jersey. The meeting had been called by Master Don Nagle, one of Master Shimabuku's first American students. While there, he took the opportunity to work out in Master Nagle's dojo. The trips to New Jersey to train became regular, and he eventually asked Master Nagle to be his sensei.

In December 1969, Sensei Cooling traveled to Okinawa to study with the founder of Isshin-Ryu karate, Tatsuo Shimabuku. Before his departure for home, Master Shimabuku promoted him to roku-dan (6th degree black belt) in March 1970.

During this time, he graduated from the University of Baltimore with a B.S. in Personnel/Labor Relations. He worked for several companies before starting his own real estate firm in 1969. He owned and operated a successful retail business, Jayco Liquors, from 1975-1989.

On August 11, 1971, Master Nagle promoted him to nana-dan (7th degree black belt). Grandmaster Shimabuku and Masters Harold Long, Steve Armstrong, and Harold Mitchum honored him with a diploma also recognizing him at this rank. On October 4, 1986, Master Nagle promoted him to hachi-dan (8th degree black belt). Master Long also recognized him as a hachi-dan with a diploma on June 21, 1987. In September of the following year, Master Cooling was inducted into the International Isshin-Ryu Karate Hall of Fame. In 1991, he received the Spirit of Isshin-Ryu award from the same organization. This award is presented to the individual who best represented and promoted Isshin-Ryu throughout the nation for that year.

Figure 86: 1972 - Elkton, MD. Toby Cooling performing Sunsu kata.

On June 14, 1992, Master Cooling was promoted to ku-dan (9th degree black belt) by Master Don Nagle, ju-dan, and Master Harold Long, ju-dan. On February 6, 1995, the World Head of Family Sokeship Council officially recognized Master Cooling as one of the heads of the Isshin-Ryu family worldwide. The Council consists exclusively of martial arts instructors who are the acknowledged heads of their martial arts systems, and the World Head of Family Sokeship Council is a world-wide organization. Master Long honored Master Cooling by presenting him with the certificate in a ceremony on March 11, 1995.

Master Cooling has continued his martial arts education, becoming proficient in Chin-na, and Kyusho. He has been active as an instructor for municipal, county, state, and federal law enforcement agencies. These include the American Society of Law Enforcement Trainers, the Maryland Police Training Commission, and private security groups. He is a former police officer from Cecil County, Maryland, has served as a reserve deputy for the Douglas County (NV) Sheriff's Department, and currently serves as a deputy constable for East Fork Township, Douglas County, Nevada.

He has served on the board of directors of the Isshin-Ryu Hall of Fame and continues to promote Isshin-Ryu Karate through seminars and his travels. He is chairman of the Order of Isshin-Ryu. Master Cooling founded the Order of Isshin-Ryu on January 15, 1971, in an effort to keep his word to Master Shimabuku, who asked him to "… go back to the States and teach good Isshin-Ryu for me, make happy family."

Master Bud Ewing
Ku-dan, 9th degree black belt

Born on Thanksgiving, 1948, Aubrey "Bud" Ewing has lived in Cecil County, Maryland all his life. His college study at Goldey Beacom College was interrupted in 1967, when he was drafted into the Army. He was trained to be a medic in Frankfurt, Germany, specializing in field emergencies, surgery, and pediatrics. He was then transferred to Viet Nam where he served until 1969. It was then that he was injured in a landmine explosion. He refused medical attention for himself until he finished attending to the seriously wounded men and they were moved to safety. This unselfish act earned him both a Silver Star and a Purple Heart. This compassion for others continues to be Bud Ewing's trademark.

After returning home to Elkton, Maryland, Bud renewed his friendship with Toby Cooling and went to work for Toby at his new enterprise, Jayco Liquors. He also acquired a passion for Toby's other life, Isshin-Ryu Karate, and began training in 1973. He was awarded a black belt in July 1975. "In those days," Master Cooling relates, "Jayco was new and business was sparse. Bud and I would pass the time playing cards, doing kata, or fighting in the store. We were together seven days a week, so we had a lot of time to work on karate. At the time, I also believed that robbery prevention included the wearing of firearms (.45 caliber to be exact)." "One night at closing time, Bud had the night deposit bag, and I was putting some bottles away. We started doing kumite near the front doors. Well, as luck would have it, a passing motorist looked in and saw the manager of Jayco fighting to keep the money bag away from a robber with a gun. He contacted the police. As Bud and I closed up and locked the doors, we were met in the parking lot by six Maryland State Police cars, whose occupants had their guns drawn and aimed at us! Fortunately, I knew one of the troopers, and we were able to explain." Bud became the owner of Jayco Liquors in 1981 when Toby went on to other business interests. Bud went on to become one of Cecil County's most prominent businessmen.

Over the years he has assisted Master Cooling with seminars for the Elkton Police Department, Cecil County Sheriff's Department, the Coast Guard, DuPont Security, and various women's groups. In 1990, Sensei Ewing became the chief instructor of the Elkton dojo. A year later, the school was voted Dojo of the Year by the Isshin-Ryu Hall of Fame. His personal achievements in martial arts include:

1992 – Male Instructor of the Year award by the Isshin-Ryu Hall of Fame
1993 – Board member of the Isshin-Ryu Hall of Fame
1997 – Outstanding Contributor to the Martial Arts award by the AOKA Hall of Fame
1998 – Induction into the Isshin-Ryu Hall of Fame

Sensei Ewing resides in Elkton with his lovely wife Ellen. Her tireless work in organizing and running the annual summer shiai picnic is nothing short of incredible. She is a treasure of the Order of Isshin-Ryu.

Bud Ewing - Reflections of Grandmaster Cooling

Bud worked his way up through the ranks quickly since he was with me seven days a week while we were both at Jayco. He made sho-dan, or 1st degree black belt, when I was building Jayco Liquors. At the time, we didn't have many customers, so we would hold impromptu training sessions continuously just to help pass the time, right in the middle of the store. He was the first ever Dai Sempai of the Order of Isshin-Ryu. The reason I picked Bud Ewing to be the 'keeper of the kata' is because Bud does not enjoy change and works diligently to maintain the kata exactly the way I taught him well over 30 years ago. Who better than to maintain the kata standards of the OI?

Master Isham Latimer
Ku-dan, 9th degree black belt

> NOTE: The bio for Master Isham Latimer is derived from the book *The Modern Day Warriors: In Their Own Words*, and has been modified slightly from the original text. This book is self-published by Professor Cleveland Robinson and is available at Lulu.com.

Master Isham Latimer has a rich background in a variety of martial arts disciplines throughout his career as both a student and teacher. His training includes Isshin-Ryu karate, Jiu-Jitsu, Arnis, Kobu-Jutsu, and Hsingi Liuhebafa Chuan Tai Chi.

Master Latimer began his martial arts training in June 1972 under Master Robert Salay (7th dan in Judo and 6th dan in Isshin-Ryu karate) and Joseph Drual (6th dan in Isshin-Ryu karate and Kodokan jiu-jitsu). Later that year, he became friends with Furman Simmons, a sho-dan in Sanuces Ryu Jujitsu under renowned Grandmaster Moses Powell. He trained diligently in Isshin-Ryu karate and earned the rank of sho-dan (1st degree black belt) on November 4, 1975, under Sensei Salay and Sensei Drual. He had begun training simultaneously in Kodokan jiu-jitsu under Sensei Joseph Drual and was awarded the rank of san-kyu in August 1975 in this system.

In the spring of 1975, Master Latimer had come to the reality that it was time to move on in order to advance his own knowledge and skill level in martial arts, and so he sought out new exchanges with other skilled martial artists. He met and trained with several students of his rank level and higher, including then Sensei Furman Simmons, who later changed his name to Makakuvu Ali El-Bey. They exchanged knowledge and techniques as they forged a great friendship that survived many sprains and bruises. Master Makakuvu was a student of both the renowned Grandmaster Moses Powell and Grandmaster Ronald Duncan. At that time, Master Latimer was also introduced to two of sensei Makakuvu's students - namely Sensei Cleveland Robinson, author of *The Modern Day Warriors: In Their Own Words*, and Sensei Hamilton Banks. Both Sensei Robinson and Sensei Banks also trained with

Grandmaster Moses Powell, and today both are master level ranked in the Sanuces ryu jiu-jitsu system. In addition, Shihan Banks works in the Kumite ryu jiu-jitsu system under Grandmaster "Little" John Davis. Grandmaster Little John Davis is a high-level master under his sensei, Doctor Moses Powell.

In the summer of 1976, Master Latimer had grown to love the Isshin-Ryu karate system because of its street combat orientation in terms of the application of techniques and rapid execution of combinations. He felt that jiu-jitsu was the perfect complement for Isshin-Ryu karate and continuously works these arts simultaneously.

Master Latimer began training under Malachi Lee (at the time 6th dan in Isshin-Ryu) in the winter of 1975. Sensei Lee was a very skilled fighter in the New York City tournament circuit. His dojo was located at East 23rd Street and 3rd Avenue, New York City. He did not like to train his students for tournament competition because of his belief that the fight on the street will never be controlled in the manner such as a tournament. Master Latimer recalls, "When Sensei Lee interviewed me, we discussed my current rank status (black belt) and my expectations. My response to Sensei Lee was that I was perfectly willing to begin training as a white belt because, in my mind, it was a new beginning for me, and I would accept whatever rank he determined I had earned at such time he saw fit. I knew that he and his students had much to offer, I would grow as a person, and my martial arts skills and knowledge would advance under Sensei Lee's leadership."

The Malachi Lee dojo had very talented students, including Maria Melendez, Jose Diaz, John McDonald, Aston Hugh, and Arthur Samson. It was an exceptional dojo as well as Malachi Lee was an exceptional instructor and martial artist. Sensei Lee's untimely death in June 1976 was a devastating jolt to Master Latimer and all of his dojo brothers and sisters. Master Latimer was received the rank of san-kyu brown belt in April 1976, by Sensei Lee.

In 1979, Master Latimer received his master's degree in social work from the State University of New York. He then began work at the John Jay College of Criminal Justice (NY) as an academic counselor and faculty advisor. In 1992, he attended the NY State Division of Parole Academy, graduating first in his class and receiving the Leroy Drake Award for Excellence. He currently works for the Specialized Warrants Unit as a warrant officer in the Absconder Search Unit. As well, for the last 9 years, he's been a Tactical Training Officer for the NY State Division of Parole.

Master Lee connected with Master Toby Cooling several years preceding his death. It was this connection and friendship that has continued to this day for which Master Latimer acknowledges and credits much of his advancement in the art of Isshin-Ryu. On February 6, 2011, Master Latimer was promoted by Grandmaster Cooling to the rank of ku-dan (9th degree black belt) during the OI shiai in

Chesapeake, Maryland. As he progressed through dan rankings to that of 9th dan, Master Latimer has been acknowledged for his dedication, skills, and loyalty to the martial arts world. He has received the following awards during his career:

1996 – Spirit of Isshin-Ryu Award presented by the Isshin-Ryu Hall of Fame
1997 – Master Instructor Award presented by Don Nagle's American Okinawan Karate Association (AOKA)
2000 – Sensei of Sensei Award presented by the Isshin-Ryu Hall of Fame
2003 – Induction into the Isshin-Ryu Hall of Fame
2017 – Visionary Martial Artist of the Year Award presented by Don Nagle's American Okinawan Karate Association (AOKA)

In 2003, Master Latimer spearheaded the development of a new system – Chi Ryu jiu-jitsu. He collaborated with his students, Master John Costanzo (8th dan) and Sensei John McDonald (7th dan). They were undeniably valuable contributors in the development of Chi Ryu jiu-jitsu... an eclectic system comprising the skills, philosophy, and principles from the Order of Isshin-Ryu karate, Kodokan Jiu-Jitsu, Sanuces-ryu Jiu-Jitsu, Hsing I Liuhebafa Chuan (Tai-Chi) and Arnis.

Figure 87: May 2017, Woodbridge, NJ. Master Isham Latimer demonstrating Chi Ryu Jujitsu technique.

Master Latimer is President of Golden Glow Investigative & Protective Services, LLC. He is a retired member of the law enforcement community after 23 years of service with the New York State Division of Parole. He has received numerous commendations for high professional standards of conduct, sound tactical judgment, and restraint under critical circumstances.

Master Latimer attributes his career achievements much in part to his martial arts training, to his family, to the accomplishments and standards set by the masters and practitioners of the arts who have preceded him, and to his contemporaries. He continues to strive for martial arts knowledge, human growth and development, and the most important purpose to him, which is his devotion to his family.

"Every Shadow is surrounded by Light."
"It is difficult to obtain new things with your hands clenched in fists."

"The difference between winning and losing is in the extent to which it affects the ego for the better or worse of the persons on either side."

--Master Isham Latimer

Isham Latimer - Reflections of Grandmaster Cooling

"A very talented, innovative martial artist. He's had the opportunity to train under something like 15 different instructors in various styles and systems, yet he's always remained loyal to me. I've seen him take various moves, experiment with them, and take them much further. He's developed a system of martial arts that he likes, but he's always been 'pro' Order of Isshin-Ryu. I've had him go many times to meetings and such in my place, and he's always represented myself and the OI extremely well."

Master Barry Smith
Ku-dan, 9th degree black belt

Master Barry Smith was born in Cambridge, Maryland in 1945. He began his martial arts studies in 1966 after he met a kid named Toby Cooling at the local drive-in. Shortly after, he joined the dojo of Master Tom Lewis. He eventually studied under Master Toby Cooling and opened his first dojo in 1969 as a brown belt. Master Smith received his 1st degree black belt in 1970. After graduating from the University of Baltimore, he joined the Maryland State Police. Over the next few years, he trained allied agencies such as the Maryland Department of Natural Resources, the Alabama State Police, and the Pennsylvania State police in defensive tactics, survival, and SWAT tactics.

Master Smith went on to many other accomplishments. He attended numerous survival schools, including the Northwestern University Survival School and the Broward County Survival School, which, at the time, was headed by Joe Hess, the 1977 Full Contact Karate Champion. He was then appointed the primary defensive tactics and physical training instructor for the Maryland State Police in 1983. In 1985, Barry entered the Police Olympics representing Isshin-Ryu karate and won four gold medals and one bronze. He was the only contestant to qualify for the International Police Olympics in Sydney, Australia. Barry also trained the governor's bodyguards. They later competed in a CIA exercise and were the only team to disarm all attackers during the exercise.

Currently a 9th degree black belt in Order of Isshin-Ryu, he received this rank on October 11, 2014. He was inducted into the International Isshin-Ryu Hall of Fame in 1996. In August 1995, his dojo won the Dojo of the Year award from the Isshin-Ryu Hall of Fame. Master Smith worked as a Defensive Tactics Instructor MPTC since 1982, Defense Tactics Instructor MSP, and currently works as a Farm Manager.

Master Smith credits Master Cooling for his martial arts growth where he states, "He stood alongside me many times when he shouldn't have. He pushed me to make me what I am today." He also credits Frank Hasting by saying, "… who left me way too soon. He taught me how to survive the tough times and tested my strength and heart when he left me standing alone. A warrior's heart he gave me."

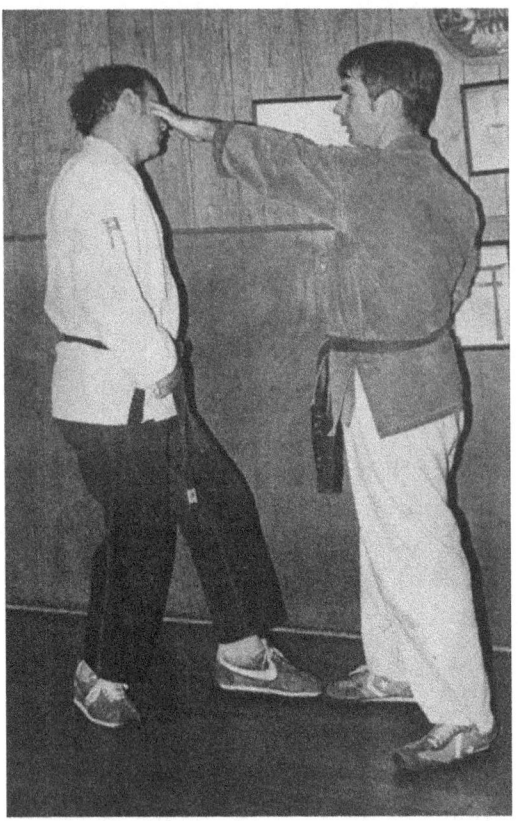

Figure 88: Early 1970s. Master Barry Smith teaching in his dojo. His uke in this photo is student, and one of his closest friends, the late Frank Hastings.

Even though Master Smith was inducted into the Isshin-Ryu Hall of Fame, he believes his greatest award was receiving his sho-dan (1st degree black belt) promotion from Master Cooling who tied his black belt around Master Smith's waist. His other greatest award is being around all his friends in the Order of Isshin-Ryu. He notes, "We were brought together by years of battle that turned into respect." And thirdly, Master Smith notes his pride regarding his wonderful sons.

When asked to provide some words of wisdom to the current kyu (student) ranks, Master Smith gave the following account:

"Go back to the old ways of training. IT IS THE ONLY WAY YOU WILL EVER KNOW WHAT I HAVE BEEN SO HONORED TO LEARN. Karate is not for everybody, so don't give it to everybody. If they don't have what it takes, let it be. Time will tell if they really want it. I have quit in my mind many times but not in my desire to stand on the line."

Barry Smith - Reflections of Grandmaster Cooling

Barry dances to a different drummer, in a different parade, in a different town. Talented martial artist. He kind of goes his own way, but he's always been loyal to the OI and loyal to me. He would come up to Chesapeake City for private instructions. On the way home, he'd stop at the bridge in Bohemia, get out of the car, face the direction of my house, give me the finger and cuss me out, get back in the car and drive back to Cambridge. Where did I get that information from? Barry Smith. One of my best friends. We both went on to college, and while I kept training, he became somewhat inactive for a time. One day on the third floor at the University of Baltimore, in my Junior year, I'm rounding a corner and here comes a roundhouse kick toward my head. My books flew everywhere. It was Smith. We've been together ever since.

Master Bill Sullivan
Hachi-dan, 8th degree black belt

Master William "Bill" Sullivan started his martial arts career in 1978 in Cambridge Maryland under the guidance of Master Barry Smith. Sensei Sullivan currently holds hachi-dan, 8th degree black belt ranking in Order of Isshin-Ryu. Prior to his martial arts training in Isshin-Ryu, Sensei Sullivan served with the United States Marine Corps from 1965 to 1969 and spent 18 months in Vietnam as an Artillery Surveyor. He credits his Isshin-Ryu abilities to the modern martial arts training provided by the Marine Corps, which included small arms training, crew-served weapons, bayonet fighting, boxing, tactics, and discipline.

After time served with the Marine Corps, Sensei Sullivan attended the Maryland State Police Academy in 1969 and served with the State Police from 1969 thru 1990, including nine years with the Special Tactical Assault Team Element, STATE Team, SWAT. From 1990 to 2000, he worked as a licensed private investigator and Accident Reconstructionist. He also was a Maryland Special Police Officer/Bailiff from 1998 to 2006 with the Maryland District Court and finally retired in 2006.

Sensei Sullivan remembers his first dojo with Master Smith as "Old School" and a school of hard knocks. It was above a casting factory with no windows and was hot and dirty. Pads were a luxury during sparring and many injuries occurred compared to today. Most of the classes were devoted to street techniques and sparring. If you wanted kata assistance, you requested before or after class. "You

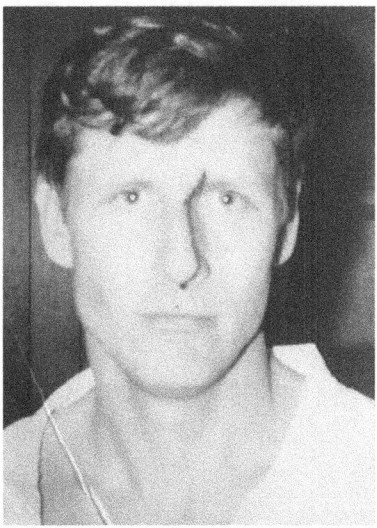

Figure 89: Master Bill Sullivan during his mudansha, or kyu rank, days of training.

had to want it back then, and there was a lot more discipline." Sensei Sullivan started the Easton dojo in 1992 at the Talbot County Community Center and eventually moved the dojo to the Easton Middle School in 2006. The Easton dojo is still active today.

In 2001, Sensei Sullivan received the Male Instructor of the Year award from the Isshin-Ryu Hall of Fame. After he attended the award presentation, he competed and won the Senior Division Kata and Kumite competition. In 2008, he was recognized by the Talbot County Council for his years of leadership running the Talbot County Parks and Recreation Martial Arts Program.

He was influenced and instructed by Master Barry Smith, Master Toby Cooling, and Master Bud Ewing. Sensei Sullivan's primary advice to his students is to study the kata. There are hidden aspects to Kata. He personally is still discovering things in his first kata after 32 years. He also advised that karate can be practiced and can be beneficial into old age. Sensei Sullivan is married to Jane, and they have one daughter, Stephanie.

Bill Sullivan - Reflections of Grandmaster Cooling

Bill Sullivan represents the Marine Corps in the Order of Isshin-Ryu. He still wears a flat top. One of the things that impressed me about Bill, when he would go to the dojo, he would go through all the kata. ALL the kata, without fail. We teach 26 kata. Like me, everything in his life is black and white. It's either 'yes' or 'no.'

Master Diane Ortenzio-Cooling
Hachi-dan, 8th degree black belt

Diane Ortenzio began training in Isshin-Ryu Karate in 1979 in Harrisburg, Pennsylvania. Her instructors were Sensei Jake Stoss, Don Monismith, and Jim Clark. After first moving to Baltimore and then Philadelphia, she became a student of Master Bud Ewing and a member of the Order of Isshin-Ryu fraternity in 1988.

Diane was a fierce competitor for 23 years, attending many events in the Northeastern part of the United States, as well as in Tennessee and Virginia. She consistently placed in the top three in women's black belt kata, kumite, and weapons. In addition, she won the Isshin-Ryu Hall of Fame's (IHOF) Women's Overall Grand Championship 3 times, and the IHOF Women's Kata Grand Championship and Kumite Grand Championships once each from 1996-2002. She retired from competition in 2003.

After moving to Nevada in 1996, she began Sierra Dojo Martial Arts to continue her own training and to introduce the OI method to others. Some of Master Ortenzio-Cooling's major awards include:

1992 – Hall of Fame Female Instructor of the Year
1998 – Hall of Fame Spirit of Isshin-Ryu Award
2003 – Induction into the OIKKA Hall of Fame
2003 – Induction into the Isshin-Ryu Hall of Fame
2017 – Woman of the Year Award presented by Don Nagle's American Okinawan Karate Association (AOKA)

She trained to become a member of Douglas County's Search and Rescue Team, earning EMT-B and POST Investigative Mantracking licenses. She has served on the Board of Directors, and as an operations leader. She also passed the Nevada POST Defensive Tactics Instructor course in 2010.

In December 2017, Grandmaster Rick Manglinong awarded Master Ortenzio-Cooling the rank of Dayang Lima (5th degree black belt) and the title of Punong Guro.

Figure 91: 2016 - Puerto Rico. Sensei Ronnie Cimorosi with sai.

Diane notes regarding her martial arts experiences, "My perception of martial arts training has changed many times in many ways in over 30 years of training. Never stop trying to learn new things and try to work with as many different people as possible."

Diane Ortenzio-Cooling - Reflections of Grandmaster Cooling

Very dedicated. One of the things that I liked about her, she emphatically has said over and over, "I am not a woman black belt in the Order of Isshin-Ryu. I am a black belt in the OI. Do not put a label on me because I'm female." She has gone out and studied other arts successfully, including Arnis where she is soon going for 5th degree black belt. That is admirable, and she sets the example for everyone, especially for all women.

Master John Costanzo
Hachi-dan, 8th degree black belt

Master John Costanzo began his martial arts training as a student of Master Isham Latimer in 1979 and continues to study with him today. Sensei Costanzo's interest in the martial arts originally started in high school where he was a gymnast who was fascinated by the athleticism, inner strength, and grace of the martial arts. After graduating high school, John served in the Army during the Viet Nam War from 1968 – 1970 where he achieved the rank of Sergeant E5 as a combat infantry squad leader for the 1st Infantry Division. He received a Bronze Star and the Army Commendation Medal for valor while serving his country.

Returning to civilian life, he graduated from Dowling College in 1976 with a BA majoring in Art Education under the GI Bill. He subsequently worked as a freelance illustrator creating storyboards and comps for various commercial firms in Manhattan, New York City. Following this, he began his career with AT&T in New York and New Jersey for 24 years. While at AT&T, Master Costanzo was promoted through the ranks to a senior management programmer information-based intranet web pages and original programs for the CEO in AT&T's WorkNet division. Lastly, he taught Computer Science AP Java classes for 12 years at St. Joseph's High School in Metuchen, New Jersey. He retired in September 2016.

While Sensei Costanzo studied under Master Isham Latimer, he simultaneously became a member of the Order of Isshin-Ryu under the direction and counsel of Master Walter "Toby" Cooling. He currently holds the rank of hachi Dan, 8th degree black belt in the Order of Isshin-Ryu.

Sensei Costanzo is proficient in Isshin-Ryu hand and weapons kata in addition to his expertise in Jujitsu, self-defense techniques, including hand, knife, and firearms. He has also honed his skills through deep breathing exercises, applying them to the ancient Chinese martial arts form known as Liuhe Bafa Chuan. From this background, Sensei Costanzo collaborated with Master Latimer and Sensei John McDonald to create the Chi Ryu Jujitsu system that melds techniques and concepts from the Order of Isshin-Ryu teachings, Jujitsu, Liuhe Bafa Chuan, and self-defense techniques developed in Master Latimer's dojo.

Master Costanzo has been a martial arts instructor under the banner of the OI for over 30 years. He teaches in Long Island, New York and currently has a non-profit dojo at the Woodbridge Community Center in New Jersey. He has a son, Matthew, and a daughter, Dawn, and five grandchildren. Sensei Costanzo resides in Union, New Jersey with his loving partner, Judith Camlin.

John Costanzo - Reflections of Grandmaster Cooling

I started calling him 'Yankee' because of where he lived, but he thought it was because the New York Yankees are his favorite team. It was simply because he lived north of the Mason-Dixon line. Very serious about the Order of Isshin-Ryu, very dedicated. A good martial artist. He has the ability to back up anything he says.

Master Mike Goodyear
Hachi-dan, 8th degree black belt

Master Michael Goodyear is known as the "quiet guy". That demeanor masks an accomplished martial artist and a fierce fighter, but those of you who've been in the ring with him already know that.

Michael began training under Sensei Bailey Russell at the Cecil Community College dojo in 1979. What impressed him the most as a new student was how real the fighting was, yet everyone had fun and there were few injuries. Michael was promoted to sho-dan (1st degree black belt) in December 1982.

In 1983, Sensei Russell's job schedule necessitated turning the dojo over to a capable blackbelt, who turned out to be Michael Goodyear. He maintained the dojo at the community college until his retirement from regular teaching in 2015. As a sensei, he has guided many students to black belt including: Kym Stanley, Richard Muhs, Rodney Manuel, Paul Heath, Glenn Fanning, and Nicki Pell. His advice for students is, "Practice. From practice comes speed; from speed comes power. Have fun in karate, for it, and life, are too short." As a student himself, Michael has progressed through the black belt ranks. He was recently awarded hachi-dan (8th degree black belt) in June 2017 by Master Cooling, and his original sensei, Bailey Russell, was there to present the obi.

A carpenter by trade, Michael was hired by the DuPont Corporation in 1987. He continues to work for DuPont as a millwright. Over the years, Mike has fashioned handsome tuifa for himself and several members of the OI. The tuifa is also his trademark weapon for kata competition.

Michael's humility and dedication to perfecting his abilities continue to inspire others. "When I think of Mike Goodyear, the words 'gentle giant' comes to mind," said Barry Smith. "Mike is always courteous, polite, quiet, and awesome. He is the type of person that steps into the ring and you think you got it made. But then, the judge's hand drops (to signify starting the match). All of a sudden, the 'quiet man' unloads his deceptive hand speed and powerful kicks all over your body. By the time you figure out what has just taken place, it's over. You turn and walk away wondering who this person was in Mike's body. You wonder where Mike went, and then you look across the room and see the man smiling at you and motioning to you that your friend is still there. He is a gentleman, a fine friend, and a fantastic sensei. I am proud to be in his corner."

Sensei Juan Lopez puts it this way, "Mike Goodyear's strongest quality is that of silence… an invaluable weapon in winning any fight. This is because the assailant will never know what's truly in your heart. If you practice this virtue — like Mike does all the time — you will end up growing in wisdom… by always pondering things first in your heart. That is why Isshin-Ryu is called the way to the 'One-heart.'"

Mike Goodyear is a devoted father to his sons, Dylan and Wyatt.

Mike Goodyear - Reflections of Grandmaster Cooling

Goodyear is very deceptive. When you fight him, it appears as if he's not really doing anything, very little effort. But when he hits you, he will rock your world. And here he is, now in his 60s, and he won't hesitate to jump into the ring with anyone and hurt you. Very loyal, to me and to the Order of Isshin-Ryu. A true asset to the OI. He's the 'Yin' of the 'Yang.' He resembles the soft side of the equation, but that ability to show force (Yang) is not far from the surface.

Master Ron Tyree
Hachi-dan, 8th degree black belt

Master Ron Tyree started his training in Isshin-Ryu karate when he was nine years old under Sensei Allan Blackburn in March 1979. He trained with Sensei Blackburn for a year before becoming a student of Master Toby Cooling. Sensei Tyree obtained his sho-dan (1st degree black belt) ranking in 1987 at the age of 16, and Master Cooling promoted him to hachi-dan (8th degree black belt) June 2017.

Ron recalls from his early days of training that even though he was nine years old, Sensei Blackburn expected the same thing from everyone, regardless of age. During one class, Sensei Blackburn instructed Ron to practice a specific technique from seisan kata. He then instructed him to move back and forth across the dojo floor for the remainder of the class with only that one specific technique. Ron states, "Of course, being nine years old, after I performed the move awhile I got bored. One time down the floor, I punched the heavy bag. Sensei came over behind my shoulder and said, 'Did I tell you to hit the bag?' I did push-ups for the rest of class. I learned how to follow directions very well that night."

Master Tyree trained exclusively with the Order of Isshin-Ryu for 20 years but was inspired and encouraged by Master Cooling to advance his martial arts knowledge. Therefore, he started studying American Kickboxing, Muay Thai, and No Gi Jiu Jitsu in 2001. Master Tyree is currently teaching at the Hombu dojo in Elkton, Maryland the grappling arts of wrestling and jiu-jitsu. Sensei Tyree also is the striking instructor at Elite Jiu Jitsu in Newark, Delaware (www.elitejiujitsu.com) where he instructs in the striking arts of karate, kickboxing, and Muay Thai. Finally, he leads an MMA fight team that competes across the country.

In September 2000, Sensei Tyree was recognized by the World Head of Family Sokeship for the Most Innovative Training Program of the Year. The program was the culmination of three years of research and experimentation. His two-week program could be taught at the middle and high school levels as a supplement to the physical education program. The training includes coaching students on awareness of dangerous situations and how to develop safety networks from student to student, teacher to student, and parent to child.

Sensei Tyree provides the following words of advice for students: *With hard work and determination and a supportive dojo family, anything and everything is possible. Train to succeed, believe in yourself, and nothing can stop you.*

He currently works as a clinical nurse supervisor for Union Hospital in Elkton, Maryland. Prior to his current position, he worked as a behavior analyst for 10 years. He earned a B.S. from the University of Delaware in Political Science with a concentration in Policy Administration. Ron currently lives in Newark, Delaware.

Ron Tyree - Reflections of Grandmaster Cooling

I think Tyree started with me when he was 10 years old. Both Ron and Danny Cross started with Al Blackburn. Very dedicated; very loyal. Even now, in his late 40s. Both he and his family are very nice people. Super fast martial artist; he only weighs about 140 pounds at the most. He'll hurt you like a .22 caliber bullet will hurt you. Doesn't have a lot of mass but has a tremendous amount of speed. And when he scores on you in kumite, you *know* you've been scored upon.

Sensei Ronnie Cimorosi
Nana-dan, 7th degree black belt

Sensei Ronnie Cimorosi started karate in the Order of Isshin-Ryu in 1984 following the suggestion of his father to study under Master Toby Cooling. Sensei Cimorosi received his sho-dan (1st degree black belt) ranking in 1989. He trained six out of seven nights every week, training with instructors such as Master Toby Cooling, Master Bud Ewing, Sensei Juan Lopez, Sensei Larry Jackson, Sensei Danny Cross and would travel two hours, one way, to train under Master Barry Smith in Cambridge, Maryland.

Sensei Cimorosi was granted permission by Master Cooling to open his first dojo in 1990 in Elkton, Maryland and since that time, he has taught hundreds of students, but has only promoted 15 to black belt ranking due to the high standards he enforces. Sensei Cimorosi spent most of his time in the 1990s running his dojo and competing in tournaments throughout the Northeastern United States. He was a member of the Order of Isshin-Ryu demonstration team performing and promoting Isshin-Ryu throughout Maryland, Delaware, and Pennsylvania.

In 1994, Sensei Cimorosi received the Isshin-Ryu Hall of Fame's Instructor of the Year award in Pigeon Forge, Tennessee presented to him by Master Harold Long. For over 10 years, Ronnie taught self-defense classes at the Cecil County Battered Women's Shelter as well as the Cecil County Rape Prevention Center. Sensei Cimorosi, upon request, has taught women's self-protection classes in major corporations throughout Maryland and Delaware as well as children's classes for the Cecil County School District. Currently, he provides a self-defense program lasting 2-6 weeks where he works. Sensei Cimorosi promotes the Order of Isshin-Ryu by teaching seminars and traveling to as many dojos as possible.

In the late 1990s, Sensei Cimorosi became a member of the Board of Directors of the Order of Isshin-Ryu. Sensei Cimorosi was promoted to nana-dan (7th degree black belt) in 2011 by Master Toby Cooling. In 2014 he was inducted into the Isshin-Ryu Hall of Fame in Gatlinburg, Tennessee. In October 2017, Ronnie was awarded *Sensei of the Year* at Don Nagle's AOKA 60th Anniversary Hall of Fame event.

Sensei Cimorosi, along with being an active member of the Board of Directors for the OI, teaches a children's class and an adult class back-to-back two nights a

Figure 91: 2016 - Puerto Rico. Sensei Ronnie Cimorosi with sai.

week along with private and additional classes on the weekends at his dojo in Elkton, Maryland. He works for Astra Zeneca as a machine technician as well as the Lead ERT Coordinator. He balances his work life and dojo time with his wife, Cheryl and his daughter, Julia.

Ronnie Cimorosi - Reflections of Grandmaster Cooling

He's the male Italian counterpart to Diane (Ortenzio). He's done more for the Order of Isshin-Ryu than anyone else, as far as activity goes and continuously doing something. Not that he's the only one by any stretch, but seemingly on a weekly basis he's involved in some type of activity to promote the OI and bring people together for training. He's very concerned about keeping the OI's high standards and keeping OI going the way I want it to go after I pass away. Helluva fighter. Like fighting a bulldozer. If you punch him hard, you'll hurt your wrist.

Sensei Jesús M. Jiménez
Nana-dan, 7th degree black belt

Jesús M. Jiménez was born in Santurce, Puerto Rico on July 27, 1960, and currently resides in Guayama, Puerto Rico. He is an attorney whose work is based in litigation involving issues in contracts, family, property, tort, corporations, and labor.

Sensei Jiménez explains his martial arts beginnings as follows: "I started martial arts at the age of 11 years old in a Judo club and practiced until I was 15 years old when my family moved to Guayama. At that time, I was brown belt. Two years later I started training in karate. The style that I started practicing, in 1978, was Order of Isshin-Ryu Karate.

My first impression of the dojo was that it was a nice place to make exercises. Sensei Juan De Dios Lopez was leading the workout on that particular day. I entered the dojo because my friend Yamil Sued took me there. The dojo was on a second floor, in a wooden building without air conditioning. My first sensei was Eduardo Gonzalez. He left the dojo to me when I was a brown belt in 1980. I inherited the dojo because Sensei Gonzalez moved to finish his career as an anesthesiologist. At this point, Juan F. "Paco" Lopez became my sensei, with the permission of Master Cooling. A year later, in 1981, Sensei Lopez came to the mainland to practice medicine. His brother, Juan de Dios Lopez, then became my sensei, and he began to prepare me for my black belt examination.

I recall going with Sensei Juan De Dios Lopez to visit other karate schools to practice kumite and training sessions with him lasting to midnight. I remember that in an Aikido seminar held by Yamada Sensei (one of Ueshiba's students) that he told me to throw a punch, so I threw a snap punch and he told me, "No! I need a thrust punch." I did what he asked, and he flew across the room. A year later, Sensei Juan De Dios Lopez moved to the mainland to pursue his career and Master Cooling became my sensei and has been ever since."

Sensei Jiménez has a very diverse background in the martial arts. He has studied Aikido with Sensei Juan Alicea; San Yama Bushi Ryu Jutjutsu with Josean Negrón; Matayoshi Kobudo with Sensei Kimo Wall and Sensei Luis Cuadrado, and Goju Ryu karate with Sensei Kimo Wall.

Figure 92: 1979 - Puerto Nuevo dojo, Puerto Rico. Sensei Jesús M. Jiménez in action.

Among his many awards are the following:

1988 – 1998: Served as a member of the Bar Examination Board – by appointment of the Supreme Court of Puerto Rico
1994: Trial Lawyer of the Year – Puerto Rico Bar of Attorneys
1995: Recognized by the Supreme Court of Puerto Rico – development of security within the courtroom
1998: Induction into the Puerto Rico Martial Arts Hall of Fame
2014: Recognized by Mayor of Guayama – work with children of the Guayama Municipality
2016: Induction into the Isshin-Ryu Hall of Fame

With regards to his personal thoughts to students, Sensei Jiménez offers these insights:

- Work often and train hard. Think on every movement your sensei shows you, and study it. Do all the movements of the kata until those movements

become natural for you. Enjoy your time with your sensei, and take full advantage of it. Always work as if training for real.
- Never stop learning. Karate has many houses (kan), and surely you can live in one of them. For the moment, we are living in the Order of Isshin-Ryu kan; in the future, we will be able to build our own house.

Jesús' wife is Doris S. Díaz, a nurse, mother and currently the administrator of his law office. They have four children: Solimar, an MD; Dorimar, a businesswoman; Maria Alejandra, a psychology student at the University of Cayey, UPR, and Jesús, who is studying secondary education with a concentration in sports.

Jesús M. Jiménez - Reflections of Grandmaster Cooling

Jesús has been very loyal and dedicated in the Order of Isshin-Ryu. He fell off a bit with training but that was because of going to law school. He started under Eduardo Gonzalez in Puerto Rico and then went on to train with Juan Lopez. Very dedicated as well. He teaches most of his students at no charge since most cannot afford lessons. He does it anyway. Again, a good fighter and an analytic fighter. He will take a move and work it relentlessly.

Sensei Kurt Kline
Nana-dan, 7th degree black belt

Kurt Kline started his training in the Order of Isshin-Ryu in 1987 at the age of 14. Prior to that, he spent two years in Kempo, which was first offered at his local YMCA and then transferred to Ed Clapp's American Karate studios. Sensei Kline worked out of the Hombu dojo in Elkton, Maryland and traveled and trained in various OI dojos coming up through the ranks. When he started, Master Cooling was the sensei of the dojo. After about two years, he turned over the dojo to Bud Ewing who then became his sensei.

Sensei Kline was quite small growing up. As an orange belt, he weighed only 85 pounds and recalls Sensei Ewing asking him why he was so little. Wrestling in high school offered a unique perspective to his training, and as a senior, he wrestled at the 130-pound weight class. As a teenager growing up in the Hombu dojo, Sensei Kline notes there were no kids' divisions at the shiai, so he sparred against the men. "There simply weren't kids in the dojo back in those days. There were a few women such as Diane Ortenzio, Carmen Grace, and Nikolina Slijepcevic. So, I had to go against the adults and figure out how to make my karate work for me. You either made it work, or you got run over."

Sensei Kline started his first OI dojo (with Sensei Ron Tyree) while a Freshman at the University of Delaware in 1990. They offered classes at the ice arena on campus where Sensei Kline worked during college. During his college years, he had various internships and lived in different locations around the country. As a result, Sensei Kline was able to train with a variety of OI senior black belts. During his time training with Sensei Juan Lopez, Kurt recalls he really got into kumite training. For two summers, he trained intensively with Master Barry Smith, as well as Sensei James Rogers in Salisbury, Maryland. These unique training opportunities and experiences ultimately helped shape his training and eventual teaching style. In October 2017, Sensei Kline was awarded the *Outstanding Contribution to the Dojo Award* at Don Nagle's AOKA 60th Anniversary Hall of Fame Ceremony.

Kurt majored in mechanical engineering and Spanish at the University of Delaware, ultimately earning his B.A. in Spanish in 1997. He then earned his MBA in 1999 at Delaware with a concentration in Finance. After working at Daimler Chrysler for a period, he then attended Widener Law School (DE) and graduated *cum laude,* earning his JD in corporate law in 2002. Finally, Sensei Kline went on to earn an LL.M., Masters in Law degree, from Villanova University School of Law in 2009.

Figure 93: Chesapeake City, MD - Sensei Kurt Kline being awarded his red/white belt by Grandmaster Cooling at the annual OI shiai.

Currently, Sensei Kline is employed as a managing partner of Bridgeforce LLC, a global consulting services firm that provides risk management, operations, compliance, and advisory services for financial institutions. He lives in West Chester, Pennsylvania with his wife Kim and three daughters.

Kurt Kline - Reflections of Grandmaster Cooling

Kurt Kline started when he was 14 years old. Turned out to be a very good fighter, and he can analyze kata to the n'th degree. The same thing, he wants to continue the Order of Isshin-Ryu for a long time and hopefully will lead the OI administratively for years to come.

Sensei John McDonald
Nana-dan, 7th degree black belt

Sensei McDonald began his martial arts training in 1972 under Sensei Malachi Lee. Shortly thereafter, Sensei Lee introduced his students to Master Cooling, and the dojo became a member of the Order of Isshin-Ryu family. Following Sensei Lee's death, Sensei McDonald along with Master Latimer, Jose Diaz, and Maria Melendez continued running Sensei Lee's dojo under the leadership of Maria Melendez who was elevated to Sensei by Master Cooling. Sensei McDonald was elevated to the rank of sho-dan on May 21, 1977, by Sensei Melendez.

Sensei McDonald has continued his training under Master Isham Latimer, utilizing his training in Isshin-Ryu, Modern Arnis, Chi'na, Liuhe Bafa, knife fighting, and firearms collaborated with Master Latimer and Sensei Costanzo to develop a new style: Chi Ryu Jujitsu.

Sensei McDonald is a 1968 graduate of Carnegie-Mellon University's School of Drama. When he graduated, he became the first African-American to receive a BFA in Acting from that institution. Going by the professional name of John Danelle, his first professional acting job was as a member of the Lincoln Center Repertory Company. His Broadway credits include Alton Scales in Lorraine Hansberry's *The Sign in Sidney Brustein's Window*, directed by Alan Schneider and the dual role of Leroy Jackson (John Amos' son) and Young Luther (John Amos as a young man) in *Tough to Get Help*, directed by Carl Reiner. Off Broadway, he co-produced and originated the role of Val Johnson in Dennis McIntyre's play, *Split Second*. The critically acclaimed play is included in the *Burns and Mantle THEATRE YEARBOOK: THE BEST PLAYS OF 1984-1985*. Subsequent productions have been mounted in Los Angeles, Chicago, Detroit, Atlanta, Miami, San Diego, and London. The play continues to be performed on various levels across the country. Sensei McDonald is known to many for his portrayal of Dr. Frank Grant on ABC-TV'S *All My Children* and Lt. Art Hindman in *Loving*. When he signed his first contract with ABC in 1972, he became only the third African-American ever to be put under contract in a daytime drama.

In the late 1980s, Sensei McDonald left acting to go into theatrical production. After several years as a freelance production manager, he became the first African-American to be named Director of Alice Tully Hall at Lincoln Center for the Performing Arts in New York City and then became the first African-American to be named Director of Operations at Carnegie Hall in New York City.

In addition, Sensei McDonald developed the concept and co-wrote the 1993 feature film titled: *By the Sword*, starring Eric Roberts and Academy Award Winner, F. Murray Abraham. As a producer, Sensi McDonald was a founding member of the company that arranged the 6.5-million-dollar financing as well as domestic and foreign distribution. The film was critically acclaimed by Variety, The Hollywood Reporter, Entre Acte, and the Los Angeles Times; he has a cult following among the fencing community as well as martial artists.

Figure 94: May 21, 1977. Sho-dan (1st degree black belt) promotion. L-R: John McDonald, Maria Melendez, Toby Cooling

Sensei McDonald is now a private acting coach who specializes in preparing high school students who wish to become professional actors for the grueling college audition process. He has a 99.5% success rate, and his students have been accepted at such prestigious schools as Carnegie Mellon University, Baldwin-Wallace, Cornich College of the Arts, Elon University, Emerson, Fordham, Ithaca, University of the Arts in Philadelphia, University of Hartford/The Hartt School, University of Michigan, Muhlenberg, Northwestern University, Marymount-Manhattan, NYU, Syracuse, and Yale.

Sensei McDonald has been married for 35 years to Cagle McDonald and has two daughters, Amanda and Mary.

John McDonald - Reflections of Grandmaster Cooling

John had to stop training for a bit due to health problems. He came back, and I treated him as if he never left. We went to a tournament in Connecticut some time ago held by Lou Lizotte. Some of the older guys only recognized bo, sai, and tuifa in Isshin-Ryu karate. But I know that Shimabuku also recognized the basic nunchaku kata because when I was on Okinawa, I taught it for him. It's a basic nunchaku kata. At this particular tournament, the first thing John did was walk right up to the judges before the tournament started and went through the nunchaku kata, practicing and warming up. But he had the attitude, 'I dare you to tell me this weapon isn't allowed for competition.' He's also a very good fighter, and he'll make you earn it. He has the "New York way."

Sensei Dan Popp
Roku-dan, 6th degree black belt

Dan began the study of Isshin-Ryu Karate in 1982 at the age of 15 under the direction of his father. With his sensei available on a continuous basis, Dan progressed to sho-dan (1st degree black belt) in just under two years at the age of 17. From there, Dan's sensei was Don Monismith, where he trained for the next twelve years reaching the rank of go-dan (5th degree black belt) in June 1996. After his sensei started to formulate his own system of karate, Dan wished to continue his Isshin-Ryu study. He recalled a seminar at his dojo years before taught by Toby Cooling, so Dan sought him out in Maryland in 1996. After petitioning to join the Order of Isshin-Ryu, Dan re-tested for his ni-dan (2nd degree black belt) and was formally accepted into the OI fraternity in October 1996.

Currently holding the rank of roku-dan (6th degree black belt), Dan was named the 2008 Male Instructor of the Year by the International Isshin-Ryu Hall of Fame. He went on to be inducted into the Isshin-Ryu Hall of Fame in July 2013, becoming the 101st member of the Hall. He has also served on the Board of Directors for the Order of Isshin-Ryu.

Dan competed heavily over the years, mainly in the Northeastern United States, winning various titles in kata and weapons divisions. He won the gold medal in black belt weapons at the Keystone Games four consecutive years – from 1989 to 1992. This annual tournament is an Olympics-style event held in Pennsylvania.

In 1990, Dan began his study of Kendo (traditional Japanese swordsmanship) under Master Duk Yeong Kim and progressed to the rank of yon-dan (4th degree black belt) awarded in December 2004. Shortly after beginning his Kendo training, Master Kim also provided Dan with instruction in the art of Shodo, or Japanese calligraphy. Although Mr. Kim passed away in 2007, Dan continues to practice Shodo to honor his teacher. Mr. Kim learned this art form in Korea from Shin Tae Sik, also known as Tei Seki. Dan has also promoted two tournaments for the World Kumdo Association (Korean Kendo) in Harrisburg, Pennsylvania. The 1st World Kumdo Association tournament was held in 1998 and the 2nd U.S. Open Kumdo Championships held in 2001 where he received the Kumdo Ambassador Award.

Dan's training in martial arts also includes Modern Arnis and Kombatan under the direction of Grandmaster Rick Manglinong, stick fighting arts originating in the Philippines, where he was awarded the rank of Lakan Isa (1st degree black belt) in

October 2012. In addition, Dan is a student of Chi Ryu Jujitsu and Liuhe Bafa Chuan under Master Isham Latimer.

Figure 95: 2015 - Chesapeake City, MD. The author about to perform sunsu kata for a judging panel of 9th dan black belts.
L-R: Don Nash, Bob Kristensen, Bud Ewing, Isham Latimer, Ralph Passero, Barry Smith.

Sensei Popp is the author of two previous books:
Sensei's Final Lessons – A Memoir, published in March 2012 by Outskirts Press.
The Floating Brush, Learning Japanese Calligraphy from a Kendo Master, published in July 2014 by Kamel Press.

A 1994 graduate of The Pennsylvania State University with a B.S. in Professional Accountancy, Dan was employed in 1999 by the National Credit Union Administration where he still serves as a federal examiner, specializing in IT audits. He holds several IT audit certifications from the Information Security Audit and Control Association (ISACA) including CISA, CRISC, and CGEIT. He resides in Harrisburg, PA with his two daughters, Britteni and Kayla.

Dan has twice held exhibitions at Mulberry Art Studios during Lancaster's First Friday; in September 2009 and July 2010. The July 2010 exhibition titled "Shodo – The Floating Brush" received a good deal of publicity. The exhibit was listed in both *Central PA* magazine and *Lancaster* magazine. His latest exhibit was held in Harrisburg, Pennsylvania at Gallery at Second in September 2012.

Dan Popp - Reflections of Grandmaster Cooling

I knew Dan Popp as a little boy (17 years old at the time). I think his Dad brought him into the dojo. He came from the same dojo as Diane Ortenzio, and somehow, they reconnected at one point, and Diane showed him how the OI does kata. From then on, Dan wanted to be a part of the OI. He and Diane are the only two outsiders who were already black belts in Isshin-Ryu and decided to start over again from seisan kata and re-learn everything according to OI standards and how I wanted the kata taught. Of the six people that were already black belts coming into the OI, the other four quit. Dan and Diane are the only two that stuck with it and excelled. I would put their knowledge up against anyone of commensurate rank.

Sensei Adam Knox
Roku-dan, 6th degree black belt

Adam Knox started his training in Order of Isshin-Ryu karate under Master Bud Ewing in September 1990. He recalls, "Sensei Kurt Kline had just received his sho-dan, and I asked if I could watch a class. During class, a man walked into the dojo with an unbuttoned shirt and a pack of cigarettes hanging out of the pocket. He had a 5 o'clock shadow. Little did I know, that man was the head of the Order of Isshin-Ryu." The next week, he started classes. He was 16 years old.

While still in high school, Adam also wrestled. Due to the training commitment needed for wrestling, his coach gave him an ultimatum: choose between wrestling and martial arts. Adam chose the Order of Isshin-Ryu. After several years of study, he developed an interest in understanding what happens between stand up and ground combat and develop a fuller understanding of balance. Therefore, he took up training in Judo under Sensei Tom Blair in Bryn Mawr, PA, all the while never having an interest in pursuing rank in Judo, but just training to garner what he could from that discipline. Adam quickly noticed similarities in training and notes, "Regardless of your position or rank, people will tend to take notice if you train hard and show respect for your fellow students."

Shortly after his promotion to 1st degree black belt, Sensei Knox was tasked to visit a black belt in Harrisburg, PA that was petitioning to join the Order of Isshin-Ryu. That happened to be Dan Popp who, at the time, held the rank of go-dan or 5th degree black belt. Due to Adam's schedule, he was able to visit often, and it became his responsibility to teach Sensei Popp the kata requirements of the OI. Adam recalls, "I was quite apprehensive *telling* a Go-dan that what he was doing was 'wrong.' Because of my lack of experience in both teaching and in my own studies, I felt I was destined for failure. If it were not for Sensei Popp's gracious nature, I may very well have failed. Sensei Popp made that process an enjoyable one. He had absolutely no ego about learning from someone who had been in the martial arts for a shorter time than he had already been as a black belt. He earned my respect and taught me a valuable lesson about being a black belt. He taught me that if you want to learn, you don't need to look up the ladder, you just have to have an open mind."

In addition, Sensei Knox studied Japanese Kendo under Master Reiun Kim in Hershey, PA traveling two hours one-way nearly every weekend for eight years.

Adam continued his studies in Kendo and Judo for over 8 years, all the while maintaining his Isshin-Ryu training. Adam earned his Sho-Dan in Order of Isshin-Ryu karate in 1995.

Adam moved to West Chester, Pennsylvania in 2002 and opened his own dojo in his home, taking on several students. He has continued to maintain that small dojo to this day. At most, the West Chester dojo has had five students at one time. Sensei Knox has never pursued having many students and never desired to have a commercial facility. Having a smaller class provides a personal aspect to his teaching and allows him to tailor the classes much more effectively. This enables the students' individual energy to shine through during training.

In October 2015, Sensei Knox achieved his greatest achievement in the martial arts to date; he was recognized by Master Toby Cooling as a Roku-Dan in the Order of Isshin-Ryu. Sensei Knox continues serving on the board of directors for the Order of Isshin-Ryu. After having several different sensei in the OI, Sensei Knox has come full circle and his sensei, once again, is Master Bud Ewing.

In 1997, Adam earned a B.S. in Physics from Muhlenberg College in Allentown, PA. Today, he is a commercial real estate broker with Geis Realty Group and lives in West Chester, PA with his wife, Bernine, and their two children.

Adam Knox - Reflections of Grandmaster Cooling

Adam started in the Order of Isshin-Ryu under Bud Ewing. The first time I noticed him was at an OI ski trip with Ron Tyree. He fell from a balcony and injured himself, so that was my first impression of him. He has been very dedicated to Isshin-Ryu karate… very loyal, and very concerned about the OI. I'm very happy about that, and he's doing an excellent job on the OI board of directors.

Sensei Chris Harris
Roku-dan, 6th degree black belt

As a kid, Chris spent a lot of time watching martial arts movies with his father. This is what sparked his love and interest in karate. His father had studied Order of Isshin-Ryu karate before, so when the time came for Chris to begin, he knew just the place to take him. In 1993, Chris began his training under Sensei Ronnie Cimorosi at the age of 10. He still remembers that first night walking into class and sitting in the back of the dojo to observe the class. He spent his beginning years working out in the adult class but would come early to help with the kids' class as well. In 1999 at the age of 16 years old, Sensei Harris received his sho-dan (1st degree black belt), one of the few Order of Isshin-Ryu black belts to receive that honor.

After graduating high school, Chris attended Salisbury University to study Clinical Laboratory Science. While in college, his martial arts training continued with various local OI dojos in Maryland from Salisbury to Cambridge, and finally in Easton. His training continued with Sensei Cimorosi during his college breaks. This additional training allowed him to earn his ni-dan in 2001. He graduated in 2004 with his bachelor's degree and began working at Upper Chesapeake Medical Center in Bel Air, MD as a Medical Technologist.

In 2008, Chris officially became a sensei in the Order of Isshin-Ryu. He currently teaches two nights a week in Elkton, Maryland and one night a week at the YMCA in Abingdon, Maryland. He spends time traveling to represent the OI at events such as the Isshinryu Hall of Fame in Tennessee, the AOKA tournament in New Jersey, the TOKI Fall Classic in Pennsylvania as well as the American Isshinryu "Day with the Masters." In 2017, Sensei Harris received the "Outstanding Instructor of the Year" award from the AOKA.

Sensei Harris currently holds the position of Dai Sempai in the Order of Isshin-Ryu and serves as a member on the Board of Directors. In February 2018, he was elevated to the rank of roku-dan (6th degree black belt) by Grandmaster Toby Cooling. When not teaching or training in the dojo, Sensei Harris enjoys spending time with his wife Danijela and daughter Nicole.

Chris Harris - Reflections of Grandmaster Cooling

Chris is a true asset to the Order of Isshin-Ryu. He recently assumed the role of Dai Sempai and is responsible for running our shai and scheduling black belt evaluations. He is doing a great job and has matured not only in the Dai Sempai role but as an overall martial artist. He is a long-time student of Sensei Ronnie Cimorosi and started in his dojo when he was very young. Chris has remained a steadfast and loyal member of the OI. He's a good fighter and a talented martial artist.

Sensei Danny Cross
Roku-dan, 6th degree black belt

Danny Cross began karate training in 1979 at the Elkton YMCA with Sensei Allan Blackburn when his son, Brian (at age 5) got bored and wanted to quit classes. Danny figured he would finish out the 8-week course, so the money wouldn't be wasted, then quit.

From 1968 – 1972 Sensei Cross served in the U.S. Navy on a destroyer and at the National Training Center in Bainbridge, Maryland. Although he had taken a year of Judo while in the Navy, it didn't affect him like Isshin-Ryu karate. "I saw these fairly large men moving like cats. Agile, but strong; soft-spoken, but confident," he recalls. Before karate, Danny describes himself as soft-spoken and afraid to speak in front of a group. He had lost both fights he had ever been in, so wasn't sure karate was for him. Luckily for all of us, he got hooked and stayed.

Figure 96: Larry Sica (in white gi) receiving his black belt promotion by Sensei Danny Cross (standing behind Larry). Larry received his sensei's obi.

When he was a blue belt, Sensei Blackburn became ill, and at his request, Sensei Cross transferred to the Hombu Dojo in Elkton, Maryland. Sensei Cross recalls his first workout at the Hombu dojo, "Everyone in the dojo was working on their sparring. A young blue belt, about 5'10" and 230 pounds called out, 'Hey you, come over here.' I hustled over and was told to rei. The young man then proceeded to work me over for what seemed like an hour. After the match, the young man provided some critiques and that was the end of it."

Sensei Cross continues, "As we progressed through the ranks, I tried to model myself after him. He taught me a lot. He reached brown belt, and then his work took him to New Jersey and New York. So, as he went on with his life somewhere else, I continued to train. I reached black belt after almost five years of training." As the story goes, Sensei Cross eventually opened his own dojo. He goes on to explain, "Master Cooling called me and said he was sending down a student he thought I could work with, who had prior training in the OI. When he walked through the door, you can imagine my amazement when the very first person who thumped me at the Hombu dojo as a beginner was willing to humble himself and be my student. As it turns out, I had the honor to promote Larry Sica to sho-dan and ni-dan. We are the best of friends."

On June 25, 2000, Sensei Cross was elevated to the rank of Roku-dan (6th degree black belt). Although inactive with the Order of Isshin-Ryu, Sensei Cross still trains in martial arts and is currently teaching safety awareness and self-defense classes at Coastal Carolina University in Conway, South Carolina. In addition, he instructs for a children's karate summer camp for Coastal Carolina.

Several people have inspired Sensei Cross in his martial arts career: Larry Sica, for his ability to adjust; Master Cooling, for his direct approach to things; Allan Blackburn, his first sensei; and Bailey Russell, for his ability to relate karate to life, and for knowing how to be a friend. Sensei Cross notes from his early years of training, "One of the most amazing things for me is that all these accomplished martial artists were always eager to teach and share their knowledge. They would take time for me or anyone who truly wanted to learn karate. It made me realize that if someone stops and gives you some of their time, they are giving a very valuable gift. I made a point to appreciate that. It is one of the reasons that it is important to me to give back to the art."

His words of wisdom for kyu ranks: You cannot execute a proper technique without balance. In life, you cannot be satisfied without balance. The samurai kept all affairs and relationships in order, knowing that he may not be alive the next day. His maxim for himself: Always be honest with yourself.

In 2013, Sensei Cross retired from Daimler-Chrysler where he was a millwright and served as a Skilled Trades Safety Trainer, where he taught employees how to safely use the machinery and equipment. He currently lives in Myrtle Beach, South Carolina with his wife Brenda. They have two grown children, Melody and Brian.

Danny Cross - Reflections of Grandmaster Cooling

First time I met Danny Cross was at a meeting at a YMCA. He kept saying, "Yes, Mr. Cooling." I thought "who is this guy?" Turns out, he was a blue belt under Al Blackburn. From then on, he excelled in karate. He took some OI guys to go into full contact fighting. He eventually moved to North Carolina. Quite a gentleman. He's one of the black belts in the OI that is shorter than me. I saw him win a shiai on pure technique, sidestepping and counterattack. He was fighting more with his mind than the body that God gave him. Impressive.

Sensei Juan D. Lopez
Roku-dan, 6ᵗʰ degree black belt

Juan D. Lopez was born in Santa Clara, Cuba in 1960. His parents fled the Castro regime, and he grew up in Bayamon, Puerto Rico. His martial arts training began at the young age of 12 in an outdoor dojo located in a parking lot behind a shopping mall. His first sensei was Eduardo Caro, under whom Juan and his older brother, Paco, studied for three years.

It was about this time that the Bruce Lee-induced karate boom began. Sensei Lopez remembers, "The goal for beginners at the time was to peel your knuckles by doing push-ups on the parking lot tar and develop big, fat callouses to show how tough you were. I still have marks on my knuckles from those days – not very wise."

Figure 97: 2012 - Puerto Rico. Sensei Juan Lopez teaching technique at dojo of Sensei Jesús M. Jiménez.

When Sensei Caro left Puerto Rico in 1974 to study medicine in the Dominican Republic, the Lopez brothers became the head instructors of the two dojos he left behind. In 1975, the brothers contacted Sensei Malachi Lee for instruction, and for a brief period before his death, studied with him. After the passing of Sensei Lee, they became direct students of Master Toby Cooling.

Although he has briefly studied Aikido and Arnis, Juan's core discipline has always been Isshin-Ryu. He has several maxims to share with students:
- Stick to the basics. They are the ones that will get you out of trouble and will remain with you for the rest of your life.
- Strive for a balance of your body/mind/spirit. These are the three stars in your patch.
- Always seek the truth, and once it is revealed to you, live by it.
- If your sensei is not practicing the above, it is time for you to move on.

His influences in the martial arts – Sensei Lopez replies, "Malachi Lee, who showed me in the brief time that he was my sensei, a great dedication for what he believed in (Isshin-Ryu), and of course Denshi, who not only polished my martial arts but molded me as a better human being."

One of his favorite stories happened around 1986. Sensei Barry Smith challenged Denshi to take his red and white belt off and compete in a Washington, D.C. tournament as a regular black belt. It didn't take long for the "Toby" temper to flare when the judges weren't paying attention to the competitors. Denshi stopped in the middle of his kata, walked up to one particular judge, and told him to wake up and watch his kata – and he even placed after doing that! He didn't have anything to prove to anybody, except to take Sensei Smith up on his challenge. "I came back convinced that day that you indeed have to be *un poco loco* to belong to this family!"

Sensei Lopez has a B.S. in chemistry and chemical engineering, as well as an M.S. in environmental engineering. He was employed by the federal government at Aberdeen Proving Ground. He is married to his wife Maria and has two daughters, Marian and Maribel.

Juan Lopez - Reflections of Grandmaster Cooling

He started Isshin-Ryu in Puerto Rico. They contacted Malachi Lee to join the Order of Isshin-Ryu. After Malachi passed away, I then went down to Puerto Rico to teach. Juan Lopez would walk into a tournament in Puerto Rico and all the black belts would turn and say, "there's first place." And they were right, every time. Juan did kata like Ron Tyree. In fact, I think Tyree modeled his kata after Lopez. He could snap a punch without a gi on. He was that good. One Christmas his father asked Juan and his brother Paco what they wanted, and they said, 'A dojo.' So, their father built a dojo on the side of their house for them.

Sensei Larry Jackson
Roku-dan, 6th degree black belt

Biographical information not available for this publication.

Larry Jackson - Reflections of Grandmaster Cooling

Nicknamed "Rambo." When he was active he was very good. A very strict disciplinarian. He would run everyone around the dojo for a mile or so, and I would ask the students, "Who's chasing you?" They just looked in Larry's direction. He worked students hard and was heavy into exercise.

Sensei Shelly Bell
Roku-dan, 6th degree black belt

Biographical information not available for this publication.

Shelly Bell - Reflections of Grandmaster Cooling

I recall one shiai where she messed up a tuifa kata. I said, "That's okay. Next competitor." Shelly replied, "No. I can do this." She didn't quit and showed everyone her toughness that day.

ORDER OF ISSHIN-RYU INDUCTED INTO THE INTERNATIONAL ISSHIN-RYU HALL OF FAME

The Isshin-Ryu Hall of Fame (theihof.com) is an international event. The Hall of Fame hosts a banquet and tournament whereby all Isshin-Ryu practitioners from around the world are welcome to compete in this annual event. The Hall of Fame recognizes outstanding Isshin-Ryu karate-ka from around the world for their contributions to the art of Isshin-Ryu Karate, regardless of their various association affiliations. The weekend event also provides the opportunity for Isshin-Ryu practitioners to come together in fellowship, exchange knowledge and ideas, compete, and to remember and honor the founder of Isshin-Ryu Karate – Tatsuo Shimabuku – who was the very first inductee into the International Isshin-Ryu Hall of Fame in 1980.

*Walter "Toby" Cooling
1988*

*Karen Bronson
006*

 Barry Smith
1996

 Dan Popp
2013

 Bud Ewing
1998

 Ronnie Cimorosi
2014

 Isham Latimer
2003

 Jesús M. Jiménez
2016

 Diane Ortenzio-
Cooling
2003

MEMORIALS

Order of Isshin-Ryu Members Who Have Passed
In alphabetical order

Allan Blackburn (1946 – 2007)

Sensei Allan Blackburn was a founding member of the OI and was instrumental in the early development of many current Order of Isshin-Ryu black belts, including Master Ron Tyree (8th dan), Sensei Dan Cross (6th dan), and Joe Ragan (3rd dan). He was a very strict, demanding instructor and was known to be all business. The term *warrior* can sometimes be overused a bit, but for Sensei Allan Blackburn, this word described him perfectly.

Allan was the owner of a trucking company and father of four boys. He served in the United States Army and was a veteran of the Vietnam War. Sensei Blackburn was the sensei of the old YMCA dojo on Rt. 40 in Elkton, Maryland. He presented an intimidating stature at over six feet tall and weighing more than 200 pounds. He demanded respect from his students. If you were not prepared to work every second, he would tell you to get out of the dojo. He would not waste time if you were not sincere in wanting to learn karate.

Sensei Dan Cross recalls training in the Blackburn dojo, "His classes focused heavily on basics. In most of his classes, 75 percent of it was focused on repetition of basic techniques. If you wanted extra training, you had to come early or stay late. His focus on the basics was because he wanted his students to be prepared for kata (forms). He demanded perfection in the execution of the kata."

Although he was a very disciplined instructor, he truly cared about the overall development of his students. Sensei Cross provides an example, "There was a dedicated student who informed Sensei Blackburn that he would have to stop coming to class because his hours at work changed and it conflicted with the dojo schedule. Without hesitation Sensei told him, 'You will not quit, you will make yourself available to come to my house and train when you are not working.' It was not a question, it was a directive."

Figure 98: 1987 - North East, MD. Sensei Blackburn watching his student receiving his black belt promotion. L-R: Grandmaster Harold Long, Master Toby Cooling, Sensei Allen Webb (tying obi), Sensei Allan Blackburn (wearing glasses), Joe Ragan receiving his black belt. Sensei Dan Cross is standing second from the left.

Joe Ragan remembers Sensei Blackburn was his instructor from 1982 to 1984. Joe recalls that one time in 1983, when he was getting ready to test for his blue belt, he asked Sensei Blackburn the question, "Does this Isshin-Ryu karate really work or am I wasting yours and my time?" Sensei Blackburn answered, "Stay after class and you can decide." After class, Joe did as instructed and remained on the floor to see what Sensei Blackburn had in mind. Allan said to Joe, "We will tap (light spar) each other and you lead the way." Joe did as instructed, and the next thing he knew, he was on the floor trying to get himself together. Sensei Blackburn had stuck his foot into Joe's solar plexus, and down he went. Joe recalls, "I didn't know what happened for about a minute. Then it all came to me, his foot hit my solar plexus, and I was out of it." Sensei Blackburn stuck around until he finally got himself back on his feet. He then said to Joe, "See you next class." Joe said to himself… this Isshin-Ryu stuff really works. Reflecting on it, Joe stated, "It was hard waiting two days until the next class. I showed up early from that day on. It was the beginning of our friendship and trust. I still think of my first sensei to this day."

Sensei Blackburn was very courageous. As a young man, he became very ill and could no longer run the dojo. During an operation, he suffered a seizure. As a result, he had blurred vision and difficulty eating solid foods. He also had slurred speech. This once large man became frail and could barely function. Yet in a more limited capacity, he continued his efforts to learn martial arts. His students recall he never complained; he was always in a positive state of mind and eager to help anyone he could. Sensei Cross remembers, "There was a time when Sensei Ronnie Cimorosi sent an email to the OI black belts asking for assistance in teaching his classes [due to an influx of new students]. The very next class, Sensei Blackburn was there and ready to help. He never let his condition get in his way."

Joe recalls, "Sensei Blackburn never gave up trying on the things he set out to do. He was very special that way. I had a nice talk with him a couple weeks before his death. He was prepared." Shortly before his passing, on August 31, 2007, he told Sensei Cross what an honor it was to have taught in the Order of Isshin-Ryu, and how rewarding it was to see some of his very first students progress through the ranks.

Karen Bronson (1955 – 2002)

Sensei Karen Bronson was born November 16, 1955, in Arlington, Virginia and lived a very full life. If you ever had the chance to meet her, you knew that she beamed with a spirit and energy very rarely seen.

Her martial arts began in 1967 under Sensei Mark Herman where she studied Judo, Aikido, and Goju-ryu karate in Palm Beach, Florida. In 1969 she started her study of Isshin-Ryu karate in Boynton Beach, Florida under Sensei Richard Ross. Her Isshin-Ryu continued in Detroit, Michigan under Sensei Lloyd Russett and John Gimpert. She was Michigan State Martial Arts Champion three consecutive years, 1975-1978.

Her background is quite interesting as she served for seven years in the U.S. Air Force where she was a jet engine mechanic. Sensei Bronson opened many dojos over the years and even taught karate while serving in the Air Force.

Figure 99: 1999 - Lake Michigan beach training. L-R: Sensei Jesús M. Jiménez, Sensei Karen Bronson

In 1991, Sensei Bronson moved to Empire, Michigan where she opened the Glen Lake dojo. In 1994, she opened a karate dojo in Suttons Bay, Michigan with the idea of inter-school competition and to pave the way for martial arts to be recognized as a sport in the area. In the same year, she created a "kids only" open karate tournament in Glen Lake, Michigan. In 1994, she petitioned to join the Order of Isshin-Ryu and in 1995 tested for her black belt and was accepted as a member of the OI. She opened several OI dojos shortly after, and her students numbered well over 200 at that time.

In 1997, she was recognized by the World Head of Family Sokeship Council in Orlando, Florida with the Silver Lifetime Achievement award. During her span of over 37 years in martial arts, she was inducted into several Hall of Fames, including the American Okinawan Karate Association (AOKA) Hall of Fame and the World Head of Sokeship Council. She received various awards from the International Isshin-Ryu Hall of Fame including: Dojo of the Year, Female Instructor of the Year, Spirit of Isshin-Ryu, Lifetime Achievement Award, and was finally inducted posthumously into the International Isshin-Ryu Hall of Fame in 2006.

Sensei Bronson earned her degree from the University of Michigan where she majored in Psychology with a minor in Sociology. She was a Duel Diagnostic Clinical Psychologist and a licensed Abuse Counselor in the state of Michigan.

Isshin-Ryu karate was Sensei Bronson's life. She often put aside her own needs to be with her Isshin-Ryu family. She never turned a student away and always made time for any student. After a long battle with cancer, she passed away in the early morning hours of January 9, 2002. She was found clutching her black belt in her hands.

Jose Diaz (dates not available)

Jose Diaz was a member of Malachi Lee's School of Isshin-Ryu in New York City prior to this dojo being accepted into the Order of Isshin-Ryu in the early 1970s.

Fellow dojo member, John McDonald, recalls Jose was born in New York City. John states, "He lived in NYC and was married, but we lost touch with his wife after he died. He had one daughter. She was very young when he died. I don't remember the year, but it was around 1975." John goes on to recall his karate abilities, "All I remember is that his technique, especially his side kick, was impeccable. He trained extremely hard and was disciplined in his daily approach to Isshin-Ryu."

Jose loved film noir. He was a big James Cagney and Richard Widmark fan and would reenact entire scenes from their movies.

Figure 100: Early 1970s - New York City: Jose Diaz.

Larry Holland (1956 - 2003)

Larry Holland started Isshin-Ryu karate at the dojo on Main Street in Elkton, Maryland in the late 1970s. His first sensei was Bucky Garret, and he eventually trained under Sensei Ronnie Cimorosi in 1991. Other than a bit of Judo training, Mr. Holland's martial arts training was only within the Order of Isshin-Ryu. According to Sensei Cimorosi, he was a very dedicated student and was knowledgeable about karate history and Japanese terminology.

Sensei Cimorosi recalls of his black belt student, "Of all my students, Larry Holland, Tony Campbell, and Jeanette McCarl did so well at their sho-dan evaluation that no questions were even asked during their evaluation before Chinto kata (Chinto is the fifth kata learned out of a total of eight empty-hand forms required for black belt in the OI). In fact, Master Cooling finally stood up and walked onto the floor, stood behind the candidates and raised his hands to the evaluation panel, suggesting to the members of the panel to start asking questions."

Mr. Holland's career background included computers and finance.

Figure 101: 1992 - Elkton, MD. Larry Holland (back row on left in black gi) with students and his Sensei, Ronnie Cimorosi, standing on far right.

Alan Jenkins (1951 - 2014)

Sensei Alan Jenkins started his martial arts training while attending the University of Maryland where he signed up for a Bando class. As he notes in his writings, "Karate was not well known in those days. I had played varsity soccer through high school and was intrigued by this athletic regimen that employed feet as well as hands. I enrolled in and attended class until I ran out of money – about two semesters' worth."

His introduction to the Order of Isshin-Ryu came very shortly after the OI's inception, in the Spring of 1972, when he investigated an on-campus free university program in karate. At this point in time, the OI was just over one year old. Sensei Jenkins noted during this training that the practical aspect of empty-handed techniques was emphasized. There was no frill or show to the training. Sensei Jenkins worked with various OI black belts around this time, including Tom Miller, Bob Burns, Buster Hash, John Remick, Charlie Deitterick, and Tom Sanson.

Figure 102: Alan Jenkins, on left, paired up with Master Bud Ewing during a seminar at the annual Isshin-Ryu Hall of Fame weekend in Pigeon Forge, TN.

Sensei Jenkins married a fellow brown belt, Julie, and shortly after focused on his marriage and his career, where he worked for NASA Goddard Space Flight Center. As such, his training in the OI dropped off but his heart never left. Around 1980 he re-dedicated to a training program of running and weight training, as well as getting back to working on his kata. A fellow OI black belt, Charlie Dietterick, started to work with him and eventually brought him back to an OI shiai where he became the student of Sensei Dan Waltemeyer from the Baltimore, Maryland dojo. Under Sensei Waltemeyer, he was eventually promoted to Sho-dan or 1st degree black belt. Sensei Jenkins went on to open his own dojo in his hometown of Olney, Maryland in September 1999, the only type of martial arts classes offered in Montgomery County, Maryland. In 2004, Sensei Jenkins left the OI and joined another karate organization.

Alan graduated from the University of Maryland in 1973 with a B.S. in Physics. He was a Principal Business Systems Analyst working as a contractor with CACI International on site with the Drug Enforcement Agency (DEA). He was also an active member of his church, where he served as a Deacon and then as an Elder.

Malachi Lee (1942 - 1975)

Malachi Lee's introduction into Isshin Ryu began in the dojo of Master Ed McGrath. In 1971, Dennis Bootle told Malachi that he had to work with this guy in Maryland, Toby Cooling. Lee hopped a plane from New York to Salisbury, Maryland and from there the two hit it off well. Lee spent the weekend training with Master Cooling and upon leaving, he told Denshi, "I've learned more this weekend than I've learned over the past 14 years in Isshin Ryu karate."

Sensei Lee trained in New York City, a literal melting pot of numerous forms of martial arts. He trained with and rubbed elbows with many of the top martial artists in the United States at that time. Lee's dojo produced several notable karate-ka, including Isham Latimer, Maria Melendez, Aston Hugh, Jose Diaz, and John McDonald. He brought PR into the OI fold. Milledge Murphy (FL), Paco contacted Denshi. Malachi had Spanish speaking students. Malachi, you take PR, and I'll take FL.

Figure 103: Early 1970s New York City tournament. Kneeling L-R: Wilfredo Roldan, Ron Taganashi, unknown. Standing L-R: Frank Ruiz (in suit - founder of Nisei Goju), Unknown, Alex Sternberg, unknown, Malachi Lee, Thomas LaPuppet (member of Black Belt Hall of Fame), last three are unknown.

According to Master Cooling, Malachi Lee could hit you with a spinning back kick *without spinning*. Being 6'7, his reach and length was a gift that not many martial artists had around this time. Master Cooling states, "He made you look short."

Malachi starred in a 1975 film, Force Four. IMDb provides the following description: When a priceless African statue is stolen, and its courier is murdered, the Force Four are called in to deal out some old-fashioned retributive action. Starring with Lee were Frank Ruiz, Alex Sternberg, and Wilfredo Roldan (*see figure 103 above*).

Frank Schwartz (1969 – 2010)

A dedicated member of the Allentown, Pennsylvania dojo, Frank Schwartz was an absolute inspiration in many ways. Not gifted with extreme talents for martial arts, he did not view this as a hurdle in his development and, in fact, worked twice as hard as the next person throughout his training. Frank projected the qualities of a genuine family man and always had time to ask how you were doing.

Figure 104: Chesapeake City, MD - Frank receiving his sho-dan ranking. L-R: Frank Schwartz, Toby Cooling, Richard Muhs (Frank's sensei), Steve Dawson.

Upon receiving his sho-dan (black belt) ranking, Frank fell victim to cancer. He fought like a true warrior. On April 6, 2010, Frank sent an email to all members of the OI explaining his illness. This email provides a glimpse of what true and absolute courage is all about. Here are Frank's words from that email:

> Hello everyone. This is the most difficult message I have ever had to post before, so here goes.
>
> I don't know how to dance around this, so I will just say it outright. I am going to die, most likely within the next month. I have been losing weight, I am now down to 128lbs (down from 212), and I am being admitted into Johns Hopkins hospital right now. My blast count has returned, and there are no other drugs or trials that will work any better.
>
> Basically, the short version of this is that the GVH has been preventing me from absorbing any of the meds I have been taking, and that includes the AC220 drug, which did a wonderful job at holding my leukemia back. However, the theory is that the AC220 did so well that the neutrofils it produced have somehow re-kindled my gut GVH, and so the vicious cycle. I was told there are no more options for me.
>
> I am not upset so much about dying as I am about leaving my wife and kids behind to fend for themselves. I don't have many regrets, as I think that I have reconciled most of my sins and past issues. I know God has forgiven me.
>
> How ironic that I would get this news one day short of the year anniversary of me being diagnosed with leukemia.
>
> While I'm here at Hopkins, they will be trying to get my blast count stabilized, and hopefully get the GVH somewhat under control. Basically, they're going to try and buy me some time, but not much.
>
> One of the biggest highlights of my life was when I received my black belt. It's unfortunate that I was only able to wear it four times before I was too sick to be able to come to classes.
>
> I have been blessed to know such a wonderful family of people. The Order of Isshin-Ryu is an organization unlike any other I have ever been exposed to. Many have called, sent cards and gifts and visited while I was in the hospital or at home during recovery periods, and I thank you all. I don't want to list names because there were so many, but Sensei Kline and Sensei Bell have since day one been there with their friendship, and very few days have gone by without an email, a call or a text message to say hi. I value their friendship so much.

I regret that I was never able to attend a shiai as a black belt (except the one where I was promoted). I would have enjoyed that, but I guess like many other things, it wasn't meant to be.

As I said, I am not very good at this sort of thing, so I will stop there. Thanks for everything. I really appreciate your friendship, prayers, and love.

Your OI brother,
Frank Schwartz

Howard Tingle (1925 – 1998)

Howard Tingle was one of the founding members of the Order of Isshin-Ryu upon Master Cooling's return from training on Okinawa. When Denshi started Isshin-Ryu karate under Sensei Tom Lewis, Mr. Tingle was a green belt. The night Master Cooling passed his black belt exam, Mr. Tingle took off his black belt and put in on Master Cooling.

According to an article in an OI newsletter written by early OI black belt John King:

> Mr. Tingle was a yon-dan (4th degree black belt) and early member of the OI. He was inspirational in the early training of Master Cooling, Master Barry Smith, and Sensei John King. Sensei Tingle began karate at the age of 29, with an extensive background in boxing and weightlifting. One of his mottos was the one who prevails gets there "… the firstest with the mostest…" He served in the U.S. Marine Corps in the Pacific theatre during World War II and was an ordained minister.

Mr. Tingle passed away on August 7, 1998.

Brenda Tome (1954 – 1992)

Brenda was a member of the Hombu dojo in Elkton, Maryland and was married to black belt Pete Tome. She was involved in a two-car auto accident in North East, Maryland driving along MD-272 on April 22, 1992. She died in the accident. She was 38 years old.

She was a key member of the Hombu dojo where she was a San-kyu, or 3rd degree brown belt. Many of the younger dojo members at that time say she was the

Figure 105: Brenda Tome

"dojo mother." She would take the time to make sure they had their uniforms in proper order with patches and red trim sewn properly on their gi. As Sensei Adam Knox recalls, "She would make the hachimaki for all students in the Hombu dojo." Brenda is honored at the Hombu dojo in Elkton, Maryland where her brown belt hangs on display in the dojo.

Black belt Nikolina Novakovic provides the following memories regarding Brenda: "She was always ready to help the dojo in any way she could, especially keeping the dojo clean. I can't remember when the dojo looked nicer than when Brenda was there. Karate did not come easy to her, but she took everything in stride. She would practice every night on the same moves and same kata and never did I see her give up. She laughed a lot about her own mistakes and how hard things were for her and how easily it seemed to come to others; however, it never discouraged her. She kept right on trying. She was always there to cheer her fellow karate students on and help when she could."

Pete Tome (1956 – 2001)

Figure 106: Pete Tome as a kyu rank.

Pete Tome was a black belt member of the Hombu dojo in Elkton, Maryland. He was married to Brenda Tome (see above). Pete worked his way up to ni-dan (2nd degree black belt) awarded by his sensei, Master Bud Ewing.

In the summer of 2001, Pete died as a result of a skydiving accident. He had been out of training for a while and had returned to classes just a few weeks before his death. This came as a shock to the OI family because he was very skilled at his passion, putting in countless hours and numerous jumps.

I met Pete Tome when I petitioned to join the Order of Isshin-Ryu in 1996. He had an impressive, muscular frame, yet he seemed as friendly and gentle as someone you've known for a lifetime. He was always smiling, always there to lend a helping hand. It wasn't until I began writing this book that I learned of his wife's tragic passing, which wasn't long before I met him in the mid-90s. Being around his OI family certainly picked up his spirits.

At one point, Pete remodeled the Hombu dojo in Elkton, Maryland. Sensei Kurt Kline recalls putting in countless reps at the makiwara board over the years at Hombu, and he wanted it for his home. However, Pete had other ideas and took it for himself. Sensei Kline remembers, "He never heard the end of that from me."

Members of the OI fondly recall the affection that Pete and his wife had for the OI family. Sensei Adam Knox mentions he and his wife, Brenda, were like 'mom and dad' to the dojo, always there to take care of the little things like sewing the red trim on the students' gi pants. Sensei Kline points out, "Pete was a pilot. One time, he took me on a ride to Pennsylvania to fly over my parent's house so I could take a picture for them. He was a good guy."

SPECIAL MEMORIALS

In alphabetical order

Walter F. Cooling (1911 – 2004)

Figure 107: L-R: Jesús M. Jiménez, Walter F. Cooling, Walter (Toby) Cooling

Walter and his wife, Hilda T. Cooling, were the parents of Toby Cooling. He was born in a time before automobiles and telephones were common, computers and television had not been invented, and business deals could be made with a handshake.

He was affectionately known as "Mr. C" to all of the karate students and was a fixture at all OI events. He started his business career as a young man by delivering milk from the dairies in Cecil County, Maryland to Philadelphia via a horse-drawn truck. He progressed to other jobs and attended Goldey College, graduating in

1931. During WWII, he worked in an ammunition plant in Kentucky. Upon returning home to Chesapeake City after the war, available jobs had already been filled by returning servicemen, so he started his own business. Cooling Hardware opened in 1945 and remained a fixture in town for 25 years. Along the way, he expanded his enterprises to include a laundromat and apartment rentals. His son, Toby, helped run the store and rehab the apartment buildings after school.

The one characteristic that everyone remembers about Mr. C is that he was one of the nicest people you could ever know. He had made shrewd choices in life and wanted to help others succeed. From allowing people to purchase appliances for $1.00 down and $1.00 a week, to serving on the board for various charitable organizations, he was a humble man who always put others first.

Karate was just a novelty when Toby started training. His son would drive 100 miles to Salisbury, Maryland to train with Sensei Tom Lewis, stay overnight for a second night's training, and then drive home. Many times, his son could hardly walk because of those workouts. For Christmas that first year, he and Hilda gave their son a bottle of Absorbine Jr. and an ice bag. Hilda was not concerned. She told Walter not to worry, that Toby would quit. Years later, he would tell people that karate was the best thing that his son ever got involved in. He was always quick with a corny joke and good business advice, when needed.

Jimmy Tyree (1942 - 2016)

Ronnie Tyree started karate at 10 years old at the YMCA in Elkton, Maryland. The year was 1980. From the moment he walked in the door, he fell in love with karate. It was the same for his dad, Jimmy. He fell in love with watching Ronnie grow up in the dojo and seeing how much he loved to train. Jimmy drove him to class every night and sat on the bench watching Ronnie train. He spent six years driving him back and forth to class until Ronnie was old enough to drive himself. Even then, Jimmy would show up night after night to watch him work out. Nothing made him prouder than to see Ronnie fighting and competing at tournaments and shiai.

Jimmy also loved talking to everyone at the shiai and at outside tournaments. He couldn't brag enough about his son and the Order of Isshin-Ryu. Grandmaster Cooling remembers a story about Jimmy from the International Hall of Fame (IHOF) tournament in Tennessee in 1993. Jimmy had walked outside to have a smoke and sat down next to this older gentleman who was also having a smoke. Jimmy struck up a conversation with the man and proceeded to tell him about his boy, Ronnie, and the fabulous organization to which his son belonged. The man nodded. Jimmy told him that the head of the organization, Toby Cooling, had been promoted to

9th degree black belt the year before. That was impressive news since there were only four 9th degree black belts in Isshin-Ryu Karate in the United States at the time. The man said, "I know." Jimmy asked, "How do you know?" The man replied, "I promoted him." Jimmy had been having a smoke with Grandmaster Don Nagle.

Black belt Nikolina Novakovic recalls fond memories of Mr. Tyree over the years. She notes, "Although I never saw him in a gi, he had the heart of a warrior. He supported the OI and dojo more than some of the students. He was of soft character but if you messed with his family, you were in for more trouble than you could imagine. He was soft spoken and most of all he loved his family with his whole heart. He would have given his own life for his family without even a second thought. He was small in stature, but his heart was bigger than some can even imagine."

Figure 108: Jimmy Tyree with his wife, Brenda.

Jimmy and his wife Brenda had great times traveling to Tennessee for the IHOF and going to Florida when Ronnie was inducted into the World Head of Family Sokeship Council's Hall of Fame. The OI was a big part of Jimmy's life, and one of its biggest supporters.

CONCLUSION

Writing this book has been an incredible journey. There was quite a bit of research involved for the various topics presented, and the history of the Order of Isshin-Ryu alone took a considerable amount of time to sort through. I had to weed through tons of pictures, newspaper clippings, written articles, and editing of various interviews with members of the Order of Isshin-Ryu. However, the time spent on this massive project was worth every minute. I had a front-row seat in uncovering quite a bit of history and had the opportunity to piece together data and information from a variety of resources. This process has truly elevated my appreciation for my karate family and what they all mean to me. Suffice it to say, I cannot put into words what that level of appreciation really is.

I'm sure I may have left out some critical information, or maybe forgotten some items of interest. Please understand, piecing together 45 years of history is no small task. Those who know me will understand my oversights are never intentional. Maybe future releases of this book will contain expanded sections with additional information and history. However, for the level of information I did present, I am pleased. I am pleased because this project allowed me the chance to revisit a part of my past that is both memorable and satisfying. I had the chance to hear many stories from my OI brothers and sisters that brought a smile to my face. It was good to be reminded of these stories and the journey the Order of Isshin-Ryu has followed.

....

Sensei Jesús M. Jiménez sums up what the Order of Isshin-Ryu family is truly about. Sensei Jiménez lives in Puerto Rico. As is well documented, Puerto Rico suffered two massive hurricanes in September 2017 – Hurricane Irma, followed by Hurrican Maria that was even more devastating to the island and the people of Puerto Rico. The island will take many years to recover from these natural disasters. The OI family, along with many friends of the OI, pulled together to send aid to our brothers in Puerto Rico. Sensei Jiménez sent a text to his OI family prior to the Fall OI Shiai and read aloud to everyone to show his appreciation. The following is that message:

> To my Order of Isshin-Ryu family,
>
> It's impossible to describe how important it is to belong to a family. The family takes care and strengthens the values, morals and interaction of its members. The family looks out for the welfare of everyone, that's why all the members are committed to each one, based on respect.
>
> The Order of Isshin-Ryu is always present in my heart. Nobody can and will not take that from me. This morning, I have all my brothers in mind and my spirit is with all of you. Today is a special day, as it's the OI shiai. An Order of Isshin-Ryu shiai isn't a competition, it's a gathering of all the members and invitees of this family to have fun and tell one another how important he or she is for this family.
>
> Today, take a second and hug every member of this Order of Isshin-Ryu family. As in every family, some of its members are more related with each other, which gives the Brotherhood an opportunity to manifest in its maximum splendor.
>
> Arigato Gozaimasu!
>
> P.S. It's easy to create a martial art style, but not a family such as the Order of Isshin-Ryu. Thank you, Grandmaster Toby Cooling.
>
> Sensei Jesús M. Jiménez
> October 7, 2017

This message sums up the Order of Isshin-Ryu. It is my hope and prayer that everyone has the chance during their lifetime to have the opportunity to belong to such a 'family' as the OI provides to its members.

> "Everything is possible for the person who has faith."
> Mark 9:23

Conclusion

Figure 109: Order of Isshin-Ryu brothers.
L-R: Jesus Jimenez, Tom Sanson, Ronnie Cimorosi, Jr.

ACKNOWLEDGMENTS

*"No eye has seen,
No ear has heard,
No mind has conceived,
What God has prepared for those who love Him."*

1 Corinthians 2:9

All credit goes to my savior, Jesus Christ. He provides all my abilities to be able to bring this book to print and honor my karate family as they most richly deserve.

Thank you, Grandmaster Cooling, my sensei, for giving me permission to document the history of your life's work – the Order of Isshin-Ryu. All my visits to your home in Nevada are enlightening; however, the visit in September 2017 was truly special. We covered a lot of ground for this publication but also many other personal topics as well at that time. I'll never forget those memorable times.

The Order of Isshin-Ryu, an amazing family of martial artists. Thank you for always being there whether it concerns karate training or helping to get me through the tough times of life. We all have difficulties, and time and again the OI family has proven how much a family should care for one another. Thank you for supporting this project with your photos, time for interviews, and ongoing encouragement. I hope I've done you all proud and met everyone's expectations with this publication.

Special thanks to those who I was able to interview in person for this publication: Bud Ewing, Barry Smith, Kurt Kline, Adam Knox, Charlie Deitterick, Isham Latimer, John Costanzo, John McDonald, Diane Ortenzio-Cooling, and Buster Hash. Many others stepped up and provided outstanding material from photos and stories to historical information. Thank you for this important historical information to: Danny Cross, Bill Sullivan, Joe Ragan, Nikolina Novakovic, Bob Foard,

Ronnie Cimorosi, Buster Hash, Tom Sanson, Aaron Walker, Bud Ewing, Diane Ortenzio-Cooling, Isham Latimer, John McDonald, John Costanzo, Larry Sica, Charlie Deitterick, Bailey Russell, and Dan Holloway. I was also able to interview several OI brothers over the telephone. Thank you all for your generous time and insights: Jesus Jimenez, Sotiere Nicholson, and Grandmaster Cooling. I'm sure there may be some others whom I unintentionally failed to mention here. You freely gave of your time, memories, historical photos, articles, personal notes, etc. Everyone brought information to the forefront that was invaluable in helping to piece together nearly 50 years of OI history.

As always, I must recognize and pay respect to each of my martial arts instructors: Toby Cooling (Order of Isshin-Ryu), Rick Manglinong (Kombatan, Modern Arnis), Isham Latimer (Chi Ryu Jujitsu), and Dave Joyner (Kendo). I always try to pattern the examples you provide over the course of my martial arts career and will always continue to do so.

Special thanks to Charlie Deitterick. The initial idea for a book to commemorate the Order of Isshin-Ryu came from you, as far back as 1998. You nudged me in the direction of taking on this project (whether you know it or not), and I couldn't be more thankful. Dropping on my lap all your historical materials regarding the Order of Isshin-Ryu, along with Master Bud Ewing, was the dose of reality I needed to get moving on this journey. Once again Charlie's wife, Deanie, provided an outstanding job for the editing and proofreading for this book. When it comes to your efforts, you are a saint!

Thank you to my OI sister, Master Diane Ortenzio-Cooling. You really stepped up and provided invaluable assistance for this project: the lineage charts, yudansha listing, bio for Mr. Cooling and Mr. Tyree, various pictures, and overall review of the various drafts.

Thank you to all those interviewed for the manuscript. Your time and input were priceless. I could see the emotions and pride in everyone's eyes as you all recalled special moments in your OI training and the brotherhood involved. Special thanks to Sensei Jesús M. Jiménez who called me from Puerto Rico, *after* suffering the effects of Hurricane Maria that devastated the island, to help me fill in the history of the Puerto Rico dojo.

A respectful *rei* goes out to the masters providing the foreword to *Order of Isshin-Ryu, One Family – One Dojo*: Butch Hill, David Joslin, Bob Kristensen, Carl Martin, and Ralph Passero. Each of you have firmly placed your mark on the history of Isshin-Ryu karate, and the OI will always treasure your friendship.

Acknowledgments

Thanks to everyone who provided their message of congratulations to Denshi at the beginning of the book. Your words added a personal touch to the life work of Grandmaster Toby Cooling.

Jerry Robinette for the front and back cover design, as well as the senior dan bio photos. Thanks also to Bill Harbold for the photos of the kanji on front and back covers along with several photos within the text. I cannot thank you both enough, for always being there for me.

To my parents Frank and Carol Popp. Thanks for your total support regarding all my efforts in life, both professional and personal.

To my wonderful daughters, Britteni and Kayla. You both are growing so fast, and I'm proud of the young ladies you have become. Although you are beyond the point of always holding my hand, you will always be able to hold my heart.

Thanks to the Kamel Press team, who are absolute professionals and so easy to work with. Bringing this publication to reality was a dream a long time in the making. Another fantastic job and I couldn't be happier with the outcome.

And finally, author Stephen King said the following about the process of writing, *"When you write a book, you spend day after day scanning and identifying the trees. When you're done, you have to step back and look at the forest."* This is certainly a fitting end to this writing journey. I could recall a good bit of OI history on my own, but I needed quite a bit of help to go back and review the early days. I am thoroughly enriched for having undertaken this endeavor, and when I step back and "look at the forest," I am honored and humbled by the talent, the people, and the spirit of the karate family to which I belong – the Order of Isshin-Ryu.

SPECIAL RECOGNITION

This book would be far from complete and woefully deficient if I didn't provide a special nod to Ellen Ewing. Ellen is the wife of Master Bud Ewing who has been there, in various capacities, for the Order of Isshin-Ryu. Her dedication and support of the OI has never failed for over 40 years! Her assistance and tireless work at the annual Isshinryu Hall of Fame weekend in Tennessee helps the event run flawlessly and efficiently.

Mrs. Ewing has the 'heart' which you often hear about and to which all of us within the OI aspire to achieve. I can honestly say the OI would not be the family that it is today without the presence of Ellen Ewing.

Figure 110: July 2017, Gatlinburg, TN. Master Bud Ewing and his wife Ellen.

APPENDIX I – Alphabetical Listing of Order of Isshin-Ryu Yudansha

The following are all black belts granted within the Order of Isshin-Ryu.

Last Name	First Name	Rank of Black Belt
Adams	Ed	2
Ankers	Gerri	3
Ankers	Pete	3
Aponte	Luis	2
Arce	Justin	1
Armani	Eleanor	1
Bear	Ian	Jr
Bear	Micah	Jr
Bell	Shelley	6
Bennett	Dave	1
Beulah	Marvin	5
Blackburn	Allan	1
Blas	Alfred	1
Bootle	Dennis	4
Bracone	Jeff	3
Bramble	Jo	3
Brittingham	Wayne	3
Bronson	Karen	2

Bullock	Andrew	1
Burig	Doug	2
Burns	Bob	3
Caballero	Wilfredo	1
Cabrera	Edwin	3
Caldwell	David	2
Calloway	Dan	1
Calman	Andrew	2
Campbell	Tony	2
Campfield	Tom	1
Cardona	Manual	1
Cimorosi	Ronnie	7
Clark	Jim	1
Clough	Gavin	1
Clough	Julie	1
Cole	Robert	3
Collins	Joshua	2
Collins	Matt	3
Cook	Jeff	2
Costanzo	John	8
Craig	Bob	1
Cross	Dan	6
Daly	Susan	2
D'Amico	Peter	1
Davis	Willie	1
Dawson	Cathy	1
Dawson	Stephen	4
DeCarli	Mark	1
deGuzman	Nathan	1
Deitterick	Charlie	2
Diaz	Jose	3
Deiter	Duane	4
Doppman	Lloyd	2
Drummond	Lois	2

APPENDIX I – Alphabetical Listing of Order of Isshin-Ryu Yudansha

Duarte	Charles	2
Duarte	Christopher	1
Duarte	Kevin	1
Durrette	Randy	1
Edwards	Oswald	1
Edwards	Ralston	1
Era	Jean	1
Era	Laura	1
Era	Richard	1
Evans	Sandra	4
Ewing	Bud	9
Fanning	Glenn	2
Fluke	Adam	1
Foard	Robert	2
Gallagher	Sean	1
Garrett	Bucky	3
Gilbert	Wendy	1
Ginn	David	3
Goding	Danny	4
Gonzalez	Eduardo	2
Gonzalez	Roberto	4
Goodyear	Michael	8
Gough	Thad	1
Grace	Carmen	5
Granger	Colleen	1
Granger	Walter	1
Gray	Mike	1
Green	Harold	1
Guzman	Joseomar	1
Guzman-Perez	Joseomar	1
Harris	Chris	6
Hash	Charles "Buster"	3
Heath	Paul	3
Hendrickson	James	1

Herd	Matthew	2
Herron	Fred	1
Heverin	Frank	3
Holland	Larry	1
Hough	Laura	1
Hugh	Aston	3
Hurt	Dale	1
Hutton	Randy	2
Iyengar	Anand	1
Jackson	Larry	6
Jackson-DeGarcia	Jacqueline	2
Jaime	Juan	1
Jenkins	Alan	2
Jimenez	Jesus	7
Jones	Curtis	1
Judway	John	3
Kadash	Bryce	1
Kaniatyn	Roman "Ray"	1
Kilmon	Shelby	Jr
King	John	3
Kline	Kurt	7
Knapp-Robinette	Rae	1
Knox	Adam	6
Kornelis	Jason	1
Krischbaum	Richard	1
Kruez	Al	1
Lane	Tony	1
Langdon	Austin	1
Langtry	Michael	2
Laporte	Antonio	1
Larrimore	Andy	1
Latimer	Isham	9
Lee	Malachi	6
Leon	Jorge	1

APPENDIX I – Alphabetical Listing of Order of Isshin-Ryu Yudansha

Lockerman	Lance	1
Lopez	Juan F.	3
Lopez	Juan D.	6
Lorden	Dan	3
MacFann	Sam	1
Magill	Mike	4
Mallon	Brian	1
Mandes	Christy	1
Manspeaker	David	Jr
Manuel	Rodney	3
Mayer	Erin	Jr
McCann	Sean	2
McCarl-Stanton	Jeanette	3
McCloskey	John	2
McDonald	John	7
McGee	Shannon	1
Merritt	James	2
Miller	Tom	2
Mills	David	1
Morrison	Robert	2
Morton	Jeff	1
Muhs	Richard	5
Murphy	Milledge	2
Nicholson	Sotiere	3
Nickle	Joe	1
Nickle	John	3
Nickle	Theresa	2
Nolen	Michael	1
Novakovic	Nikolina	3
Ortenzio	Diane	8
Pell	Nicki	2
Phillips	Art	3
Phillips	Tom	1
Pierce	Hank	1

Pioreck	Brian	2
Poalillo	Shawn	1
Popp	Dan	6
Ragan	Joe	3
Remick	John	2
Rivera	Edgar	1
Rivera	Efrain	4
Robertson	Rod	2
Robinette	Jerry	4
Rodriquez	Juan Jaime	1
Rodriquez	Randy	2
Rodriquez	Maria	4
Rogers	Doug	3
Rogers	James	1
Rose	David	4
Rossini	John	2
Rudd	Scott	2
Russell	Bailey	3
Russell	Jeannie	1
Sanchez	Gregorio	2
Sanson	Tom	4
Schade	Shannon	1
Schalk	Ryan	2
Schwartz	Frank	1
Scott	Greg	2
Sica	Larry	3
Simmons	Dicky	4
Slijepcevic	Mico	1
Smith	Barry	9
Smith	Daniel	2
Smith	Terry	1
Snapp	Kevin	1
Spence	William	2
Spiker	Don	3

APPENDIX I – Alphabetical Listing of Order of Isshin-Ryu Yudansha

Sposato	Samuel	4
Stallings	Mark	2
Stanley	Kym	1
Stanton	Dale	1
Stare	Todd	1
Stone	Clara	2
Stone	Joshua	1
Sullivan	William C.	8
Taggart	Christopher	3
Taylor	G.P.	1
Tome	Pete	2
Townsend	Harold	1
Tyree	Ron	8
Varney	Ken	3
Waldridge	Larry	3
Walker	Aaron	2
Walker	Dennis	1
Wallace	Mark	3
Waltemeyer	Dan	3
Watson	Mike	1
Webb	Alan	2
Weber	Bert	2
Weber	Jeff	3
Whited	Bob	2
Wolf	Steven	2
Wright	Christine	1
Zurolo	Joe	1

APPENDIX II – Lineage Tables

The following tables represent the lineage of various black belts over the years by the sensei under which they achieved their sho-dan ranking. The listings are provided in alphabetical order by each respective sensei.

* Denotes no longer a member of the Order of Isshin-Ryu

Sensei Shelley Bell

Wayne Brittingham

Dickie Simmons

Matt Collins*

Marvin Beulah*

Matt Herd

Sensei Marvin Beulah

Andy Larrimore

Shelby Kilmon

Sensei Alan Blackburn

Allen Webb

Joe Ragan

Danny Cross

Sensei Jeff Bracone

Dave Bennett

Dan Waltemeyer

John McCloskey

Sensei Karen Bronson

Jason Kornelis

Joshua Collins

Rod Robertson

Scott Rudd*

Susan Daly*

Kevin Snapp

Sensei Ronnie Cimorosi, Jr.

Larry Holland (d. 2003)

Tony Campbell

Jeanette McCarl

Chris Harris

Frank Heverin, Jr.

W. Mark Wallace

Eleanore Armani

Fred Herron III

Walter Granger*

Colleen Granger*

Joe Zurolo

Larry Waldridge

Laura Hough

Mike Watson

Thad Gough

Andrew Bullock

Austin Langdon

Grandmaster Toby Cooling

Richard Krischbaum

Barry Smith

John King

Malachi Lee (d. 1975)

Allan Blackburn (d. 2007)

Edwin Cabrera

John Remick* (d. 1987)

Juan Francisco Lopez

Juan DeDios Lopez

Bob Burns

Tom Miller

Charles "Buster" Hash

John Nickle

William Spence

Bucky Garrett*

Bob Craig*

Tom Sanson

Dale Stanton

Lois Drummond

Theresa Nickle

Bud Ewing

Larry Jackson

Aston Hugh*

Eduardo Gonzalez*

John Judway

David Rose

Hank Pierce

Joe Nickle

Larry Sica

Jeff Bracone

Ken Varney

Bob Whited

Danny Cross

Dennis Walker*

Dennis Bootle*

Pete D'Amico

Milledge Murphy*

Randy Hutton*

Ron Tyree

James Merritt

Curtis Jones

Sean McCann

Ronnie Cimorosi, Jr.

Anand Iyengar

Doug Burig

Karen Bronson (d. 2002)

Dan Popp

Master John Costanzo

Justin Arce

Bryce Kadash

Sensei Duane Dieter

Bert Weber*

G.P. Taylor*

Lance Lockerman*

Jeannie Russell*

Master Bud Ewing

Diane Ortenzio

Carmen Grace

J. Kurt Kline

Pete Tome (d. 2001)

Mico Slijepcevic

Nikolina Slijepcevic-Novakovic

David Mills

Joe Ragan

Samuel Sposato

Dan Lorden

Ryan Schalk

Shannon McGee

Mike Gray

Doug Rogers

Robert Foard

Michael Nolen

Tony Lane

Sensei Danny Goding

Andrew Calman*

Michael Langtry

Daniel Smith*

Terry Smith*

Sensei Aston Hugh

Oswald Edwards*

Harold Green*

Ralston Edwards*

APPENDIX II – Lineage Tables

Sensei Larry Jackson

Sotiere Nicholson

Randy Durrette

Robert Morrison

Sensei Jesús M. Jiménez

Alfred John Blas

Manuel Cardona

Luis F. Aponte

Antonio Laporte

Edgar Rivera

Joseomar Guzman Perez

Efrain Rivera

Juan Jaime

APPENDIX II – Lineage Tables

Sensei John Judway

Bailey Russell

Sensei Kurt Kline

Christopher Taggart

APPENDIX II – Lineage Tables

Master Isham Latimer

Willie Davis

John McDonald

Rose Roales

Shawn Poalillo

John Costanzo

Brian Piorek

Harold Townsend

Sensei Malachi Lee

Maria Melendez Rodriquez

↓

Isham Latimer

Jose Diaz

John McDonald

Willie Davis

Tom Campfield

Ray Kaniatyn

Jim Hendrickson

Randy Rodriquez

Sensei Juan F. Lopez & Sensei Juan D. Lopez

Jesús M. Jiménez

Wilfredo Caballero

Roberto Gonzalez

Sensei Tom Miller

Charlie Deitterick

APPENDIX II – Lineage Tables

Sensei Richard Muhs

Adam Knox

Stephen Dawson

Cathy Dawson

John Rossini

Frank Schwartz (d. 2010)

Master Diane Ortenzio

Adam Cooper

Mark Stallings

Charles Duarte

Christopher Duarte

Kevin Duarte

APPENDIX II – Lineage Tables

Sensei Dan Popp

Jacqueline Jackson-DeGarcia

Jerry Robinette

Aaron Walker

Sensei James Rogers

Jeffrey Cook, Sr.

APPENDIX II – Lineage Tables

Sensei Larry Sica

Todd Stare

Christy Mandes

Master Barry Smith

Frank Hastings (d. 1981)

Duane Dieter*

Perry Hall

Bill Sullivan

Art Phillips

Jeff Weber

Shelley Bell*

Christine Wright

Sandy Evans

Jim Clark

Richard Era

Laura Era

Jean Era

Dale Hurt

Greg Scott

James Rogers

Master Bill Sullivan

Jo Bramble

Mike Magill

Gavin Clough

Julie Clough

Dan Calloway

Danny Goding*

Robert Cole

Clara Stone

Joshua Stone

Gregorio Sanchez

Sean Gallagher

Nathan deGuzman

Master Ron Tyree

Wendy Gilbert

Ed Adams*

Steven Wolf

Shannon Schade

Brian Mallon

APPENDIX II – Lineage Tables

Sensei Ken Varney

Al Kreuz

APPENDIX III – Photo Credits

Figure 1: see internet sources; *Figure 2*: see internet sources; *Figure 3*: Bud Ewing; *Figure 4*: Bud Ewing; *Figure 5*: author – photo by Bill Harbold; *Figure 6*: see internet sources; *Figure 7*: see internet sources; *Figure 8*: OI pamphlet; *Figure 9*: author – photo by Bill Harbold; *Figure 10*: Toby Cooling; *Figure 11*: Danny Cross; *Figure 12*: Dan Holloway; *Figure 13*: Diane Ortenzio-Cooling; *Figure 14*: OI pamphlet; *Figure 15*: Bud Ewing; *Figure 16*: Bud Ewing; *Figure 17*: author – photo by Bill Harbold; *Figure 18*: see internet sources; *Figure 19*: Toby Cooling; *Figure 20*: Charlie Deitterick; *Figure 21*: Diane Ortenzio-Cooling; *Figure 22*: Danny Cross; *Figure 23*: John McDonald; *Figure 24*: Charlie Deitterick; *Figure 25*: Charlie Deitterick; *Figure 26*: Charlie Deitterick; *Figure 27*: Charlie Deitterick; *Figure 28*: Toby Cooling; *Figure 29*: Isham Latimer; *Figure 30*: Toby Cooling; *Figure 31*: Danny Cross; *Figure 32*: Bill Sullivan; *Figure 33*: Luis Aponte; *Figure 34*: Jesus Jimenez; *Figure 35*: Toby Cooling (published in Who's Who in Isshinryu); *Figure 36*: Toby Cooling; *Figure 37*: OI pamphlet; *Figure 38*: author; *Figure 39*: see internet sources; *Figure 40*: Jesus Jimenez; *Figure 41*: Diane Ortenzio-Cooling; *Figure 42*: Charlie Deitterick; *Figure 43*: Tom Sanson; *Figure 44*: see internet sources; *Figure 45*: Diane Ortenzio-Cooling; *Figure 46*: Bill Sullivan; *Figure 47*: Bill Sullivan; *Figure 48*: Charlie Deitterick; *Figure 49*: Bud Ewing; *Figure 50*: author; *Figure 51*: Jesus Jimenez; *Figure 52*: Diane Ortenzio-Cooling; *Figure 53*: Nikolina Novakovic; *Figure 54*: author; *Figure 55*: Toby Cooling; *Figure 56*: Bill Sullivan; *Figure 57*: Bud Ewing; *Figure 58*: Diane Ortenzio-Cooling; *Figure 59*: Diane Ortenzio-Cooling; *Figure 60*: Diane Ortenzio-Cooling; *Figure 61*: Bill Sullivan; *Figure 62*: author; *Figure 63*: author; *Figure 64*: author; *Figure 65*: Bud Ewing; *Figure 66*: Isham Latimer; *Figure 67*: author; *Figure 68*: Bud Ewing; *Figure 69*: Ronnie Cimorosi; *Figure 70*: Tom Sanson; *Figure 71*: author; *Figure 72: author; *Figure 73:* Bud Ewing; *Figure 74:* Diane Ortenzio-Cooling; *Figure 75:* author – photo by Bill Harbold; *Figure 76:* Diane Ortenzio-Cooling; *Figure 77:* Diane Ortenzio-Cooling; *Figure 78:* Diane Ortenzio-Cooling; *Figure 79:* Isham Latimer; *Figure 80:* author; *Figure 81:* Toby Cooling; *Figure 82:* Diane Ortenzio-Cooling; *Figure 83:* Ronnie Cimorosi; *Figure 84:* Ronnie Cimorosi; *Figure 85:* author; *Figure 86:* Toby Cooling; *Figure 87:* author; *Figure 88:* Bill Sullivan; *Figure 89:* Bill Sullivan; *Figure 90:* Diane Ortenzio-Cooling; *Figure 91:* Ronnie Cimorosi; *Figure 92:* Jesus Jimenez; *Figure 93:* Kurt Kline; *Figure 94:* John McDonald; *Figure 95:* Diane Ortenzio-Cooling; *Figure 96:* Danny Cross; *Figure 97:* Jesus Jimenez; *Figure 98:* Joe Ragan; *Figure 99:* Jesus Jimenez; *Figure 100:* Isham Latimer; *Figure 101:* Ronnie Cimorosi; *Figure 102:* Bud Ewing; *Figure 103:* Isham Latimer; *Figure 104:* Diane Ortenzio-Cooling; *Figure 105:* Nikolina Novakovic; *Figure 106:* Bud Ewing; *Figure 107:* Jesus Jimenez; *Figure 108:* Brenda Tyree; *Figure 109:* Ronnie Cimorosi; *Figure 110:* author.

All portrait photos in **Senior Dan Bios** chapter – courtesy of Jerry Robinette.

APPENDIX IV – Sources

Various sources were utilized and supported the topics provided in this book. Being an avid reader and understanding how many areas relate to my martial arts growth, I enjoy utilizing the material from other authors which assisted in the writing of this manuscript. Topics utilized cover a broad spectrum, including non-martial arts related sources. I encourage all aspects of life from which to pull information in your own training and research. You never know from where a lesson or usable information may come.

Book Sources

Order of Isshin-Ryu (student manual & black belt manual)

A Stroll Along Ryukyu Martial Arts History, by Andreas Quast - ©2015 Andreas Quast, published by Andreas Quast (www.ryukyu-bugei.com)

Because of Bethlehem, by Max Lucado - ©2016 Max Lucado, published by Thomas Nelson

Clouds in the West – Lessons From the Martial Arts of Japan, by Dave Lowry - ©2004 by Dave Lowry, published by The Lyons Press

Daily Readings From Every Day a Friday, by Joel Osteen - ©2012 Joel Osteen, published by FaithWords

Ego is the Enemy, by Ryan Holiday - ©2016 Ryan Holiday, published by Penguin Random House LLC

Focus, by Daniel Goleman - ©2013 Daniel Goleman, published by HarperCollins

Following the Martial Path: Lessons and Stories from a Lifetime of Training in Budo and Zen, by Walther G. von Krenner with Ken Jeremiah - ©2016 Walther G. von Krenner, published by Tambuli Media

Glory Days, by Max Lucado - ©2015 Max Lucado, published by Thomas Nelson

God Will Carry You Through, by Max Lucado - ©2013 Max Lucado, published by Thomas Nelson

In the Dojo, by Dave Lowry - ©2006 Dave Lowry, published by Shambhala Publications, Inc. (Weatherhill)

Isshin-Ryu Karate – The Ultimate Fighting Art, by Harold Long and Tim McGhee - ©1997 Isshin-Ryu Productions, Inc.

It's How You Play the Game – The 12 Leadership Principles of Dean Smith, by David Chadwick - ©2015 David Chadwick, published by Harvest House Publishers

APPENDIX IV – Sources

Japanese Swordsmanship – Technique and Practice, by Gordon Warner and Donn F. Draeger - ©1982, 2001 by Warner and Draeger. Published by Weatherhill, Inc.

Karate: Beneath the Surface, by Roy Kenneth Kamen - ©2017 by Kamen Entertainment Group, Inc. Published by Kamen Entertainment Group, Inc.

Kodo: Ancient Ways, by Kensho Furuya - ©1996 Ohara Publications, Inc.

Modern Arnis – The Filipino Art of Stick Fighting, by Remy Presas - ©1983, 2004 Black Belt Communications LLC

No Wonder They Call Him the Savior, by Max Lucado - ©1986, 2004 Max Lucado, published by Thomas Nelson

Okinawa: Island of Karate (rev. ed.), by George W. Alexander, Ph.D. - ©1980 by George W. Alexander and Yamazato Publications

Okinawan Kobudo, by Andrea Guarelli - ©2015 by Andrea Guarelli, published by Skyhorse Publishing

Old School, Essays on Japanese Martial Traditions, by Ellis Amdur - ©2002 Ellis Amdur, published by Edgework

On the Anvil, by Max Lucado - ©1985, 2008 by Max Lucado, published by Tyndale House Publishers, Inc.

Persimmon Wind, A Martial Artist's Journey in Japan, by Dave Lowry - ©1998 by Dave Lowry, published by Charles E. Tuttle Co., Inc.

Resisting Happiness, by Matthew Kelly - ©2016, published by Beacon Publishing

Sacred Calligraphy of the East (3rd Ed.), by John Stevens - ©1981, 1995 (rev) John Stevens, published by Shambhala Publications, Inc.

Shotokan's Secret, The Hidden Truth Behind Karate's Fighting Origins, by Bruce D. Clayton, Ph.D. - ©2010 Cruz Bay Publishing, Inc.

Steal My Art – The Life and Times of T'ai Chi Master T.T. Liang, by Stuart Alve Olson - ©2002 by Stuart Alve Olson, published by North Atlantic Books

Sword and Brush, The Spirit of the Martial Arts, by Dave Lowry - ©1995 by Dave Lowry, published by Shambhala Publications, Inc.

Tales from the Western Generation – Untold Stories and Firsthand History from Karate's Golden Age, by Matthew Apsokardu - ©2015 by Matthew Apsokardu, published by Apsos Publishing.

The Essence of Budo, A Practitioner's Guide to Understanding the Japanese Martial Ways, by Dave Lowry - ©2010 by Dave Lowry, published by Shambhala Publications, Inc.

The Essence of Karate, by Gichin Funakoshi – English translation 2010 by Richard Berger, published by Kodansha International Ltd.

The Heart of the Brush, The Splendor of East Asian Calligraphy, by Kazuaki Tanahashi - ©2016 by Kazuaki Tanahashi, published by Shambhala Publications, Inc.

The Karate Dojo – Traditions and Tales of a Martial Art, by Peter Urban - ©1967 by Charles E. Tuttle Publishing Company, published by Charles E. Tuttle.

The Karate Way, Discovering the Spirit of Practice, by Dave Lowry - ©2009 by Dave Lowry, published by Shambhala Publications, Inc.

The Last Lesson – The Go-kui of Isshin-ryu, by James C. Burris Jr., Ed.D - ©2008 by JC Burris, published by JCBPublishing.

The Road to Sparta, by Dean Karnazes - ©2016 by Dean Karnazes, published by Rodale, Inc.

The Secrets of Isshin-Ryu Karate, by Joel Chandler - ©1989 by Joel Chandler, published by National Paperback Books, Inc.

The Sword of No-Sword – Life of the Master Warrior Tesshu, by John Stevens - ©1984, 1989 by John Stevens, published by Shambhala Publications, Inc.

APPENDIX IV – Sources

The Twenty Guiding Principles of Karate, by Gichin Funakoshi and Genwa Nakasone, ©2003 Japan Karate-do Shotokai, published by Kodansha International, Ltd.

The Weaponless Warriors, by Richard Kim - ©1974, Ohara Publications, Inc.

The Writing Warrior, by Laraine Herring - ©2010 Laraine Herring, published by Shambhala Publications, Inc.

Wabi Sabi, The Japanese Art of Impermanence, by Andrew Juniper - © 2003 Andrew Juniper, published by Tuttle Publishing

Who's Who in Isshinryu, by Long, Manis, and McGhee - ©1993 by Harold Long, published by National Paperback Book Publishers, Inc.

Zen Word Zen Calligraphy, by Eido Tai Shimano and Kogetsu Tani, ©1990, 1995 Theseus Verlag, Zurich, Munich, published by Shambhala Publications, Inc.

Internet Sources

Google searches and internet sources provided historical photographs, articles and maps presented in this text.

Map of Okinawa
https://goo.gl/gMhJGn

Map of Okinawa and Surrounding Countries
https://goo.gl/R8BqRJ

Black Belt Magazine Cover
http://ma-mags.com/showmag.php?CatCde=BB60

Itsukushima Torii
https://en.wikipedia.org/wiki/Itsukushima_Shrine

Gichin Funakoshi (1868 – 1957)
https://goo.gl/fhtzQE

Choki Motobu (1870 – 1944)
https://goo.gl/iFgLpq

Chojun Miyagi (1888 – 1953)
https://goo.gl/ZHZRFn

Chotoku Kyan (1870 – 1945)
https://goo.gl/mwhdKA

Shinken Taira (1897 – 1970)
https://goo.gl/TASPk6

Eizo Shimabuku
https://goo.gl/92twaW

Kichiro Shimabuku
https://goo.gl/km9X1W

APPENDIX IV – Sources

Shinso Shimabuku
https://goo.gl/SrL1mM

Angi Uezu
https://goo.gl/s9AXaa

Jigoro Kano (1860 – 1938)
https://goo.gl/KVt3e7

Remy Presas (1936 – 2001)
https://goo.gl/tRiuU1

Ernesto Presas (1945 – 2010)
https://goo.gl/3LkSwR

www.ingramcontent.com/pod-product-compliance
Lightning Source LLC
Chambersburg PA
CBHW080531170426
43195CB00016B/2529